The Fundamental Practices

The Fundamental Practices
A Modern Ngöndro Guide

His Holiness the Forty-Second Sakya Trizin,
Ratna Vajra Rinpoche

Foreword by His Holiness the Sakya Trichen

Wisdom Publications
132 Perry Street
New York, NY 10014 USA
wisdom.org

© 2025 H. H. the 42nd Sakya Trizin, Ratna Vajra Rinpoche
All rights reserved.

No part of this book may be reproduced in any form or by any means, electronic or mechanical, including photography, recording, or by any information storage and retrieval system or technologies now known or later developed, without permission in writing from the publisher.

Library of Congress Cataloging-in-Publication Data
Names: Rat-na Vaj-ra, Sa-skya Khri-'dzin XLII, 1974– author.
Title: The fundamental practices: a modern ngöndro guide /
　　His Holiness the Forty-Second Sakya Trizin Ratna Vajra Rinpoche.
Other titles: Modern ngöndro guide
Description: First edition. | New York, NY: Wisdom Publications, [2025] |
　　Includes index. | Includes bibliographical references and index.
Identifiers: LCCN 2024021629 (print) | LCCN 2024021630 (ebook) |
　　ISBN 9781614299554 (paperback) | ISBN 9781614299790 (ebook)
Subjects: LCSH: Sa-skya-pa (Sect)—Rituals.
Classification: LCC BQ7672.6 .R56 2025 (print) | LCC BQ7672.6 (ebook) |
　　DDC 294.3/438—dc23/eng/20240805
LC record available at https://lccn.loc.gov/2024021629
LC ebook record available at https://lccn.loc.gov/2024021630

ISBN 978-1-61429-955-4　　ebook ISBN 978-1-61429-979-0

29　28　27　26　25
5　4　3　2　1

Cover design by Gopa & Ted2. Interior design by Tony Lulek.

Printed on acid-free paper that meets the guidelines for permanence and durability of the Production Guidelines for Book Longevity of the Council on Library Resources.

Printed in the United States of America.

Please visit fscus.org.

CONTENTS

Foreword		vii
Introduction		1
1.	The Buddha and His Teachings	17
2.	The Guru	33
3.	Ngöndro: The Preliminary Practices	47
4.	The Right Motivation	59
5.	The First Common Ngöndro: The Shortcomings of Samsara	69
6.	The Second Common Ngöndro: A Precious Human Birth	85
7.	The Third Common Ngöndro: The Impermanence of Life	91
8.	The Fourth Common Ngöndro: The Law of Karma	99
9.	The First Uncommon Ngöndro: Refuge	113
10.	The Second Uncommon Ngöndro: Bodhichitta	147
11.	The Third Uncommon Ngöndro: Vajrasattva Practice	159

VI | THE FUNDAMENTAL PRACTICES

12. The Fourth Uncommon Ngöndro:
    Mandala Offering   165
13. The Fifth Uncommon Ngöndro:
    Guru Yoga   177
14. Dedication   181

Appendix 1. Practice Questions   183

Appendix 2. Mandala Offering Illustrations
    and Figures   199

Notes   213

Index   217

About the Author   227

Foreword

This work, authored by His Holiness the Forty-Second Sakya Trizin in collaboration with the Sakya Tradition organization, presents a clear and complete introduction to the Sakya ngöndro.

This book on the preliminary practices is of great value not only for students in the Sakya lineage, but also for practitioners of all traditions. The preliminary practices are of enormous importance as they constitute the foundation for all further practices.

I am very pleased that his guide is being published, and I am confident that it will greatly help countless practitioners to pursue their path to enlightenment.

With blessings,

The Sakya Trichen
June 27, 2021

INTRODUCTION

According to Buddhism, the true nature of the mind is primordially pure and unstained by defilements or afflictive emotions or obscurations. Another way to express this, in Buddhist terms, is to say that all of us possess buddha nature. At the moment, however, we cannot see the true nature of our minds. They are covered over with two kinds of obscurations: the *obscuration of defilements* and the *obscuration of knowledge*. Because the nature of the mind is primordially pure, we can attain buddhahood by removing these obscurations. This is why we engage in the spiritual practices that were taught by Buddha Shakyamuni and transmitted by his authentic disciples and teachers.

The practices described in this book, called *ngöndro*, or preliminary practices, are authentic, vast, and profound, and they will have enormous benefit for those who are ready to undertake them. It can be said that no one attains buddhahood except through these practices. These are the practices that were followed by all the buddhas to enlightenment and that were taught by Shakyamuni Buddha for the benefit of beings.

The preliminary practices are divided into two sets: the *common* and the *uncommon*. The common preliminary practices are the four thoughts that turn the mind away from samsara and toward the Dharma:

- Remembering the shortcomings of samsara
- Remembering the preciousness of a human rebirth

2 | THE FUNDAMENTAL PRACTICES

- Remembering impermanence
- Remembering the law of karma

These thoughts are essential for motivating us to follow the path all the way to complete enlightenment. They will help us practice Dharma without any delay, with a strong sense of renunciation, and with profound effect. We don't "finish" thinking about these four thoughts and then set them aside, like how one finishes the first grade and then moves on to the second grade. These thoughts will accompany us all the way to buddhahood. They are called *common* because they correspond to Buddhist teachings common to the Hinayana and the Mahayana; the order of presentation of these four can vary, but the meditations remain the same.

The *uncommon* preliminary practices are five: refuge, bodhichitta, Vajrasattva practice, mandala offering, and guru yoga. These practices correspond more particularly to the Mahayana and the Vajrayana. The uncommon preliminaries represent an indispensable practice on the path to enlightenment. In traditions such as the Sakya school's Lamdré tradition, these preliminaries embody four key qualities: the unwavering flow of essential empowerment, unbroken blessing lineage, organized levels of oral instruction, and the ability to fulfill devotional aspirations. The initial step of going for refuge is paramount, serving as the foundation of all Dharma and distinguishing Buddhists from non-Buddhists. By seeking refuge, one enters the direct guidance of the Triple Gem— the Buddha, Dharma, and Sangha. Progressing toward the higher path of seeking buddhahood for all sentient beings requires the cultivation of *bodhichitta*, the enlightened mind, as personal happiness poses a significant obstacle to enlightenment. Clearing negative karma and obscurations through practices like Vajrasattva purification is essential, alongside accumulating merit through practices like mandala offering. In Vajrayana practices, the guru plays a pivotal role, facilitating the realization of the nature of mind. Thus, these uncommon preliminaries serve as the fundamental groundwork for buddhahood.

Given the profound importance of both common and uncommon preliminaries on the path to buddhahood, I will be sharing insights on these topics in this book. Even for those not yet aspiring for liberation or buddhahood, many aspects discussed here offer valuable insights for leading a happier life, as Buddhism is ultimately a way of life. While some of the uncommon preliminaries of the Sakya school require prerequisite teachings from qualified teachers and may not be suitable for public dissemination, the content covered in this book is accessible to all, and some parts can even be practiced independently. Practical instructions are provided to support your practice, along with common questions related to ngöndro and general Dharma practice in the appendix, addressing concerns you may have. Don't be deterred by technical details or Buddhist terminology; this book aims to inspire and encourage everyone, from beginners to seasoned practitioners, and even those yet to embark on the Buddhist path. It's important to note that one doesn't need to be skilled to begin practice; Dharma practice itself is what helps us improve. While it may seem daunting at first, taking the first step makes subsequent steps easier. Remember, practice makes perfect.

Throughout the exploration of these preliminary practices, my aspiration is that you will also develop a deeper understanding of what Dharma practice truly encompasses and how we can authentically engage in it. May you come to appreciate its profound significance and experience the transformative benefits it offers for both ourselves and all sentient beings.

All the authentic Buddhist teachings that we study and practice today—whether they are Hinayana, Mahayana, or Vajrayana—were taught by Shakyamuni Buddha, the fourth of one thousand buddhas that will manifest in our fortunate eon.[1] His teachings were transmitted in a pure, unbroken lineage that began with his original disciples, who gathered in councils to recite the different discourses they had memorized after hearing the Buddha speak them. In this way, they preserved the teachings of Buddha and transmitted them to others. These discourses, called *sutras*, were later preserved in written form. All the major schools of Buddhism acknowledge this history of transmission and rely on it for the authenticity of the teachings.

In addition to the sutras, we are fortunate in the Tibetan tradition to have received the texts and teachings of the *tantras*, which form the basis of the Vajrayana, which we will be exploring more in depth in this book.

4 | THE FUNDAMENTAL PRACTICES

Like the sutras, the tantras were taught by the Buddha, though they were kept and practiced in secret for hundreds of years. The teachings of the Vajrayana have also been transmitted from teacher to disciple in unbroken lineages that carefully preserve the authenticity of the teachings.

The teaching transmissions and the practice lineages of the Sakya have preserved the essential teachings of the sutras and tantras in a pure form and transmitted their blessings. These transmissions and lineages are like the channels through which the liberating waters of the authentic Buddhadharma, or Buddha's teaching, flows. Because studying the great teachers inspires confidence in the teachings and is a source of blessing, the history of the Sakya school will be briefly described here. The great masters of the Sakya can stand as examples and as sources of blessing for all practitioners of the Dharma.

THE EARLY PERIOD AND THE KHÖN CLAN

Buddhism entered Tibet in two diffusions. The first was during the reign of the Tibetan king Trisong Detsen (ca. 740–98 CE), when the great abbot Shantarakshita (725–88) was invited from India and began building Buddhist temples and monasteries. Shantarakshita encountered resistance from local divinities and spirits who, by generating storms, lightning, and other forces, destroyed the structures built under Shantarakshita's guidance. Shantarakshita was unable to tame these spirits himself, so he invited Guru Padmasambhava to accomplish this. Thanks to his clairvoyance, Padmasambhava already knew that he was needed there and, unbeknown to Shantarakshita, had already set out on the journey from India to Tibet; Shantarakshita's messengers met him halfway. Guru Padmasambhava was a powerful practitioner who was able to subdue the spirits that hindered the spread of the Dharma in Tibet, exacting from them a pledge to become Dharma protectors.

Among the disciples of Padmasambhava and Shantarakshita were several members of the Khön clan, the family that would later become the progenitors of the Sakya order of Tibetan Buddhism. Even today, the position called Sakya Trizin (Sakya Throne Holder), the head of the Sakya order, is held by descendants of the Khön family. According to legend, the Khöns were descended from celestial beings who had come down from the sky to the mountains of Tibet in ancient times before written records. Although most of them returned to their heavenly realm, one of them stayed in Tibet and established a hereditary lineage. At that time, Buddhism did not exist in Tibet. Until the time of Shantarakshita and Padmasambhava, when the Khöns converted to Buddhism, they were Bönpos, or followers of the autochthonous religion of Tibet called Bön.

In addition to his work building temples and monasteries, Shantarakshita introduced the full monastic ordination to Tibet. Initially, he ordained just a small group of seven Tibetans as a trial. This group consisted of three old men, three young men, and one middle-aged man. One of the three young men was a Khön. In the same period, another Khön, named Nagendrarakshita, or Khön Lui Wangpo Sungwa in Tibetan, translated Dharma from Sanskrit to Tibetan. He and his younger brother Dorjé Rinchen, who was a householder, received an enormous number of important empowerments and teachings from Guru Padmasambhava. Both of them attained high realization.

Having converted to Buddhism in this way, the Khöns were practitioners of the Nyingma lineage from that time onward for about thirteen generations. *Nyingma* means "old" school, in contrast to the new schools that arose later during the second diffusion of Buddhism into Tibet.

THE SECOND DIFFUSION

The second diffusion of Buddhism to Tibet began in the middle of the tenth century. This was an exciting period for Buddhism in the Himalayan regions, with many great Indian translators and teachers making the epic journey over the mountains. The teachings and translations of the second diffusion produced the *Sarma* schools, the new schools of Dharma in Tibet. The Sakya school is a jewel of the Sarma; its founding was one of the outcomes of the second diffusion.

This diffusion began during the reign of Yeshé Ö (ca. 947–1019), the king of Gugé—a kingdom in western Tibet in what is now called the Ngari Prefecture. He sent twenty-one Tibetans to the Kashmir region of India to study Sanskrit, in addition to Buddhist scriptures, Indian logic,

6 | THE FUNDAMENTAL PRACTICES

language arts, and medicine. Yeshé Ö was a devout Buddhist. He later abdicated the throne to become a lama, which is why he is sometimes called Lha Lama Yeshé Ö.

Nineteen of the twenty-one scholars died on their journey from disease, the climate, and other causes. The two who survived were Rinchen Sangpo (958–1055) and Drakjor Sherab, who is also known as Ngok Lekpai Sherab. Rinchen Sangpo became one of the greatest scholar-monks of his time. He was a pioneer of the extraordinary translation activities for which the second diffusion is known. He made two separate trips to India, where he studied at Vikramashila, the great monastery and university.

His companion from this first seminal journey, Ngok Lekpai Sherab, had a nephew named Ngok Loden Sherab (b. 1059). In 1076, this nephew participated in a conference devoted to the Dharma sponsored by one of Yeshé Ö's successors, King Tsedé of Gugé. The conference was attended by some of the most important Tibetan teachers of the time, and it also included sages from Kashmir and other regions of India. An important outcome of the meeting was a commitment to produce new, accurate translations of the Buddhist scriptures in the Tibetan language. In order to fulfill this mission, Loden Sherab set out with a group of others to Kashmir to study Sanskrit—just as his uncle had done before him. This time, they were a group of six, and they all became accomplished and famous translators. Among them were Lotsawa Tsen Khawoché, Khyungpo Chötsön, Ra Lotsawa Dorjé Drakpa, and Nyen Lotsawa.

Prior to this, however, there was another mission that had been sent from Gugé to India. Yeshé Ö's nephew and immediate successor to the throne, Jangchup Ö, sent a group in 1037 headed by Naktso Lotsawa Tsultrim Gyalwa (1011–64). Their aim was to convince the very famous scholar Atisha (982–1054) to come to Tibet. Because Atisha was one of the most revered figures of the era, this was a major "ask." However, Atisha had already spent twelve years in Sumatra spreading the Dharma there, both Mahayana and Vajrayana, so he was known to be a dedicated missionary of Buddhism. Atisha agreed to come to Tibet, and he arrived in Gugé in 1040. His most influential work, *Lamp for the Path to Enlightenment*, was composed there, in the monastery of Tholing, the capital city of Gugé.

Drokmi Lotsawa: Bringing the Lamdré to Tibet

Drokmi Shakya Yeshé (992–1072), also called Drokmi Lotsawa, lived in this time of renewal and flourishing of the Dharma. Drokmi is important because, thanks to yet another mission to India to study and receive texts and transmissions, he transmitted the precious Lamdré to Tibet. The Lamdré, originating in the teachings of the ninth-century *mahasiddha* Virupa, is the most important system of teachings and practice for the Sakya. Lamdré, meaning "Path and the Result," is the foremost teaching in the Sakya tradition, passed down from Vajradhara through Mahasiddha Virupa. It comprises two parts: the *Triple Vision*, elucidating Sutrayana, and the *Triple Tantra*, expounding the esoteric Hevajra teaching. Inspired by the Dharma activity of the great teachers and translators of the era, Drokmi Shakya Yeshé traveled to India and Nepal. He lived in India for many years, where he mastered Sanskrit and studied epistemology or logic, language arts, astrology, and tantric systems. One of the famous translators, there are about seventy Tibetan translations of tantric texts attributed to him.

On his first journey, Drokmi stayed for one year in Nepal. There, he met the teacher named Shantabhadra, from whom he received teachings on the *Hevajra, Samvara, Guhyasamaja, Yamantaka,* and *Mahamaya* tantras. After this, Drokmi traveled to India, stopping at Bodhgaya along the way. In India, he studied for eighteen years at the monastery and university called Vikramashila. He was fortunate to receive teachings from many masters. Of special interest for the Sakya, he studied the *Hevajra* and *Samvara* tantras and the Prajnaparamita, or "Perfection of Wisdom," with Shantipa.

A master from Vikramashila named Viravajra, also called Prajnendraruchi, introduced Drokmi to the Lamdré system. Viravajra taught Drokmi the root tantra of *Hevajra* and its two explanatory tantras, called the *Vajrapanjara* and *Samputa*. Altogether, while he was in India, Drokmi received the transmissions of about eighty important tantras, making him one of the most accomplished tantric teachers of his era.

Back in Tibet, Drokmi stayed at a hermitage in Mugulung, where a monastic university had arisen. Drokmi became a celebrated teacher with many students, teaching masters like the great Marpa Chökyi Lodrö

8 | THE FUNDAMENTAL PRACTICES

(1012–97). One day, the Indian master Gayadhara (994–1043), who had received the Lamdré from Avadhutipa in India, arrived at Mugulung. Unable to stay because of a prior commitment, the two men made arrangements to meet in the future. Two years later, Gayadhara returned to Mugulung and accomplished the transmission of the complete Lamdré, including commentaries, to Drokmi over a period of three years.

Drokmi Lotsawa is thus the font of the Lamdré teachings in Tibet. He transmitted them to Khön Könchok Gyalpo (1034–1102), who built Sakya Monastery in 1070, and the monastery's founding is understood to formally mark the beginning of the Sakya order.

DROKMI AND THE KHÖNS

During the time of Drokmi, there were two Khön brothers named Khön Sherab Tsultrim and Khön Könchok Gyalpo who had developed concerns that the long-held practices of the Khöns, the Nyingma practices that they had performed since the time of the first diffusion of Buddhism into Tibet, were no longer effective. They believed that this was so because the pledges were not being upheld—in particular, the pledge to secrecy. The brothers set out to find a teacher for the new transmissions, and this is how they came into contact with Drokmi Lotsawa. Thus, they became firmly established in the transmissions of the new diffusion and went on to found Sakya Monastery.

The precipitating event for the Khöns' break with the old systems and their eventual establishment of the Sakya order came when Khön Könchok Gyalpo, the younger brother, attended a large public gathering with many ritual dances. When he came home, he told his older brother that he enjoyed the entertainment very much, but the most impressive performance he saw was a sacred dance performed by twenty-eight yogis. He asked his brother whether it was appropriate for the dancers to display their ritual in public, and Khön Sherab Tsultrim answered that it was not right that the sacred dances should be performed in front of an audience; they should only be performed in secluded places and with a small number of people.

Sherab Tsultrim told his brother that although he himself was old and not able to learn new things, Könchok Gyalpo was both young and bright. Sherab Tsultrim instructed him to seek out the new teachings, which were said to be advanced and efficacious. Under his brother's direction, Könchok Gyalpo sealed up his collection of old ritual materials inside a stupa, as they had decided not to practice them anymore. Out of respect, this was deemed the appropriate way to seal them, rather than disposing of them elsewhere. He then began to seek out the Vajrayana transmissions that had recently arrived.

First he studied with a translator named Khyin Lotsawa, and later he requested teachings from Drokmi. Within just a few years of Drokmi's death, Könchok Gyalpo built the famous Sakya Monastery and founded the glorious Sakya order, of which he is recognized as the first throne holder, or Sakya Trizin.

Sakya Monastery

Sakya Monastery is situated in an area named Sakya near Shigatse in Tibet. The nearby Ponpori Mountain was distinguished for its deposits of white or gray earth in formations that appeared in the shape of a lion. The name *Sakya* means "gray earth" in Tibetan.

There are three accounts of special signs that indicated the importance Sakya would have for the flourishing of Buddhist teachings in Tibet and beyond. First, Guru Padmasambhava blessed the Sakya land and erected stupas there in the eighth century. He also prophesied that a major monastery would be built there, which would cause the teachings of the Buddha to flourish in all directions. This was hundreds of years before the Sakya school was established. Second, when Atisha once passed by the land of Sakya, he prostrated and told his attendant that he could see the syllable *hrih* (ཧྲཱིཿ), seven *dhi* (དྷཱིཿ) syllables, and one *hum* (ཧཱུྃ) on the mountainside. This meant, he said, that an emanation of Avalokiteshvara, seven emanations of Manjushri, and an emanation of Vajrapani would all arise here. He added that there would also be many more emanations of these three bodhisattvas who would benefit all sentient beings.

The third sign occurred during the life of Sachen Kunga Nyingpo (1092–1158), the third throne holder of Sakya and one of the five founders of the lineage. Sachen fell seriously ill at one point in late life, and he

10 | THE FUNDAMENTAL PRACTICES

required very powerful medicine. As a result, he forgot most of the Lamdré teachings that he had studied and memorized. Because the teacher from whom he had received them, Shangtön Chöbar (1053–1135), had already passed away, it would have been nearly impossible for him to receive the teachings again. At his age, making the journey to India to receive them from another master was unthinkable. So Sachen Kunga Nyingpo prayed earnestly to his guru, and as he did this, he started remembering the teachings. He prayed more, and his guru appeared as if in person and bestowed the teachings on him again. He was able to remember nearly all that was lost. Still, he continued to pray. One day, Mahasiddha Virupa appeared and, leaning toward a circle of gray earth, his body covered the entire Sakya Valley. Virupa then announced that the site of Sakya belonged to him.

THE EARLY FLOURISHING OF SAKYA

The early years of the Sakya order correspond to the period of the Five Founders: Sachen Kunga Nyingpo, Lopön Sönam Tsemo (1142–82), Jetsun Drakpa Gyaltsen (1147–1216), Sakya Pandita (1182–1251), and Drogön Chögyal Phakpa (1235–80). Khön Könchok Gyalpo, who received Lamdré teachings from Drokmi and founded the monastery at Sakya, was the father of Sachen Kunga Nyingpo. Sachen in turn received the famous mind-training teaching known as *Parting from the Four Attachments* directly from Manjushri when he was only twelve years old.

The twelfth century was another exciting time for the Dharma in Tibet. In this period, great teachers like Milarepa and Sachen Kunga Nyingpo traveled the country and could sometimes be found teaching in the same area. Sachen received the Lamdré from Shangtön Chöbar, a disciple of Seton Kunrik who was himself a disciple of Drokmi. Sachen also received the Lamdré and many blessings directly from Mahasiddha Virupa in a sequence of visions. His sons, Lopön Sönam Tsemo, called the master of the five sciences, and Jetsun Drakpa Gyaltsen both held the throne of Sakya. They are counted as the second and third of the Five Founders.

Sakya Pandita was the fourth of the Five Founders and the son of Drakpa Gyaltsen's nephew, Palchen Öpo. He was one of Tibet's greatest luminaries, and his influence on the Dharma in Tibet and on Tibetan culture and society is difficult to overstate. He was a scholar, translator, poet, and politician. Some of his writings, like *A Precious Treasury of Elegant Sayings*, the *Treatise Distinguishing the Three Vows*, and the *Treasury of Valid Cognition*, are classics of Tibetan scholarship and literature. The *Treasury of Valid Cognition* was the only book written in Tibetan that is known to have been translated into Sanskrit and circulated in India.

Sakya Pandita's exceptional skill as a spiritual and political leader shaped Tibetan history and culture in lasting ways. His writings—and his example—inspired centuries of Tibetan literature, philosophy, and medicine. Sakya Pandita negotiated with the Mongols, who were then expanding their rule, and his diplomacy saved Tibet from experiencing a violent invasion and established an important role for Tibet within the Mongol Empire.

Sakya Pandita's nephew, Drogön Chögyal Phakpa (1235–80), succeeded him as the throne holder of Sakya. Phakpa became the *dishi*, or imperial preceptor, to the Mongol emperor Kublai Khan in 1260, a position that gave him—and his successors—both spiritual and temporal leadership over all of Tibet. As a result, Tibet was united under one ruler for the first time in the three hundred years since the king Langdarma ruled over a since-dissolved Tibetan empire. The concept of the dishi—a position that combined religious and political authority—prefigured Tibet's unique Dalai Lama system that would emerge centuries later. Chögyal Phakpa spread the Dharma widely in his travels across the Mongol Empire, not only by giving teachings, but by ordaining many thousands of monks. Among them were Hans, Koreans, Indians, Uyghurs, and more.

During the years he lived at the Mongol court of Kublai Khan, Chögyal Phakpa spearheaded political reforms to benefit living beings. He also innovated a Mongolian script and, under his direction, many Buddhist scriptures were translated into Mongolian.

Many later saints and masters arose in the Sakya order. A traditional grouping of six Sakya luminaries is known as the Six Ornaments of Tibet. They are Yaktön Sangye Pal and Rongtön Sheja Künrig, famous for their mastery of the sutras; Ngorchen Kunga Sangpo and Songpa Kunga Namgyal, famous for their mastery of the tantras; and Gorampa

12 | THE FUNDAMENTAL PRACTICES

Sönam Sengé and Shakya Chokden, famous for their mastery of both. Gorampa Sönam Sengé introduced the formal study of logic into the Sakya monastic tradition. His explanation of the Madhyamaka philosophy of Nagarjuna is foundational for the Sakya understanding of the view. He has been influential among the Kagyü and Nyingma, too.

THE SAKYA TEACHINGS

The Sakya school follows the complete Buddhist teaching of sutras, tantras, and the outer sciences. The Sakya teachings are characterized by their descent from the four great translators: Drokmi Lotsawa, Bari Lotsawa Rinchen Drakpa (1040–1111), Mal Lotsawa Lodrö Drakpa (ca. eleventh century), and Lotsawa Rinchen Sangpo (958–1055).

The Sakya are masters of many important sutra and tantra teachings and lineages. These include, among others, the Yangdak Heruka and Vajrakilaya practices of Padmasambhava, the Lamdré of Virupa, the transmission of Guhyasamaja and Chakrasamvara from Mal Lotsawa, and the Madhyamaka and pramana teachings of Ngok Lotsawa.

As already noted, the most important teaching of the Sakya is the Lamdré, an extensive system derived from the *Hevajra* root tantra and the pith instructions of the mahasidda Virupa. The Lamdré is a systematic teaching of the entire Buddhist path. It presents the essence of the Buddhist Tripitaka, or "Three Baskets" of teachings: the Vinaya, or instructions on ethics and discipline; the Sutra Pitaka, or discourses of the Buddha; and the Abhidharma, which are teachings on psychology, cosmology, and metaphysics. A gradual system of learning and yogas, it coordinates both sutra and tantra, and the teachings of the Lamdré have been passed down in an unbroken line of transmission since the time of Virupa in India. The body of Lamdré scriptures, commentaries, and additional teachings has grown over the centuries so that today it comprises thirty large volumes. Key to the Lamdré is its view of the non-differentiation of samsara and nirvana, a framework for realizing perfect enlightenment.

Other important teachings held by the Sakya and popular today among followers are the *Eleven Yogas of Vajrayogini* according to the

Naropa tradition, the Thirteen Golden Dharmas, and the pith instruction called *Parting from the Four Attachments*.

SAKYA SUBSCHOOLS

Over time, subschools emerged within the Sakya. The Ngor lineage is associated with Ngor Monastery, founded in 1429 by Ngorchen Kunga Sangpo (1382–1450), one of the luminaries of the Sakya tradition. It is also called Ngor Ewam Chöden and is the monastery second in importance after Sakya Monastery. First located in the Ü-Tsang region of central Tibet, Ngor Monastery relocated to Manduwala, India, in 1959 under the guidance of its abbot, His Eminence Luding Khenchen Rinpoche. Like Sakya Monastery, the original Ngor Monastery in Tibet was famous for its ancient library of Sanskrit texts. It was also home to a collection of important fifteenth-century Newari *thangka* paintings, some of which are now in major museums around the world. Ngor Monastery became the major center for monastic and tantric training among the Sakya. It has historically conducted an important annual Lamdré teaching, and it is famous for the annual Drubchot Vajrayana rituals. The Ngor subschool refers to the teachings and transmissions associated with Ngorchen Kunga Sangpo, Ngor Monastery, and successive masters in this lineage like Könchok Lhundrup, Thartsé Namkha Palsang, and Drubkhang Palden Dhöndup.

The Tsarpa subschool was founded by Tsarchen Losal Gyatso (1502–56) with the establishment of the monastery called Dar Drongmoché in Lhartsé, Tsang. It is known as the Whispered Lineage of Tsar and includes the secret teachings of Mahakala, Vajrayogini, and others. The cycle of teachings called the Thirteen Golden Dharmas is associated with Tsarpa. The subschools of Ngor and Tsar have flourished into the present day. A lesser-known subschool called Dzongpa has recently been revitalized. It was founded by Ngakchang Sungkyi Palwa (1306–89), a disciple of Lama Dampa. It is associated with the Dzongchung palace at Sakya Monastery and with Gongkar Chödé, a monastery founded in 1464.

The subschools called Jonang, Buluk, and Bodong have ceased to exist as separate traditions, but their contributions remain in the form of treatises, commentaries, and other writings. Some of them have had

14 | THE FUNDAMENTAL PRACTICES

a profound influence on the course of Tibetan Buddhism. For example, the Jonang school, established by Dölpopa Sherab Gyaltsen, a thirteenth-century Sakya monk, stands out as the only school that emphasizes this unique doctrine and upholds its lineage of Shentong Madhyamaka philosophy. This philosophy is recognized as the highest view by many of the most realized Tibetan masters. The *Kalachakra Tantra* is considered the most comprehensive and effective system within Tibetan Buddhism; the Jonang tradition is unique in holding the entire Kalachakra system, which includes the distinctive completion practice known as the six *vajra* yogas.

The Sakya were involved in the *rimé* movement in the nineteenth and twentieth centuries, a lively effort to create an ecumenical awareness among the different Buddhist traditions of Tibet by sharing, collecting, and synthesizing teachings. Luminaries like Jamyang Khyentsé Wangpo, Loter Wangpo, Ngawang Lekpa, and Dezhung Rinpoche were prominent figures in this movement.

The Sakya Tradition in the Modern World

Beginning in the 1950s, the Sakya order began to flourish around the world under the skillful leadership of the Forty-First Sakya Trizin, Ngawang Kunga, born in 1945. At the age of six, he was designated the throne holder of Sakya by His Holiness the Dalai Lama in Lhasa, but the official three-day enthronement ceremony only occurred in 1959. Shortly thereafter, however, he left Tibet for Sikkim and later, India. Although he was still a boy when he departed Tibet, he already held a great reputation for the depth of his Dharma practice.

The Forty-First Sakya Trizin was the longest-serving Sakya Trizin in Sakya history. He retired from the position in 2017, and he continues to teach. Now known as His Holiness Kyabgon Gongma Trichen Rinpoche (the Sakya Trichen), he is a renowned teacher of Tibetan Buddhism respected for the clarity of his teachings.

In 2014, a new succession system was instituted for the Sakya Trizins. By mutual agreement between the Dolma Phodrang and the Phuntsok Phodrang, members of each *phodrang*, or palace, will hold the position of Sakya Trizin for three years, alternating between phodrangs. The first

Sakya Trizin under the new system was me, as the Forty-Second Sakya Trizin, and I was succeeded by my younger brother, the Forty-Third Sakya Trizin, Gyana Vajra Rinpoche, in 2022.

Since the 1950s—especially during the long and eventful period of the Forty-First Sakya Trizin's wise reign—the Sakya order has flourished, aptly fulfilling the prophecies Padmasambhava and Atisha made about Sakya. The ancient Sakya Monastery was reestablished in India as the Sakya Centre in 1964. The Sakya Centre is the main seat of the Sakya order, and the personal monastery of the throne holders of the Sakya. The two subsects, Ngor and Tsar, are also thriving. In addition to the colleges and monasteries that were founded in India and Nepal, the Sakya order is active in North and South America, Asia, and Europe with numerous temples, retreat centers, and Dharma centers.

In the spirit of this flowering of the Sakya teachings around the globe, this book of ngöndro instructions is offered as a precious guide to attaining liberation from suffering and perfect enlightenment. The following chapters present the ngöndro in an authentic, traditional manner according to the Sakya school. They also give advice that might be helpful for contemporary lay practitioners. May it benefit all beings.

CHAPTER 1
THE BUDDHA AND HIS TEACHINGS

All Buddhist traditions derive from the teachings of Buddha Shakyamuni. About two thousand five hundred years ago, the great Buddha Shakyamuni descended from the heavenly realm of Tushita and entered the womb of Queen Mayadevi. At that time, Queen Mayadevi dreamed that a white elephant with six tusks entered into her body. Throughout the pregnancy and during labor Queen Mayadevi experienced no pain, only bliss.

Buddha Shakyamuni took birth in Lumbini as Prince Siddhartha, the son of King Suddhodana and Queen Mayadevi of the Kapilavastu kingdom. This birth was the first, most important noble activity of the Buddha.

As soon as Prince Siddhartha was born in the Lumbini garden, he took seven steps. At each step, a lotus appeared on the ground, and the infant prince said, "I am the most excellent being of this world." At the same time that Prince Siddhartha was born many auspicious and wondrous signs appeared, including the birth of noble sons to many other kings. This was a strong indication of Prince Siddhartha's extraordinary nature. Thereafter the child prince continued to demonstrate his excellent qualities. At the royal ceremony for baby Siddhartha, seers predicted he could become either a buddha or a wheel-turning monarch, indicating great potential for Kapilavastu's expansion under his secular leadership. Determined to protect Siddhartha from discomfort, King

18 | THE FUNDAMENTAL PRACTICES

Suddhodhana ordered guards to shield him from any unpleasantness, decreeing that no aged, sick, or sad people be near the prince.

Siddhartha enjoyed a seemingly perfect life with his beloved wife, Princess Yashodara. However, as time passed, Siddhartha matured, and his father, King Suddhodana, sought to involve him more in the affairs of the kingdom. Siddhartha expressed a desire to tour the kingdom to better understand his future role as king. Although granted permission by his father, Prince Siddhartha made his first venture outside the palace at the age of twenty-nine, accompanied by his charioteer Channa. Siddhartha's tour was carefully orchestrated to shield him from any potential disturbances or unpleasant sights, in line with the prophecy concerning his destiny. During this journey, he came across an elderly person, which was his first encounter with the effects of aging. Witnessing this sight for the first time in his life, Siddhartha was deeply shocked. Suddenly, he felt the physical pain and psychological suffering associated with old age, not only within himself but also in those he loved and cared for.

During his second excursion outside the palace, Siddhartha encountered a sick person on the city streets. Immediately he felt the physical and mental distress the sick man was experiencing. He actually felt that suffering himself and became determined to find a solution for such suffering. He considered the possibility of studying medicine. Soon he realized that medicine could cure physical illness, but could never end suffering altogether.

The prince wondered if there were a way to eliminate all suffering. Once again, he left the palace. On this excursion he saw a corpse, and immediately experienced the suffering of death and dying himself.

Those three encounters caused the young prince to reflect, "Just being a prince with a magnificent kingdom does not suffice to comfort and benefit all living beings." This contemplation deepened when he encountered a *shramana*, a non-Buddhist monk, immersed in profound meditation. The peaceful scene briefly eased his inner turmoil and ignited his curiosity, prompting him to ponder whether these seekers of truth held the solution to the sufferings he witnessed. For that reason, Siddhartha renounced his kingdom and left the palace in search of the truth and a path to freedom from suffering.

Subsequently, after years of spiritual practice, he sat meditating under the Bodhi Tree. Many evil spirits, or *maras*, tried to disrupt his meditation, attacking him with weapons and emanating in front of him as beautiful dancing girls. With the power of his loving-kindness and compassion, Siddhartha defeated all these evil beings, transforming the hail of harmful weapons into a shower of flowers. All that was possible by the power of practicing loving-kindness, compassion, and bodhichitta.

THE PURPOSE AND GOAL OF BUDDHIST TEACHINGS

Generally speaking, the Buddha's teachings are methods for training the mind. By practicing the Buddha's teachings, we can tame, subdue, and control the mind; then we can experience genuine happiness. The *Dhammapada* says,

> To avoid all evil, and to cleanse one's mind—this is the teaching of the Buddha.[2]

Just as a skillful doctor prescribes different medicines to cure various diseases, in order to accommodate the various mentalities of living beings, the Buddha turned the wheel of Dharma to impart an immense number and variety of different teachings. The many different teachings the Buddha bestowed were designed to suit our different personalities. His teachings are methods, or paths, that lead us from dissatisfaction and suffering toward temporary and final happiness. So, we should regard the Buddha as a skillful doctor and his teachings as medicine. We should regard sentient beings and ourselves as patients, and our defilements and negative thoughts as illness. Receiving and practicing Dharma teachings are like seeking a doctor's advice and then following it. With these considerations in mind, we can properly practice the Buddhadharma.

On the other hand, if a patient merely listens to the doctor's advice but does not follow it, the patient's illness will not be cured. The patient must follow the doctor's advice, for example, by taking the prescribed medicine at the right dosage, by following a prescribed diet, or by abandoning harmful diets or medicines. Only by following a doctor's advice can a patient cure their own sickness.

20 | THE FUNDAMENTAL PRACTICES

Accordingly, listening to Dharma teachings is beneficial but alone it is not enough. After listening to teachings, we must follow them. If we follow them or put those teachings into action, then we can make an impact; we can change our own minds. We can make our minds more peaceful. Once we control our minds, we can control our physical and verbal activity.

It is crucial that each of us practice the Dharma to see change in ourselves; this change doesn't come from elsewhere. The practice of Dharma involves training the mind, and this training can only be accomplished by us. Neither someone else nor even the Buddha can train our minds for us. If, for example, a wealthy patient sponsors the medical care of poorer patients, those poorer patients are helped. However, sickness will not be cured by the wealthy patient's generosity alone; each patient will still have to take their own medicine. Only then can each patient cure his or her illness.

THE WHEEL OF DHARMA AND THE THREE YANAS

The Buddha gave an enormous number of teachings to suit the different mentalities of followers. We say he gave eighty-four thousand teachings, but this is only the number that was heard by the disciple Ananda; there were other teachings he did not hear. The Buddha's teachings are categorized under the *three turnings of the wheel of Dharma*. The first turning is comprised of his discourses on personal liberation, such as the teaching on the four noble truths. The second turning consists of teachings on emptiness, the ultimate view. We can also say that teachings of the first turning are interpretive, and those of the second turning are definitive.

The third turning of the wheel of Dharma, which is the Vajrayana, is *both* interpretive and definitive. There are different explanations for this according to the various schools or traditions of Buddhism. Some Buddhist schools do not accept that there were three turnings of the wheel. Vaibhashika, for example, is a school that did not accept the second and the third turnings of the wheel. Also, within the Paramitayana, or Perfection Vehicle, there are different ways of understanding the third turning of the wheel of Dharma. All Tibetan Buddhist schools accept that there were three turnings of the wheel of Dharma, but their explanations of these three turnings are not identical. In the Sakya tradition, we understand the third turning of the wheel of Dharma to be both clarifying and distinguishing, meaning it contains both interpretative and definitive teachings.

Another way to talk about the three turnings of the wheel of Dharma is in terms of the three *yanas*. *Yana* is a Sanskrit term usually translated as "vehicle," but it also means "the path" and "the result." The distinction of vehicles or conveyances is just one among several classification schemes applied to the Buddha's teachings. The primary distinction is that of the Lesser Vehicle, also known as Shravakayana, the Hearer Vehicle—in recognition of the outcome of following this path, where followers become "hearers"[3]—and the Great Vehicle, or Mahayana. Lesser Vehicle here loosely corresponds to the Pali-language tradition of Buddhist scriptures, and Great Vehicle corresponds more or less to the Sanskrit-language traditions. We should understand that such names do not imply any disrespect for practitioners of the Lesser Vehicle, nor are they supposed to boost the pride of practitioners of the Great Vehicle. All are followers of the Buddha. The distinction of Great and Lesser Vehicles is just one way of classifying Buddha's teachings according to paths and results. It's important to note that all the vehicles were taught by the Buddha himself. While ordinary human beings may perceive some vehicles as superior and others as inferior, this distinction is often influenced by our own negative thoughts and emotions. In reality, all vehicles were taught by the Buddha as methods to lead sentient beings from suffering to happiness, both temporary and ultimate. When we delve into the unique characteristics of each vehicle, we can discern their differences without assigning superiority or inferiority based on mundane thoughts.

Mahayana is a generic term that includes Paramitayana, or Vehicle of Perfections, as well as Vajrayana, which is also called Tantrayana, or Adamantine Vehicle. This understanding is commonly held among scholars. However, in contemporary usage, when people refer to Mahayana, they typically only consider the Paramitayana. Generally speaking, Mahayana practice is based on the attitude of renunciation toward all of samsara, which is common to all the Buddhist schools. It

22 | THE FUNDAMENTAL PRACTICES

is also based on loving-kindness and compassion for all sentient beings, and bodhichitta; bodhichitta is the main essence of all the Mahayana teachings. And the ultimate goal of Mahayana practice is to attain buddhahood. These are the common characteristics of both Paramitayana and Vajrayana. While they share many aspects in common, there are a few special characteristics of the Vajrayana. Generally speaking, the Paramitayana focuses on gradual cultivation of the six *paramitas*, or perfections (see chapter 12), and thus is often referred to as the Causal Vehicle. In contrast, Vajrayana emphasizes the direct realization of the enlightened state as already present within oneself, requiring the removal of obscuration rather than the gradual accumulation of merit; hence it is known as the Resultant Vehicle. There are five other specific characteristics of Vajrayana:

- Within Vajrayana, there are supplementary techniques aimed at understanding the genuine essence of reality. All practices from Paramitayana are incorporated into Vajrayana, alongside unique methods such as the transmission of primordial wisdom during empowerment ceremonies.
- In Vajrayana, there are a greater number of methods available to achieve both temporary and ultimate outcomes. Temporary outcomes encompass aspects such as longevity, wisdom, and wealth. While Paramitayana offers methods for achieving these objectives, Vajrayana introduces additional, specialized approaches. For instance, practitioners in Vajrayana can engage with long-life deities, involving processes such as receiving proper empowerment, undertaking sadhana and retreat practices, participating in fire *pujas*, and more. Similarly, for wisdom cultivation, practitioners can connect with wisdom deities like Manjushri, utilizing methods such as empowerment and retreat practices. Regarding wealth—which should be pursued not for personal gain but for the benefit of all beings—Vajrayana offers practices involving wealth deities such as Jambhala. While Paramitayana primarily focuses on the six paramitas, which are also present in Vajrayana, the latter

places particular emphasis on the two stages of generation and completion.

- Vajrayana offers a more expedient path to achieving buddhahood compared to Paramitayana. While Paramitayana is indeed a straightforward route to buddhahood, Vajrayana is considered even more accessible.
- Vajrayana is regarded as a swifter path to achieving buddhahood. It is believed that with proper practice and under the right conditions, one can attain buddhahood within a single lifetime.
- The Causal Vehicle, Paramitayana, primarily focuses on mental practices, while the Vajrayana places a strong emphasis on physical aspects. In the Paramitayana, virtues like generosity and moral conduct are primarily concerned with the mind and motivation. For instance, generosity in Paramitayana is not solely about alleviating poverty but entails cultivating the altruistic wish to give to all sentient beings unconditionally. Even in the absence of poverty, one can practice generosity as it is rooted in the mind. Conversely, Vajrayana incorporates numerous practices involving the body, such as those centered on the four inner elements.

In short, the Shravakayana, Paramitayana, and Vajrayana are like three different modes of transport: a bicycle, a car, and an airplane. Although they go to the same destination, some are slower and some faster.

VAJRAYANA

The Sanskrit term *Vajrayana* has two parts: *vajra* and *yana*. *Vajra* denotes a buddha's body, speech, and wisdom (Sanskrit: *kayavajra, vagvajra*, and *chittavajra*). In English, I prefer not to use the terms *body, speech*, and *mind* when referring to the Buddha; the Buddha is not characterized by a conventional mind, for example. Instead, the Buddha embodies wisdom. Our conventional mind transforms into wisdom upon attaining buddhahood. The Tibetan term *sem* typically refers to the mind. However, it's important to note that the *alaya* consciousness is distinct from *sem*, or the mind. According to Buddhist teachings, there are eight consciousnesses: the first five pertain to our sense consciousnesses, the sixth is the consciousness of the mind, the seventh encompasses our afflictions or defilements, and the eighth is the alaya consciousness. While both the mind and the alaya consciousness are forms of consciousness, they are not identical. Therefore, in Vajrayana, the term *vajra* signifies the Buddha's body, speech, and wisdom, representing the ultimate fruition, which is none other than buddhahood or the state of Buddha Vajradhara. The term *yana* is commonly translated as "vehicle," but it also carries the meanings of "path" and "result." *Yana* means "the path or way to attain"; hence Vajrayana means "the path to buddhahood." Regarding the origin of the Vajrayana teachings, it is important to know that there are two types of buddhas who give teachings: *sambhogakaya*, the body of enjoyment, and *nirmanakaya*, the body of emanation, buddhas. In the tantra *Chanting the Names of Manjushri* (*Manjushrinamasangiti*), it says that past, present, and future buddhas will give Vajrayana teachings again and again. This is referring to the sambhogakaya buddhas. Sambhogakaya buddhas always give Vajrayana teachings. However, in our eon, in which one thousand buddhas will appear, only the fourth buddha—Shakyamuni Buddha—gives Vajrayana teachings. He did so in a nirmanakaya form.

Why is this so? In his previous life, Shakyamuni Buddha prayed that he would become a buddha in the worst of times, in a degenerate age greatly afflicted by negative emotions. In order to tame such beings, he needed to give them the most excellent teachings. He wanted to give the best methods for gaining enlightenment in such a degenerate time. This is why we believe that only the fourth buddha of this age, Shakyamuni Buddha, has given the Vajrayana teachings in nirmanakaya form to common followers in this world.

Regarding the path, in Vajrayana, the guru introduces the fact that our body, speech, and mind are none other than a buddha's body, speech, and wisdom. Our body, speech, and mind and a buddha's body, speech, and wisdom are based on the same stream or continuum, the alaya, or ground consciousness. So, the guru introduces our true nature to us as being the same as a buddha's nature. Once introduced, the identity of our body, speech, and mind with a buddha's body, speech, and wisdom gradually becomes clearer. Regarding the result, by following the Vajrayana path one reaches the same level of enlightenment as Buddha Vajradhara, or Vajra Holder. In short, the Vajrayana is both the path to attain buddhahood and the result itself; these two are inseparable.

Tibetan Buddhists practice all three yanas: Shravakayana, Paramitayana, and Vajrayana. Primarily, however, Tibetan Buddhism emphasizes the Vajrayana, with some Shravakayana and Paramitayana elements. Practically speaking, when we keep Vajrayana vows, we also need to keep the bodhichitta vow of the Paramitayana and the individual liberation vows, or *pratimoksha* vows, of the Shravakayana, too. This is because the base of any Vajrayana vow is the bodhichitta vow, and the base of the bodhichitta vow is the refuge vow, which is part of the pratimoksha vows. Because we have to keep all these three levels of vows, we practice the teachings of all the three vehicles, although the main emphasis of Tibetan Buddhism is on the Vajrayana path.

Within Tibetan Buddhism, all schools are the same in that they have the same motivation and the same objects of refuge: the Buddha, Dharma, and Sangha. The regard for bodhichitta is the same, and so is the ultimate view, or emptiness, *shunyata*. The two heaps—the accumulation of merit and wisdom—are the same. The five Buddhist paths are the same. And the ultimate result, buddhahood, is the same. The only differences between the schools of Tibetan Buddhism are their distinct lineages and their styles of explanation.

Paramitayana and Vajrayana are both based on wisdom and compassion—that is to say, based on the accumulation of the two heaps of merit and wisdom. However, their approaches to wisdom are a bit different. In Paramitayana, there are five paths: accumulation, application, seeing, meditation, and no more learning. These paths represent the progression of wisdom rather than physical pathways. Advancing along these paths entails deepening one's understanding and realization of wisdom. When traversing the first two of the five paths (the paths of accumulation and application), one can only understand emptiness through one's thoughts and imagination, not through direct nonconceptual wisdom. In Vajrayana, however, one can see emptiness directly on the first two paths. This is like seeing the light of the moon reflected

26 | THE FUNDAMENTAL PRACTICES

in water—you know it is not the moon, but you are still able to see it, rather than only using your imagination or your thoughts. In later stages, such as when a practitioner reaches the first *bhumi*, or level of a bodhisattva, and can see emptiness directly like seeing the real moon in the sky, there is not much difference between Paramitayana and Vajrayana.

Vajrayana methods are called skillful means. Without skillful means, a poison is simply that, poison; it will cause harm. If a person takes that poison, it will cause them pain or even take their life. However, through skillful means, a poison can be transformed into medicine. If the poison is mixed with other things, for example, or if it is used in a small dose, or undergoes some special procedure, the poisonous ingredient can be a medicine that helps people and cures sickness. Similarly, mental afflictions are harmful to us. They are the cause of our suffering, and they bind us to samsara. But through the skillful means of Vajrayana, these mental afflictions can be transformed into the path so that we can gain liberation and even the enlightened state of Vajradhara through them. This is the primary way that Vajrayana is a path of skillful means. Other Vajrayana methods include such things as increasing wisdom through the practice of wisdom deities, prolonging life through the practice of long-life deities, and so on.

In the Vajrayana tradition, we sometimes speak of attainments, or *siddhis* in Sanskrit. This refers to the results that we wish to attain. There are two types of siddhis: common and excellent. Common siddhis vary and include having pacifying, increasing, magnetizing, and wrathful abilities. Excellent siddhi refers to the attainment of the state of Buddha Vajradhara, which is the ultimate attainment.

VAJRAYANA TRANSMISSION

In the Vajrayana tradition, it is essential to receive transmission from an authorized guru before performing Vajrayana practices. For example, if one does not own a parcel of land, to use it one first needs to get permission or authority from the landowner. Similarly, except through empowerment we have no authority or permission to practice the Vajrayana path. In order to practice the Vajrayana path, it is essential to receive the necessary transmissions and empowerments first.

Practically speaking, a Vajrayana empowerment is not just a doorway to enter the Vajrayana path; it is the main practice of the Vajrayana path. Therefore, given that empowerment is most important for all Vajrayana followers, I will briefly explain the different empowerments and initiations according to the Sakya school.

Empowerment

Generally, according to the Sakya tradition, those who have received no previous Vajrayana teaching must, upon entering the Vajrayana path, receive a major empowerment *wang*—or *wangchen* in the Tibetan language (Sanskrit: *abhisheka*), which is the most crucial Vajrayana teaching, typically spanning two days. It is believed to ripen disciples, preparing them for the Vajrayana path. For example, suppose there is fresh land to be converted to cropland. Since the land is uncultivated, the farmer has to prepare it by removing vegetation and stones, to make the soil conducive to growing crops. Likewise, for anyone who has never received any Vajrayana teachings, the first major empowerment given to them is like planting seed in fresh land. The first day involves preliminary rituals like throwing the tooth stick to determine one's attainments and observing significant dreams. If the signs are favorable, the actual empowerment takes place on the second day, starting with entering into the mandala, a symbolic offering of the entire universe, to establish a karmic connection with Vajrayana deities. This is followed by receiving the empowerment itself, such as the Hevajra cause empowerment, which grants practitioners the authority to engage in Vajrayana practices. Without this empowerment, practitioners are not empowered to perform visualizations, recitations, or meditations. Just as cultivating a new farmland requires thorough preparation, receiving the major empowerment involves clearing obstacles and establishing the foundation for spiritual growth. Hevajra, a primary tantric deity meditation in the Sakya school, is an exceptionally powerful method for achieving complete buddhahood. Representing the union of boundless compassion and profound wisdom, the Hevajra cause empowerment, a two-day empowerment of the highest class of the tantra, is bestowed upon those commencing Vajrayana practices within the Sakya tradition, and is often received prior to engaging in the ngöndro practices of the Lamdré tradition.

Moreover, empowerment also serves as permission to practice the Vajrayana teachings. To return to the analogy of the farmland, using someone's land without permission is illegal. To use someone else's farmland, we must secure the owner's permission, which is like receiving an empowerment. If we practiced the Vajrayana teachings without receiving empowerment, we would face negative consequences; no matter how diligently one practiced, it would not yield any results. It would lead us away from the correct path, creating additional obstacles and difficulties in gaining the right understanding and view of the truth. However, by practicing the Vajrayana teachings only after receiving empowerment from a qualified guru, we will be able to gain both temporary and ultimate results, or realizations.

An empowerment is also a method that allows us to plant the seed of buddhahood in our psychophysical aggregates,[4] opening the possibility of attaining buddhahood in this very life. The great Sakya Pandita said there is no Paramitayana practice without bodhichitta, and there is no Vajrayana practice without empowerment. Hence, empowerment is not just a gateway to the Vajrayana path; it is also the main practice of the path. Empowerment is the special Vajrayana method to reach buddhahood in this very life.

Permission

Permission (Tib. *jenang*; Skt. *anumati*) is part of an empowerment, which we commonly refer to as "initiation." It means "permission" or "subsequent permission," and gives one authorization to practice this particular deity for which you have received an initiation. Compared to an empowerment that requires two days to complete, a permission ritual is usually short.

Blessing

A blessing, or *chinlab* in Tibetan (Skt. *adhisthana*), such as the Vajrayogini blessing or guru yoga blessing, is given to enhance our practice. It is like fertilizing the ground, making it so that not much work is required to further improve the condition of the land for growing abundant crops. After receiving an empowerment, receiving a blessing can further enhance our spiritual practice. However, to receive a blessing, one must have already received an empowerment.

Oral transmission

Oral transmission—known as *lung* in Tibetan (Skt. *agama*), and sometimes referred to as reading transmission—is imparted by a teacher who has received the transmission of a text or mantra. This transmission, which can occur without the need for an initiation or empowerment, serves to establish a connection with a text or mantra. In the case of tantric texts, the transmission typically follows the reception of the relevant empowerment. During the transmission, it is essential for students to attentively listen, even if the teacher is reciting the text in Tibetan, Sanskrit, or a language unfamiliar to them, or if they do not fully comprehend the content. By focusing on listening, it plants an imprint on our minds, which is what we refer to as receiving the full blessing.

Instructions

In general, instructions, *tri* in Tibetan, refers to explanations, which serve as elucidations or interpretations. A tri can be applied across a spectrum of teachings, including *sutras*, the discourses of the Buddha; *shastras*, or commentaries; Vajrayana texts, or *sadhanas*; and pith instructions. In the Sakya school, it is common to receive explanations on the sadhanas of deity meditation after students have received the empowerment. This aids them in understanding how to perform that specific practice.

Pith instructions

The collection of Buddhist scriptures in Tibetan translation are known as the Kangyur. The collection of commentaries on the teachings of the Buddha by various masters in Tibetan translation are known as the Tengyur. In these collections, teachings that best explain how to gain

30 | THE FUNDAMENTAL PRACTICES

higher rebirth, liberation, and enlightenment for beginners on the path are known as pith instructions, or *mengak* (Skt. *upadesha*). Pith instruction is usually shared subsequently with students in the correct sequence.

There are different types of pith instructions. For example, *Parting from the Four Attachments* is a pure Perfection Vehicle pith instruction. *Triple Vision*, also commonly known as *The Three Levels of Spiritual Perception* (*Nangsum*), is another type of pith instruction that is a preliminary to a Vajrayana teaching, the Lamdré. Although the *Triple Vision* is a pith instruction on Vajrayana teachings, it belongs to the Perfection Vehicle. The *Triple Tantra* is an uncommon Vajrayana pith instruction. Uncommon Vajrayana pith instructions should never be shared with those who have not received the empowerment of the related teaching. If we practiced the pith instructions without required empowerments, it would do more harm than good.

KEEPING THE VAJRAYANA TEACHINGS SECRET

It is incorrect to practice the Vajrayana teachings or study them from books without receiving the relevant empowerment or without having any guidance, explanation, or teaching from a qualified guru. This is like using someone else's house without permission, which is a punishable offense. If someone attempts to practice Vajrayana teachings or read the Vajrayana teachings in books without first receiving empowerment, they could experience great harm or face severe consequences. Without proper initiation, one might misunderstand or lack sincere faith and devotion to the Vajrayana teachings, and thus criticize the profound and precious teachings. This would give them the opportunity to commit severe unwholesome deeds.

For those who have received the Vajrayana teachings, it is essential to keep the teachings secret and not share with those who have not received empowerment. Disclosing Vajrayana teachings to them will not generate good results. Rather, they will fall down to the lower realms in a future lifetime. For instance, when a homeowner leaves their house, they keep a key in a secret place and do not disclose its whereabouts. This is to avoid the house being invaded by someone who might commit negative deeds in the house. Moreover, if we disclose Vajrayana teachings to the uninitiated, the power of one's blessing or the empowerment will not remain.

The great Sakya Pandita said that no matter how hard we squeeze sand, it will never yield oil. It is not correct for a guru to give Vajrayana teachings to a disciple who has not received the requisite empowerment. Not only will such teachings not yield any great result, but both guru and disciple will face severe consequences. Therefore, it is important to receive empowerments and not disclose Vajrayana teachings to the uninitiated.

Chapter 2
The Guru

The Sanskrit word *guru* means "heavy"—in particular, someone who is heavy with knowledge. It refers to someone who has amassed great knowledge that they can teach to others.

When we fall ill, we need to consult a physician for medical advice and treatment until we recover from our illness. At present, as ordinary beings we are afflicted with the "illness" of our negative emotions and unwholesome actions. To overcome this illness, as patients we must consult the right Dharma teacher, who, like a genuine doctor offering advice and prescriptions, can provide us with Dharma teachings. In this way, we can be free from negative emotions and unwholesome actions.

Today, just as in ancient times, even though it is possible to read Dharma books without depending on a teacher, without one we will not comprehend the genuine and complete sense of the teaching. Dharma is endowed with profound and deep meaning; it cannot be understood only by the words used to express it literally. The Buddha's teachings are generally categorized as provisional or definitive. Provisional teachings cannot be understood only by reading books because they have hidden meanings, which are not apparent without the help of a trained guide.

Without genuine Dharma teachers, we are like blind people walking alone on roads with traffic. We cannot walk alone on the road without prior training, guidance, and help. A guide is essential to help us arrive at the destination. A genuine Dharma teacher is the guide who will

34 | THE FUNDAMENTAL PRACTICES

help us to listen, contemplate, and meditate on the teachings properly. Without the guidance of a teacher, we are unable to know what to adopt and what to abandon. And without relying on a teacher, we will not be able to obtain wisdom. Without wisdom, it is impossible to accomplish results.

At the moment, we do not have the fortune to see Buddha Shakyamuni with our eyes and receive teachings directly from him. Through the guru, however, we can receive the unbroken lineages of the Buddha's teachings. These have been passed down from the Buddha, through the lineage masters, and finally to one's present master. The teacher is the one who passes the Buddha's teachings and blessing to us in our mental process. It is impossible to receive the unbroken lineage of blessing from the Buddha reading Dharma books. This is why we need to depend on a genuine teacher to receive proper teachings and unbroken blessings. Although the sun always radiates heat, using its energy to heat water is not very efficient. However, a solar panel efficiently collects and concentrates the sun's energy. Coupled with a hot water system, it can heat water to scalding temperatures. Without such panels, even if there is sun in the sky and a tank of water sitting in the sun, the water will not get very hot. A genuine teacher is like that solar panel, connecting us with the Buddha.

DIFFERENT TYPES OF DHARMA TEACHERS

All Dharma teachers, generally speaking, are considered gurus. There are teachers of various traditions such as those who bestow the monastic vows, refuge vows, Shravakayana teachings, bodhichitta vows, Mahayana teachings, and so forth. Each teacher has his or her own characteristics that are described in the teachings. Some teachers are excellent masters able to bestow teachings of all the yanas, including the highest yoga tantras in the Vajrayana tradition. Other teachers are qualified to teach Paramitayana teachings but not qualified to give Vajrayana empowerments or teachings. There are still others who can give empowerments but are not able to teach such Paramitayana topics as Madhyamaka philosophy or the Abhidharma. The important thing for a disciple to look for is a qualified master who can teach the specific teachings that they seek, whether Paramitayana or Vajrayana.

In the Vajrayana tradition, there are six types of gurus. There are those who (1) teach and bestow *samaya* commitments or precepts; (2) give verbal transmission of the mantra; (3) give teachings on tantra; (4) bestow pith instructions; (5) bestow empowerments; and (6) explain the ritual, or puja, such as consecration puja, fire puja, and so on. A guru in the Vajrayana tradition is known as a *vajra master*.

It is possible to have many teachers and gurus. In the Vajrayana tradition, *guru* and *root guru* are synonymous; they impart Vajrayana teachings, making them all root gurus or gurus. However, these days, some individuals with multiple gurus tend to designate one of them as their primary and refer to them as their "root guru." But in actuality, they are the same. Most importantly, a guru is the one from whom we have received teachings on the view. For example, the teacher who really introduces the mind to us—in the Sakya tradition, that is the nondifference of samsara and nirvana—is the guru. We would refer to the teacher who directly bestows us with empowerments and pith instructions of the Vajrayana teachings and so on as our root guru. A *lineage guru* is the guru of our guru, and so on. For clarity, I'm introducing a new term, *grand guru*, solely for the purpose of this book: lineage gurus encompass all the gurus tracing back from the original guru who transmitted this specific Vajrayana teaching, extending through successive gurus to our "grand guru" (the guru of our guru), and then finally to our own guru, in an unbroken lineage. We would not call a lineage guru simply "my guru," since that would imply we have directly received teachings from them. A Dharma master who does not have any dharmic relationship with us is not considered our guru because we have not received any teachings from them.

The Guru-Student Relationship

It is essential to find the right teachers, especially in the Vajrayana tradition. Ideally both the guru and the student should examine each other before entering a guru-student relationship. In any case, as students we must examine a potential teacher thoroughly before receiving Vajrayana teachings from them and thus accepting them as our teacher. When you purchase a car, you will spend an incredible amount of time and effort

36 | THE FUNDAMENTAL PRACTICES

to research about the type of car that interests you, comparing the make and model, the price, various features, and so on. Choosing a guru is much more serious than choosing a car. You are not only relying on the guru for the next ten or fifteen years, as you would a car, but for the rest of this life. In fact, the guru will remain your field of refuge and protector for many lives to come, until you attain liberation and perfect enlightenment.

THE QUALITIES AND CHARACTERISTICS OF A QUALIFIED GURU

When you are evaluating a potential teacher, there are several qualities and characteristics to look for based on the teachings you wish to receive. Overall, a Dharma teacher should have good discipline, keep their vows intact, and have knowledge of the teachings they are giving. The teacher should have positive qualities and be endowed with learning, kindness, compassion, bodhichitta, and so forth. The teacher should be able to remove the doubts of listeners. The teacher should also have a sincere motivation to teach. Just giving teachings does not mean a teacher is accumulating great merit, because accumulating great merit depends on motivation. If a teacher teaches to gain wealth, fame, followers, power, and so on, then they will fail to accumulate merit given that they lack the right motivation. Giving teachings under such circumstances will obstruct the teacher's own liberation. We should depend on a teacher who is a good person, free of arrogance, pride, and afflictive emotions.

Teachers of the Vinaya tradition in particular should have pure moral conduct, keeping their Vinaya or pratimoksha vows intact, as well as be knowledgeable of and familiar with the rituals of the Vinaya. He or she should have great compassion toward beings who are ill or suffering, should aspire to help others with the Vinaya teachings, and be capable of giving precious and profound teachings.

Teachers of the Mahayana tradition should have tame minds and be well trained and knowledgeable in the general Mahayana teachings. They should hold the pratimoksha and bodhisattva vows and the general Mahayana precepts as being more precious than their own lives.[5] In short, they must uphold pure moral conduct. When a teacher's physical and verbal actions are pure, their wisdom is pure. When their wisdom is pure, they can master sutras and related topics; if possible, they will also master tantric teachings. That mastery means they've mastered both the words and the meanings of the teachings they give.

A teacher should be capable of clarifying students' doubts using logic, explanation, and scriptural citation. He or she should not expect material gifts in return for giving teachings; in other words, they do not give teachings just to gain material things. Thus, the teachings they give become antidotes for afflictive emotions, an expression of their wish to bring all sentient beings to buddhahood. With such compassion, they develop bodhichitta. Such a master is regarded as a teacher according to the Mahayana tradition. So according to the Mahayana tradition, teachers must possess three primary traits: pure moral conduct, pure wisdom, and great compassion. With these three they develop bodhichitta.

A qualified teacher of the Vajrayana tradition must meet many criteria; most importantly, they must hold an unbroken lineage of empowerments. If an empowerment has no lineage, then it is not genuine and proper. If the guru holds an unbroken lineage from Vajradhara up until now, then one receives the empowerment of an unbroken lineage. Such a guru will know the meaning of tantra.

Once they have such knowledge, the teacher should engage in all the necessary practices and retreats according to the tantra. They must regard the samaya of the four empowerments[6] as more important than their own life. They will know many pith instructions related to the tantric teachings. They should always have great loving-kindness, compassion, and bodhichitta. Their mental continuum will be sealed by this loving-kindness, compassion, and bodhichitta. In brief, a Vajrayana teacher should be well versed in many sutras, tantras, and treatises. As it is taught in scriptures, these qualifications must be fulfilled by all Vajrayana gurus.

For the sake of sentient beings, a Vajrayana guru appears in ordinary human form, bestowing the Vajrayana teachings as the embodiment of all buddhas' compassion and wisdom; we should rely on such a guru. The guru is the root cause for us to accomplish all ordinary and supreme accomplishments. In fact, all siddhis, or realizations, can be realized through the practice of guru yoga or by pleasing the guru, such as putting

38 | THE FUNDAMENTAL PRACTICES

the Dharma teachings into practice. If one desires, they can offer their time, skills, money, and other resources to support the guru's Dharma activities, benefiting more beings. Thus, the guru is most important. Through the guru, one can realize the view.

THE QUALITIES OF A STUDENT

In addition to teachers, students should possess certain qualities to ensure that they are ready to receive the teachings at this time. First and foremost, one should have a sincere wish to receive teachings, not merely to listen out of curiosity. A student should be intelligent and able to understand the teachings. By listening to teachings, one gains knowledge and understanding, but these alone are not enough; one must actually practice the Dharma. For example, a sick person will not be cured of illness simply by receiving a doctor's advice. In order to cure their illness, after learning about medical treatments, a sick person needs to follow the doctor's advice. Similarly, we must apply Dharma teachings in daily life in order to become an authentic spiritual being.

MAINTAINING A GURU-STUDENT RELATIONSHIP

Once one has received an empowerment, a guru-student relationship is established. At that point, one should not change one's mind and discard the teacher. We should always respect the teacher and have faith in him or her. The surface of the earth can support all things, animate and inanimate, from a skyscraper to an earthworm equally. Similarly, our perception of the teacher should not waver. While listening to teachings, our minds should be like the earth, even and equanimous. What is more, we should develop a vajra-like mind, meaning it should be stable, powerful, and not liable to change or deterioration—like the adamantine diamond. With such a vajra-like mind we should perceive the teacher and receive the teachings accordingly.

We should not criticize and should always be respectful of the guru. If we perceive anything negative in the guru, we should understand this is our own impure flawed perception, and not indicative of the true nature of the guru. Because of our impure perception, we will see various faults in the guru. Because the guru is Buddha Vajradhara in reality, in reality the guru is flawless—in the ultimate view. This is how we should think.

Even after awakening to buddhahood, we retain the utmost respect and devotion for our gurus. Fervent, unchanging regard for the guru is essential to the Vajrayana tradition. That is why, on the crown of the *yidam* deity's head there is a second head, that being the lord of the Buddha family.[7] The lord of the family is none other than one's own guru.

Once we have received teachings, we cannot break the guru-student relationship. Doing so entails serious consequences later on. For this reason, disciples should always respect the guru. If it is a Vajrayana guru, then the disciple should see the guru as the real Vajradhara and as their refuge, and they should have sincere and unshakable faith in and devotion to the guru. The disciple should follow the guru's advice and guidance.

It is important to note that this does not mean that the disciple should do absolutely anything that their guru tells them. If a guru asks a disciple to do something that is obviously against the Buddha's teachings, or something against one's vows, then the disciple can leave that teacher, in equanimity, without either following or criticizing the guru.

There have been well-known cases in the West of gurus abusing their authority. This is a complex topic. From the disciple's side, once you have accepted someone as your guru, once you make that Dharmic connection, then you should never lose your faith in your guru. This is not to defend any particular lama, but we can look at the lives and teachings of past masters and learn from them. The great Marpa asked Milarepa to build a nine-story building. Milarepa worked very hard to do this, and then Marpa asked him to demolish it and rebuild it. This happened several times. It might seem cruel or arbitrary; Marpa did not need this building, and he did not need Milerapa to do this for him. The objective was for Milarepa to purify his own negative karma, and Milarepa did not lose faith in Marpa even when facing this great difficulty.

One of our great translators, Drokmi Lotsawa Shakya Yeshé, said that even if your guru falls into the hell realm, as a disciple, from our perspective as students, we should still not lose faith in or think anything negative about them. We must continue to regard the guru as the real Buddha.

Another example is the mahasiddha Tilopa, who performed an action that in appearance seemed negative. When his disciple Naropa saw it, he did not lose faith. Thanks to his unshakable devotion, Naropa gained realization. In short, just by seeing *outer* actions, we cannot always tell whether the guru's actions are right or wrong.

Still, there are some masters who are not acting in a proper way in the present world, and this is why you need to be extremely careful about choosing a guru and investigating a teacher before receiving Dharma teachings from them. Once you receive the teaching, especially an empowerment in the Vajrayana, you have made a Dharmic connection as guru and disciple. From that point onward, even if you later see something that does not seem right to you, you cannot lose your faith in the guru as being of the same nature as Vajradhara without facing karmic consequences.

Students often want to do things to please their teachers. They give gifts, they volunteer to clean the temple, and so on. From the disciple's point of view, these things are good because the most important thing is to please the guru. However, it is important to know how to please one's guru in the right way. There are three types of offerings to a guru: superior, mediocre, and inferior. The superior offering is to practice the Dharma—offering one's authentic and sincere practice to applying the teachings we've learned in our daily lives, both during formal meditation sessions and in our activities off the cushion. Genuine Dharma practice should permeate our day-to-day lives at all times. The mediocre offering is to follow the guru's advice and guidance on other mundane activities. The inferior offering is to make an offering of wealth. An authentic guru is most interested in their students making the superior offering, the offering of their practice. If the disciples engage in proper Dharma practice and they gain realization, then this will truly please the guru much more than any material gift.

We are fortunate to have some very qualified, genuine masters in our present time. It is less important, however, to receive many teachings or empowerments from many great gurus than it is to keep the samaya—a commitment taken when receiving empowerment to awakening—of the guru, to keep one's devotion to the guru intact at all times and without any obscuration. When this is done, then one can receive teachings from all qualified and authentic masters. But if we cannot keep the samaya, then it is better to have fewer gurus. This will depend on the individual characteristics of each student.

It might be difficult for new students to understand the nature and importance of the guru-student relationship. First, for a student, it is important to know the meaning of the fundamental teachings of the Dharma. This includes the difficulty of obtaining a precious human life, impermanence and death, the law of karma, the faults of samsara, the thought of renunciation, refuge, loving-kindness and compassion, and bodhichitta. We should know all these things properly. Then, it will be easier to understand the relationship with the guru. When we do not yet have this basic knowledge, it will be difficult to understand the importance of the guru-disciple relationship.

The famous models of the guru-disciple relationship—such as the example of Marpa and Milarepa—depict personal relations. However, it is not necessary for students to make efforts to have a personal, close relationship with their guru. The guru-disciple relationship is made through the Dharma. Because it is a Dharmic connection, it does not need to be a personal relationship.

In fact, for beginners, it is actually better not to be close to the guru. There is a famous prayer that we recite called Calling the Guru from Afar; it helps us see that it is easier to develop a genuine, sincere, and unshakable faith when it is done from a distance. After all, a person becomes our guru because we receive teachings or initiations from them, not because we have a personal relationship with them. Even if one has a close relationship to a teacher but no Dharmic connection, then this person is still not one's guru.

For beginners who do not yet have strong and unshakable faith, it is better to stay at a distance. Such students can attend and receive the teachings, and this is close enough proximity. As ordinary beings, we have strong obscurations and impure vision, and this can cause us to see many faults in the guru. When we see these as faults of the guru rather than the product of our own impure vision, this will cause us to lose faith, which is the greatest obstacle to keeping the guru-disciple relationship.

If our human bodies were to get too close to the sun, they would burn. For disciples without strong faith, being too close to the guru would be similarly destructive. Their impure vision, arising from our own

42 | THE FUNDAMENTAL PRACTICES

ignorance and mental afflictions, will impact their faith and devotion in a way that will be harmful for them. We should train our minds to have pure perception of the true nature of the guru, such that even if the guru were to be born in a hell realm because of their misdeeds, we would not lose faith at all, at any time or in any way. This is how we accumulate merit and purify our negative deeds and obscurations.

In ancient times, to reach exotic destinations one would have to travel by ship, depending on the prevailing winds and trusting an expert captain to navigate the course. Similarly, to quickly reach the destination of buddhahood, our devotion is a driving force like the wind, samsara is the ocean to be crossed, buddhahood is our ultimate destination, and our authentic teacher is the captain. With a captain, a ship can arrive safely at port; without him, a boat cannot reach the destination all by itself. Similarly, with a teacher one can safely cross the ocean of samsara. Therefore, we must rely on a genuine guru; they cannot be replaced by anyone else or even by information in Dharma books, such as this.

Practical Advice for Evaluating a Guru

Now that we understand how to relate to the guru and the role the guru plays on the path to buddhahood, we can explain more thoroughly how to go about evaluating a teacher as we set out on the path. As students, we need to examine potential teachers carefully before accepting them as our gurus. This is true above all in the Vajrayana tradition, in which the guru is indispensably important, just like the Triple Gem itself—that is, the Buddha, Dharma, and Sangha we take refuge in. Sometimes students are unclear about how they should go about examining a potential teacher, or they lack practical experience, or they have other concerns.

First of all, a potential student should look at a guru's physical and verbal activities. This means not only his public Dharma activities and teachings, but also his conduct. The most important thing is to check whether this master teaches the authentic Dharma according to the Buddha's teachings. Then, if possible, one should consider their mental activities—that is, whatever we can understand about their intentions and motivations. If this is beyond our ability, we can try to ask honest and sincere practitioners who are familiar with that particular guru. Then, we can listen to the guru and try to hear him or her directly before accepting them as a teacher and receiving empowerments or Dharma teachings.

At first, it can be difficult to know very much about a guru. Although we can and should ask others whom we trust to give us knowledgeable opinions and judgments, it is also true that reputation is not necessarily sufficient to judge if a person is an authentic master or not. There have always been renowned teachers who were not authentic. This is not new to our modern era. Even one or two thousand years ago, there were renowned masters who were not authentic.

Those who do not have the opportunity to have personal interactions with a potential guru should take their time and try to judge a teacher through different means. It is not necessary to interact with a master personally because we can learn about them through many channels— nowadays, even through social media. The important thing is to try to know and understand their qualities. For example, when we want to buy a house, we spend time examining it. We would not buy a house immediately, or without thinking carefully about it. When we look for a life partner, we do not marry the first person we meet. A guru is even more important; once you accept someone as your guru, once you have generated sincere faith and received teachings and initiations from them, that person is your guru not only for this life but all the way to buddhahood. In the prayers that we recite, we pray to meet our guru again in lifetime after lifetime until we attain buddhahood.

When a student does personally interact with a potential teacher, it would not be practical to ask that person directly about their qualifications to be a teacher. This is different from other kinds of evaluations you might make of people, houses, or other things in your life. It would not be practical because, generally speaking, authentic gurus will not broadcast their qualities, even when they possess extraordinary qualities. Authentic gurus are not prideful. It is much better to investigate them in the ways described here.

Many people live in places where there are no Dharma centers or temples. In terms of general Dharma teaching, today we are fortunate that we can receive teachings from authentic masters through watching videos or reading teachings on the internet. We can also incorporate these avenues when we are choosing a Vajrayana master, after careful investigation.

44 | THE FUNDAMENTAL PRACTICES

If someone visits an unfamiliar Dharma center, then the primary thing to look for is that they teach the genuine Dharma—meaning authentic teachings imparted by the Buddha, and not just teachings bearing the Buddha's name or containing Buddhist terms that sound authentic. It is also important to look at the resident teacher and determine whether or not the person is genuine, and then decide whether or not you can have faith in them if you take them as a guru.

The key thing is to have unshakable faith and belief in the teacher once you accept them as your guru. If this is the case, and if that unshakable faith is maintained, then even if someone has not done a thorough examination but accepts a person as their guru and receives the teachings, they will receive the blessing of the guru. But if we lose faith in, disregard, or criticize the guru, there will be severe karmic consequences, such as rebirth in the hell realm. These heavy consequences arise because we are breaking samaya. For this reason, whenever we have impure vision regarding the guru, we should remember that it is due to our own mistaken perceptions of the guru's true nature.

In short, it is important to investigate and examine a teacher before accepting them as your guru because there are karmic consequences if you change your mind or lose faith afterward. If we can maintain strong faith and keep our samaya intact, then we will have great benefit, not only in this life, but all the way until buddhahood is attained.

THE FOUR RELIANCES

In a Mahayana sutra called the *Teaching of Akshayamati*, the Buddha taught what are called the *four reliances*. These four reliances are important because they give guidance for practitioners on what we should accept or adopt. As new students of Buddhism approaching a guru and the Buddha's teachings, these four reliances can be helpful guideposts to lead you on your path.

The four reliances are:

Rely on the meaning, not on the words.
Rely on dharma, not on the individual.
Rely on wisdom, not on the ordinary mind.

> Rely on the definitive meaning, not on the provisional or
> interpretative meaning.[8]

The Buddha's four lines of advice are very important as they offer a framework for discerning the authenticity of teachings and nurturing wisdom. Their relevance spans across time, remaining as crucial today as they have been throughout history. In fact, these pieces of advice are applicable not only in spiritual pursuits but also in various aspects of mundane life and endeavors. They have been explained by many great scholars, like Jayananda, who also wrote a commentary on Chandrakirti's treatise *Introduction to the Middle Way*. Many other great Indian and Tibetan masters have also explained the four reliances.

The first reliance says to rely on the meaning, not on the words. To depend, trust, and believe in what is true, we must rely on the truth—not on words alone. An attractive expression is not a basis for our reliance; it is not necessarily a fact. We must check to see if what they say comports with reality, if is true or not. If it is true, then yes, we should believe, accept, and trust what they say—regardless of whether the words are presented nicely or not. We should also study the words of a teaching, for example by examining the context in which words are used, so that we can discern the meaning.

The second reliance says to rely on dharma, not on the individual. Here, *dharma* means "reason."[9] If there is a logical reason for a statement, then we should accept it. It does not matter who said it; what matters is what is said, and whether it is true. We should not accept the truth of a statement because it came from a powerful, famous, or rich person. A poor and homeless person may just as well speak something that we should accept, trust, and believe. We cannot decide the truth of statements based on who said them; if we judge this way, then we are relying on the individual, not on dharma.

As for our Vajrayana guru, however, we must maintain clear, unshakable faith, and hold a pure view of the guru's activities. In some situations, a guru might say something wrong or against the Buddha's teachings; if this happens, we must check carefully. The guru could be doing this intentionally to help us purify our negative thoughts or strengthen our faith. But if what is said is without any genuine reason, then it does go against the Buddha's teachings. In this case, we should leave, and do so in equanimity. However, if such a thing was said to strengthen our faith, then we should not lose that faith, whatever the guru does or says.

The third reliance says to rely on wisdom, not on the ordinary mind. Through meditation and experience, wisdom is gained. Our ordinary mind can make false decisions, but wisdom cannot; it will always make a good and right decision. There are different levels of wisdom. Ordinary people like us might have some wisdom, although it is not the wisdom of the noble beings, like the bodhisattvas. But we must try to rely on the wisdom that we have and diminish our ordinary thoughts.

The fourth reliance says to rely on the definitive meaning, not on the provisional or interpretative meaning. The Buddha's words or teachings can be classified in many ways. One is to classify them into two categories: those of definitive meaning and those of provisional meaning. *Provisional meaning* means that we cannot understand a statement based on just the literal sense of the words. If we do that, then we do not understand. We need to know the difference between teachings of definitive meaning and those of provisional meaning. In English, we say, "It's the icing on the cake" when something good happens and then, on top of that, another good thing happens. We cannot take that statement literally. In the Buddha's teachings, words of provisional meaning are things that we similarly cannot take literally; these words indicate another meaning. In Buddhism, we must learn the difference between the relative and ultimate truth. And as to relative truth, we should learn the difference between outer appearances and the actual or true meaning.

Teachers can help us ascertain which words or teachings are of interpretative meaning, and which are of definitive meaning. We need our teachers to show us the path, guide us, and explain the teachings. In the Buddhist tradition, we do not encourage people to practice Dharma without a teacher. Especially in the Vajrayana, to practice without a teacher means to practice without receiving empowerment. This is a great fault, the cause of being reborn in the hell realm in the future.

If we know these points, they can help us to move forward on the right path and avoid the wrong path.

CHAPTER 3
NGÖNDRO:
THE PRELIMINARY PRACTICES

Ngöndro, a Tibetan term meaning "what goes before," refers to the preliminary or foundational practices of Vajrayana Buddhism. To build a stable high-rise building, a solid foundation is essential. Likewise, a strong ngöndro practice is of utmost importance in Vajrayana. If we pursue deity practice or any higher practices without engaging in the ngöndro practices, our practice will not be genuine and fruitful, and it will be impossible for us to gain liberation and buddhahood.

To enter the Buddhist path and progress upon it until we reach the state of buddhahood, we must complete the accumulations of merit and wisdom. The two accumulations are like the wings of a bird that can fly across rivers or oceans; without them, buddhahood is impossible. If just one wing is damaged, it is impossible for a bird to fly. Similarly, if we want to cross the ocean of samsara and reach our ultimate destination—the state of complete enlightenment—we must have these two wings of merit and wisdom, each perfectly accumulated.

COMMON AND UNCOMMON PRELIMINARIES

Common preliminaries encompass fundamental Buddhist teachings that are shared across all vehicles and traditions of the Buddhist path. These teachings are vital for attaining liberation and buddhahood, serving as crucial elements guiding practitioners in the right direction. The four common preliminaries include contemplation on the shortcomings

48 | THE FUNDAMENTAL PRACTICES

of samsara, the preciousness of human rebirth, impermanence, and the law of karma. Even for those not pursuing liberation or buddhahood, reflecting on these thoughts can lead to greater temporary happiness and reduced suffering in mundane life, fostering healthier relationships and success in various endeavors.

On the other hand, uncommon preliminaries are foundational practices specific to Vajrayana Buddhism, essential for attaining buddhahood. These practices, such as refuge, bodhichitta, Vajrasattva practice, mandala offering, and guru yoga, serve as skillful means to swiftly cultivate wisdom, compassion, and other positive qualities necessary for awakening. Taking refuge in the guru, who embodies the Triple Gem, helps generate unshakable faith and devotion, while also demolishing pride and ego. Genuine bodhichitta, the altruistic intention to benefit all sentient beings, serves as the catalyst for attaining buddhahood, bringing about happiness, peace, and the cessation of suffering. Merit accumulation, facilitated through practices like mandala offering, is crucial for advancing on the path to buddhahood. Strong devotion to the guru, representing the Triple Gem, brings immense blessings and accelerates the journey toward enlightenment.

Notably, in the Sakya ngöndro, what is common or uncommon depends on context. Generally, the four thoughts that turn the mind to the Dharma—namely, the shortcomings of the samsara, the difficulty of obtaining a precious human life, impermanence and death, and the law of karma—are common ngöndro. This order is according to the *Triple Vision*, or *The Three Levels of Spiritual Perception*. But in other texts, the order of the four thoughts is different; they are first the difficulty of obtaining a precious human life, impermanence and death, the law of karma, and the shortcomings of the samsara.

In the Hevajra sadhana practiced in the Sakya school, however, the common ngöndro means refuge, bodhichitta, and Vajrasattva practice. Even with the common preliminary practices, not only can we accumulate merit; if our practice is sealed with the ultimate view, we can accumulate wisdom as well. In fact, there are no other practices to perfect the two accumulations besides the preliminary practices, just as for a bird to fly there is no substitute for wings. So, we cannot replace the preliminary practices with other practices to accumulate

Just a Preliminary Practice?

merit and wisdom. If we desire liberation and buddhahood, we must do ngöndro.

All followers of the Buddha's teachings, or Buddhists, must practice the preliminaries. In the past, those who have attained buddhahood, have practiced ngöndro when they were on the path.

According to the Mahayana teachings, Buddha Shakyamuni is the supreme nirmanakaya, or emanation body. In reality, he attained buddhahood countless eons before he was born as Prince Siddhartha in Lumbini. He was already a buddha, but in the eyes of common people, he first lived as a prince, and only later renounced his kingdom and eventually attained buddhahood. Buddha Shakyamuni's noble activities are understood across various Buddhist traditions. He practiced common preliminary practices over the course of many lifetimes, such as practicing loving-kindness and compassion, and so on. For example, as a child, when his cousin shot a bird with an arrow, Prince Siddhartha showed great compassion to the bird. Any such practice of loving-kindness or compassion is considered a preliminary practice. Although we might not have many stories of young Prince Siddhartha's preliminary practices, that does not mean he did not practice them.

The great Indian mahasiddhas, too, practiced the preliminaries. For example, in our Sakya tradition, the most precious and profound teaching is the Lamdré teaching, based on the *Vajra Verses* by the great mahasiddha Virupa. In his text, Mahasiddha Virupa explains the *Triple Vision*, of which the first vision, impure vision, explains refuge and the four thoughts that turn the mind to the Dharma. The second vision, the vision of experience, concerns infinite loving-kindness, infinite compassion, and bodhichitta. These are the so-called preliminary practices, or ngöndro, that Mahasiddha Virupa taught based on his practices and experiences. If he had not practiced the preliminaries and had no experience of them, he would not have explained these teachings, since his explanation was based on experience from practice.

Lamdré teachings are said to have the four authenticities: the authenticity of the Buddha's teachings, the authenticity of treatises, the authenticity

50 | THE FUNDAMENTAL PRACTICES

of gurus, and the authenticity of experience. These pillars ensure the integrity and reliability of the teachings passed down through the lineage. In Lamdré teachings, adherence to these four authenticities is paramount. The core sequence of receiving instructions from a teacher and engaging in personal study, contemplation, and meditation remains consistent, maintaining the tradition's authenticity. While certain aspects such as origin, translation, and practice methods may vary, the fundamental teachings remain unchanged. Through meditation practice, practitioners acquire unique and profound experiences. These experiences serve as a litmus test for the authenticity of their teacher. If the teacher is authentic, practitioners are able to attain remarkable experiences that validate their authenticity. This process reinforces a practitioner's confidence in their teacher's authenticity and the teachings they bestow. Furthermore, the authenticity of the teachings is reinforced by their lineage, which traces back to Mahasiddha Virupa and other ancient masters. The teachings are based on authentic commentaries and teachings, ensuring their alignment with the Buddha's words and principles. This lineage-based validation further solidifies a practitioner's conviction in the authenticity of the teachings, affirming their reliability and trustworthiness. It is certain that Mahasiddha Virupa practiced the preliminaries and then, based on his practice and experience, taught them to his students. We might not read about how these great masters practiced in their biographies, but that does not mean that they did not practice the preliminaries or that they gained no experience from them.

Preliminary practice should not be considered just a foundational practice for total beginners or something for "lesser" practitioners. The preliminary practices are vast; from a broader perspective, all Dharma practices performed before buddhahood can be defined as preliminaries. So, all the Dharma practices that we do to attain buddhahood can be defined as preliminary practices. Preliminary practices are not just the four common and uncommon foundations, infinite loving-kindness, infinite compassion, bodhichitta, and so on—those we commonly refer to as *ngöndro*. Apart from these, practicing the ten virtuous actions and abstaining the ten nonvirtuous actions can be considered preliminary practice, too. Sometimes the common and uncommon preliminary practices are taken as one's main practice, depending on the time you want to devote to them and the type of practice you are pursuing. For instance, in the teaching of *Triple Vision*, the preliminary part is to practice refuge, the main part is the different topic of the day, and then the dedication is the conclusion of the practice. But on the first day of the *Triple Vision* teaching, the main topic that is taught is refuge, therefore, taking refuge is not only the preliminary practice but also the main practice, at least for that day. As such, depending on the topic we practice, the preliminary practices can also be the main practice.

The preliminary practices are special because they train one's mind— that is, they tame and subdue our wild unruly minds, transforming them in a positive way. If our mind is positive, then our physical and verbal actions become positive. If those actions are positive, it is certain that we will only gain happiness. We will not experience suffering by performing good deeds. Gradually, as our actions and minds gradually improve, we will gain higher and higher realization and eventually attain enlightenment. These preliminary practices are thus special and effective; we must practice them. It is impossible for us to gain a high realization or inner qualities without focusing or putting effort into them.

Traditional teachings often speak of so-called lesser, mediocre, and superior individuals, a categorization of practitioners based on their various capacities for practice or learning. However, the so-called superior individuals are not superior from beginningless time. First, they were ordinary individuals, then they became lesser practitioners, and then mediocre practitioners, and then superior practitioners. One is not instantly a superior practitioner at birth. A so-called superior practitioner, at a particular time, might not practice the preliminaries, but they would have done so in a prior lifetime when they were a lesser or mediocre practitioner. But all Buddhists should practice ngöndro, even superior practitioners, because they have yet to attain buddhahood.

The Preliminary Practices according to the Sakya Tradition

All Dharma traditions originate with Buddha Shakyamuni. The Sakya lineage also derives from the Buddha—passing through Manjushri, Mahasiddha Virupa, and the lineage masters up until now. For example,

52 | THE FUNDAMENTAL PRACTICES

Manjushri gave the precious and profound *Parting from the Four Attachments* teaching to the great Sachen Kunga Nyingpo directly, in a pure vision. *Parting from the Four Attachments* directly explains the four common foundations: the shortcomings of samsara, the difficulty of obtaining a precious human life, impermanence and death, and the law of karma. Mahasiddha Virupa taught the Lamdré teaching that contains *Triple Vision*, which likewise explains the four thoughts that turn the mind to the Dharma, as well as loving-kindness, compassion, and bodhichitta, which are also preliminary teachings. There is a preliminary practice lineage based on the Hevajra deity and the *Hevajra Tantra*, and on the basis of those, there are common and uncommon Lamdré preliminary practice lineages. There is also a preliminary practice lineage based on the *Chakrasamvara Tantra*, and then based on that tantra, we have the preliminary practice lineage of Vajrayogini. While there exist diverse lineages of preliminary practices, even within the Sakya school, their essence underscores their essential nature; otherwise, they would not be upheld and transmitted.

Overall, there is no distinctive difference between the Sakya ngöndro lineages and other traditions. Interestingly, within the Sakya ngöndro lineages, the order of presentation may differ. For example, in the *Triple Vision*, first, Lamdré students are taught to generate the thought of renunciation, and for this purpose, the teaching first explains the shortcomings of samsara, the preciousness of human life, impermanence and death, and the law of karma. In contrast, *Parting from the Four Attachments* first explains the difficulty of obtaining a precious human life, followed by impermanence and death, the law of karma, and, lastly, the shortcomings of samsara. The Vajrayana Sakya ngöndro practice is unique to the extent that this practice is sealed with the view of the nondifferentiation of samsara and nirvana, which is the view of Lamdré.

THE STRUCTURE OF THE PRELIMINARY PRACTICE

Preliminary practices are classified as common and uncommon, depending on the context. Generally speaking, the four thoughts that turn the mind to Dharma—the difficulty to attain a precious human life, impermanence and death, the law of karma, and the shortcomings of samsara—

are considered common preliminary teachings. Taking refuge, generating bodhichitta, Vajrasattva practice, mandala offering, and guru yoga are considered uncommon preliminary practices. However, in some contexts—such as the uncommon meditation of Vajrayogini according to the Naropa tradition—taking refuge, generating bodhichitta, and Vajrasattva practice are considered common preliminary teachings, whereas the accumulation of merit and wisdom are considered uncommon preliminary teachings. Thus, the classification of common and uncommon preliminary practices depends on the context of a particular teaching.

It may not be necessary to distinguish between the various types of practices, whether they are common or uncommon, as such distinctions may not be practically beneficial and may not directly enhance our practice. However, I'm sharing this information to provide a general understanding of common and uncommon practices, as practices extend beyond mere labels. Being aware of these distinctions can be helpful for understanding the practices you are engaged in, enabling you to have a clearer understanding of your spiritual journey.

QUANTITY VERSUS QUALITY

Preliminary practices can be performed through our three doors: body, speech, and mind. However, preliminary practice should mainly come from one's mind—the mental practice. Relying on physical and verbal preliminary practices alone, without engaging in the practices mentally, will not help us accumulate great merit. Through relying on physical and verbal practices only, we cannot become real Dharma practitioners, or even earn the name of one. Dharma practice should always concern the mind—not just recitation, sitting in a crossed-leg position, making prostrations, and so on.

Dharma practice is a method for us to become better people temporarily—the moment we start practicing Dharma, we see positive transformations in ourselves—and eventually to gain liberation and the enlightened state. The mind of a good person, a one hundred percent positive mind, can neither be bought nor given by others. This positive mind has to be developed by oneself through one's practice. The whole purpose of Dharma teaching is to tame the mind and to develop a positive mind.

A genuine preliminary practice begins with having the right motivation and reflecting on the four thoughts that turn the mind to the Dharma. "Reflecting" means we not only contemplate the teaching but, after that, practice it—and in this way, we embody the meaning of the four common preliminary practices. Whatever Dharma practices we do must be done with a good motivation. Hence, there is a cause-and-effect relationship between our knowledge, intentions, and practice. By means of our knowledge, we should practice; without acquiring knowledge, we are not able to perform a practice properly. There is also a connection between practice and experience. Practice results in having inner, personal experience. Establishing such cause-and-effect connections between our Dharma knowledge and Dharma practice, as well as our Dharma practice and Dharma experience, will make our practice effective and be greatly impactful. Our very wild minds will be subdued and tamed.

We should develop the right motivation—practicing for the sake of all sentient beings—at the start of any practice and then again when we commence the accumulation of the preliminary practices. This way, our practice will be an effective method for us to accumulate merit within a short duration; it will be the real method to purify our negativities and obscurations, and we will thus be able to attain liberation and buddhahood. All these are possible through engaging in the preliminary practices on the mental level. If we just recite the words without visualization and attention—if we recite with a distracted mind, or if we merely focus on the words of the recitation—even reaching a milestone such as one hundred thousand recitations will not bring us great benefit. Counting the numbers of practices one accumulates is good, but if only they are done with proper visualization, attention, and concentration. According to the authentic teachings, we should not be distracted from practice; the number of recited words is not that important. Most important are the visualization and concentration. Even parrots can recite the *mani* mantra—*om mani padme hum*—or the refuge prayer. Having accumulated a large number of recitations is good, but it is more important to have a high number of recitations along with the visualization. As His Holiness the Forty-First Gongma Trichen always emphasizes, the quality of our practice is more important than the quantity.

One Hundred Thousand Accumulations

We must practice ngöndro until there is some impact on our minds, when there is some result that we can really feel. The "result" is that after the practice, we become a better person; our mental attitude improves. We become less angry. We develop more positive thoughts. We reduce negative thoughts further and further. These are the signs of progress in one's practice. It is also mentioned in the teachings that there are some signs, like purifying negative actions. So, ideally, until these signs appear, we must practice.

Traditionally, we are meant to accumulate each of the ngöndro practices one hundred thousand times. If we can have signs of a successful practice before achieving a hundred thousand recitations, then it is a very good indication that our practice is progressing in the right direction. Even if we do not have signs after completing one set of ngöndro, or after one hundred thousand recitations each of refuge, bodhichitta, Vajrasattva, mandala offering, and guru yoga, respectively, we should try to practice until there is some sign. An accomplished Sakya practitioner named Jamgön Ngawang Lekpa performed preliminary practices for decades. He only counted the practices he did that were accompanied by visualizations, yet he performed the refuge with prostration several hundred thousand times and recited the seven-heap mandala offering one million times with the visualization. He did not include any practice that was done with a distracted mind. In short, this means that most of his life was spent doing the preliminary practices.

Many signs showed his mastery and comprehension of teachings during his twelve-year retreat, diligently practicing both common and uncommon preliminary practices. His experience of auspicious dreams and signs underscored his profound understanding and realization. Yet, even after completing this extensive retreat, he remained committed to rigorous engagement with preliminary practices, highlighting their importance and necessity for genuine progress. This shows how important it is for us to perform the preliminary practices with concentration and visualization. Until there is some sign of improvement, we need to practice.

TRANSMISSION FROM A QUALIFIED GURU

It is good to have received teachings on the ngöndro practices from a qualified teacher, because through the teacher we can understand the real meaning of the practices and also gain the blessing of an unbroken lineage. The practices we receive teachings for become more powerful, especially if we practice the uncommon Vajrayana ngöndro, like uncommon Vajrayana refuge, Vajrasattva, mandala offering, or guru yoga. For these, we must have a guru from whom we can receive empowerment, blessing, and oral transmission, and then we can subsequently practice. Even for the common preliminaries, it is beneficial to have a teacher from whom we can receive instruction—not only to gain knowledge, but for instruction on how to practice properly.

Teachings on the preliminary practices are not ordinary teachings, topics for learning or gaining knowledge about. They are profound teachings that can benefit us in this life as well as future lives. These are the teachings that can really help us gain liberation and enlightenment. Hence, we must study well with qualified gurus and then practice properly and diligently with the right motivation.

Some might think these preliminary practices are not so profound, while the main practices of the Vajrayana are more profound. This is untrue. Whether a practice is profound or not depends on how we practice. If we practice in a profound way, then preliminary practice becomes a profound practice. If we do not know how to practice in a profound way, even though we are practicing the Vajrayana, our practice is not profound. Therefore, whether one's practice is profound depends on the practitioner, not on the teachings being practiced. It is essential to practice in a proper and profound way so that our preliminary practice will also become a profound practice.

PREPARING FOR THE PRELIMINARY PRACTICES

In Maitreya's *Mahayana Sutralamkara*, it is said that in order to practice, first we need the basic facilities for living, such as being able to find food and shelter without difficulties. Next, we need to be able to find a conducive place to practice—somewhere in solitude, without disturbance, with clean water, and in an environment that will not cause us to fall sick. We also require good spiritual friends who share the same view and whose conduct is in accordance with the Dharma. The above environment coupled with right motivation, visualization, practice, and dedication is the right setup for our practice.

Shrine setup

If you've spent time in a temple or Dharma center, you will know that practices are usually conducted in front of a shrine. You may benefit from having a dedicated space to practice the preliminaries in your own home. There are two ways to approach engaging in the preliminaries: proceeding with the practice with a shrine or without a shrine.

If you are doing ngöndro based on a particular deity, it would be appropriate to have that particular deity's statue, thangka, or picture on the shrine. Decorate and set up the eight offerings on the shrine: two water offerings, flowers, incense, a light or butter lamp, scented water, food, and music. Sometimes, seven bowls of water and a candle are used to represent these eight offerings. It is important to keep the offering objects clean and fresh. If you are doing a few sessions a day, if possible, before each and every session you should change the offerings objects to keep them fresh, or you may add a small amount of new offering objects before the start of each session. For example, in the morning before we start the session, we change the offering objects, so before we begin the second and third sessions of the same day, we can just add some new offering to the existing ones. Then the next morning, we replenish the offering objects.

This is a simple setup for the shrine. However, we have to keep in mind that simply having a shrine does not make our practice better. Whether our practice is properly done or whether our practice is improved does not merely depend on the outer shrine; it mainly depends on what kind of motivation we have developed before we practice. It depends on whether we really understand the meaning of what we are practicing, whether we can really apply the meaning into practice, whether we can visualize during the practice. If we know the meaning but do not apply its meaning or visualize properly when we practice, our practice will not be so helpful or impactful.

Some practitioners prefer a simple style; the great Indian mahasiddhas from ancient times did not have a physical shrine set up when they engaged in the preliminaries and other sacred practices. If we are not able to physically set up a shrine, we should still visualize a shrine with the Buddha statue or thangka and offerings in front of us, conceive the right motivation, apply our understanding of the meaning of the practice, and then seal the practice with a proper dedication at the end. In this way, our preliminary practices will be complete. Yet even those who have the material resources to set up a physical shrine should still visualize the shrine with the Buddha and offerings.

Once we gain realization, our minds become stable; nothing in the environment will disturb our practice. Even if we are in the most crowded place, we can still pay attention single-pointedly to our practice, without any distraction. The outer environment might affect a beginners' practice, so we should find a conducive environment, as mentioned earlier. But once we have higher realization or our mind is very stable, it does not matter what environment we are in or who is surrounding us—it will not affect our practice.

Mental preparedness

In addition to these outer preparations, we must be mentally prepared to commence practice. Preparedness here means you are not obliged by others to do the practice; you have a sincere and genuine wish to perform the preliminaries as your practice. This is the right motivation. Having the right motivation indicates you are ready to go forward with the ngöndro practices; without the right motivation, or with only a superficial or artificial wish to practice, one's practice will not be genuine. Therefore, we should examine our motivation. With the right motivation and a sincere wish to practice, we should first learn the meaning of the preliminary practices; on that basis, we can study and contemplate these teachings that we have received from genuine masters. Then we meditate and practice.

CHAPTER 4
THE RIGHT MOTIVATION

In his pure vision, the great master Sachen Kunga Nyingpo saw Manjushri, who gave him a pith instruction known as *Parting from the Four Attachments*. This teaching is the essence of the Mahayana, and it has special significance for understanding the right motivation for approaching one's practice. The underlying motivation behind all Mahayana practices is to benefit all sentient beings. The first line of the instruction says, "If you have attachment to this life, you are not a spiritual person."[10] If we study, contemplate, and practice the Buddhadharma for the purposes of our present lifetime, then whatever practice we do will not be a genuine Dharma practice.

Sometimes we might think, "I have to perform Dharma practices because I need to gain merit," or "I have to engage in virtuous deeds because I need to purify my negative karma." At those times we have to check whether we are performing Dharma practices or virtuous deeds for our own benefit or for others. If we just think about "I myself"—"I need to do practice," "I have to develop virtues," "I want to gain merit," "I have to purify my nonvirtuous deeds"—it indicates our practice stems from self-cherishing thoughts and thus is not based on a proper motivation. Whatever we practice, we should not imagine we do so only for our own benefit. If our practice is only based on our own agenda, then our Dharma practice cannot be genuine, nor are we to be considered spiritual persons, following Maitreya's guidance. Accordingly, in *Parting from the Four Attachments*, the great Jetsun Drakpa Gyaltsen points out that

60 | THE FUNDAMENTAL PRACTICES

to uphold moral conduct and practice or to listen, study, contemplate, and meditate on the Dharma with attachment to this life is a mistake.

Practicing the Dharma with attachment to this life is like eating delicious food that has been contaminated with poison. If food is contaminated with poison, no matter how good it may taste, it is still inedible because it will make you suffer great physical pain and might even threaten your life. If we practice Dharma with wrong motivation—that is, with attachment to this life—then no matter what we practice and how much effort we invest into our practice, it will not be genuine and therefore will not bring us great benefit.

It is said that centuries ago, while a Kadampa practitioner was diligently circumambulating a stupa, the great Kadampa master Dromtönpa happened to be there and advised him, "It is good for you to circumambulate, but you must practice the Dharma."

This practitioner pondered what would rightly be considered "Dharma practice," and so he decided to study Dharma texts. Dromtönpa saw this, too, and made another remark, "It is good to read Dharma texts, but you should practice the Dharma."

Upon hearing this, this practitioner went on to meditate. Dromtönpa, again, further remarked, "It is good that you meditate, but you must practice the Dharma."

This time, the practitioner decided to consult with Dromtönpa and clarify what he should be doing exactly to be considered as Dharma practice. Dromtönpa directly pointed out to him, "You must renounce this life!"

Dromtönpa's point is that if whatever we are doing—any virtuous deed or Dharma practice—is done with attachment to this life, then it is not considered correct and genuine Dharma practice. Therefore, we must develop the right motivation.

This was as true then as it is now, in our modern era. If we study the Dharma thinking that we are doing so in order to be a Dharma teacher in the future, for example, such intention indicates that we are studying for this life, which is not correct. Moreover, if we wish to learn the Dharma so that we can be free from suffering or avoid taking birth in the lower realms, such intention is based on "I" or "myself," which is not right either.

Sometimes we might think since we have met many great masters, have received many profound teachings, and have been practicing Dharma for many years, we are thus considered "real" Dharma practitioners. In actuality, a genuine practitioner is neither determined by the number of great masters they have met, the amount of teachings they have received, nor the number of years they have been practicing. Rather, it is the type of motivation that decides whether a Dharma practitioner is "real." We have to check our motivation constantly; only those harboring the right motivation are really practicing the Dharma. Hence, it is essential to develop the right motivation for whatever virtuous deed or Dharma practice we pursue.

With the right motivation, we will earn greater merit, and our virtuous activity will generate a greater result. Our virtuous activities can be the real antidote to remove negative thoughts and their result, which is none other than suffering. Our mental processes will also receive the blessings of the guru, deities, buddhas, bodhisattvas, Dharma protectors, and so on.

The Goals and Intentions of the Buddha

The Buddha gave many profound teachings in order to suit the different mentalities of all beings. However, the purpose of all these precious teachings is the same: to free us from suffering, leading to a state of liberation from both samsara and nirvana, and ultimately to the state of buddhahood. The Buddha did not teach a single word just for the sake of benefiting this life. Therefore, as followers of the Buddhadharma, if we practice merely for this life—that is, if the purpose of our study and practice is to remain in samsara—we are actually endeavoring toward the opposite of the Buddha's intent, which is to lead us out of samsara.

If we want to remain in samsara, we are not required to practice Dharma, because the Buddha's teachings are meant to free us from samsara. The Dharma is a profound method to assist us in this way. If we harbor a purpose that is opposite to that of the Buddha when we engage in practice, it is just impossible to achieve a great result from it.

In secular fields such as sports, politics, or business, to be considered a loyal follower, one would not go against the goals and objectives of a coach, leader, or CEO. Similarly, as a follower of the Buddha, if our purposes differ from the Buddha's, it means that we are not following the Buddha's teachings correctly and genuinely. That being said, we should cultivate the right motivation, beginning with generating the thought of renunciation of all of samsara, and on the basis of that, cultivating loving-kindness and compassion toward all sentient beings, without exception. This is followed by generating bodhichitta, the awakening mind, which means that we aspire to attain buddhahood for the sake of all sentient beings. And to that end we should engage in Dharma practice in general and, particularly, the preliminary practices.

The Thought of Renunciation

Because the right motivation begins with having the thought of renunciation—a sincere wish to gain liberation from all of samsara—this thought is most essential. If one does not wish to be liberated from samsara, one will not make any effort to overcome the suffering of samsara. If we really like a place, and we really wish to stay there as long as possible, then we will not even try to leave or go somewhere else. Similarly, if one really wishes to be free from samsara, then one will make an effort to do so and engage in the path of liberation.

Why do we need to develop the thought of renunciation toward samsara? Why is gaining liberation so important? It is because samsara as a whole has the nature of suffering, which we cannot avoid. As long as we are in samsara as ordinary beings, we cannot avoid suffering, since it is the very nature of samsara. We cannot avoid heat without avoiding fire—if there is a fire, then obviously there is heat. We cannot differentiate fire from heat. Similarly, we cannot differentiate samsara from suffering, since the nature of samsara is suffering. Therefore, we all need to gain liberation.

To gain liberation means our mind needs liberation from samsara; it does not mean our physical body needs to gain liberation, or that we go somewhere else that is beyond samsara. Even if our body remains in samsara, we can still gain liberation, because liberation is a mental state, not a physical achievement.

We sometimes say we are in the "prison" of samsara, but this prison and an ordinary prison are not the same thing. In an ordinary prison, authorities confine a person's body, but they cannot keep a person's mind in the prison. Although one is physically imprisoned, one's mind can still think of many different things that are beyond the walls of the prison. On the other hand, the so-called prison of samsara does not necessarily confine one's body; it is mainly a prison of the mind. The mind has obscurations and mental afflictions, which keep us trapped in samsara. No matter where the physical body is, samsara has to do with one's mental state because it is the mind that is caught up with negative thoughts and actions.

Whenever our mind becomes free from mental afflictions or obscurations of mental afflictions, we are liberated at that moment. At that time, we are not necessarily going to a physical place beyond samsara. The body could still be in samsara, but the mind has reached a state free from all afflictive emotions. This is what we mean by "gaining liberation from samsara."

Just wishing to gain liberation is not enough. Wishing and fulfilling our wishes are two different things. Nevertheless, first, we need to wish, because without this wish we will not make an effort to embark on the path of liberation. No matter how good we are, how well we behave, or how much practice we do, if we do not have the attitude of renunciation, or if we have attachment to this life, we are still not a truly spiritual person or a Buddhist.

How to generate the genuine thought of renunciation

To generate the genuine thought of renunciation, the sincere wish to gain liberation from all of samsara, we must know the faults of samsara and not have any attachments, whether that's attachment to people, food, clothes, a house, car, and so on. Of course, there are necessities we need to live and we can use those, but we should do so without attachment. Similarly, we can love people without fostering unhealthy attachment to them, avoiding the misconception that our relationship dynamics are static and permanent, which inevitably leads to suffering for both ourselves and those we are attached to. Instead, Dharma teaches us to nurture unconditional love that is genuine, boundless, and limitless, leading to genuine and enduring happiness. When we are without attachment, it is easier to generate the genuine wish to gain liberation from all of samsara without any difficulties and obstacles. For example, if a stone is tied to a bird's leg, it will be a great obstacle to the bird's ability to fly. Likewise, if we have strong attachment, it will prevent us from gaining liberation. If we genuinely seek to transcend suffering, we must transcend samsara or attain liberation from it entirely. But liberation from samsara does not entail freeing our physical bodies; rather, it involves freeing our minds from affliction, liberating them from afflictive thoughts and emotions. Attaining such a state grants us liberation and freedom from the suffering inherent in samsara. Buddha Shakyamuni—who came to this world in a nirmanakaya form as a prince and then became enlightened when he was thirty-five years old—has shown us how a worldly being can attain buddhahood. He set an example for all followers.

The Buddha was an enlightened being, but he spent most of his life in India. This shows that while his physical body was in samsara, he was not a samsaric being. After he attained buddhahood, which is the ultimate mental state, he then went on to teach for decades. Based on the right understanding of what real liberation is, we are able to generate the thought of renunciation toward all of samsara and to develop the genuine wish to gain liberation, just like him.

Immeasurable Loving-Kindness and Compassion

On the basis of having developed the thought of renunciation, we need to cultivate infinite loving-kindness and compassion. We already have loving-kindness and compassion, but at the moment they are limited; we cannot extend them to all sentient beings without discrimination. What we need is limitless, immeasurable loving-kindness and compassion. Developing limitless loving-kindness and compassion depends on the object to which they are directed. Subject and object are dependently originated generally speaking, but especially here, in relation to an infinite number of sentient beings. We call it "limitless" loving-kindness and compassion because the object of loving-kindness and compassion is all sentient beings, without limit.

As Buddhists, we do not study and practice Dharma only to gain knowledge and wisdom; neither do we do so just to preserve the Buddha's teachings, nor just for the sake of fellow Dharma friends or Buddhists. Rather, we are studying and practicing the Dharma for the sake of all sentient beings, which includes Buddhists as well as non-Buddhists, like non-believers and all beings of the six realms—humans, gods, demigods, animals, hell beings, and hungry ghosts. Sentient beings are limitless because we cannot count them, just as we cannot measure space.

The reason we study and practice the Dharma is for the sake of all sentient beings, without any exception. If we can imagine this, and there is no barrier or demarcation in our mental image, then we can extend that loving-kindess and compassion as wide as possible, like space. First it is important to know for whom we are going to develop loving-kindness and compassion; if we can recognize the object is limitless sentient beings, then it is easier for us to develop limitless loving-kindness and compassion. After recognizing that our object is limitless sentient beings, then while focusing on those beings we wish them temporary and ultimate happiness and the causes of happiness. This is limitless loving-kindness.

Next, we focus on the same sentient beings, wishing them to be free from suffering. This is not just the suffering they experience in their present lives, but the suffering of suffering, the suffering of change, and the suffering of the conditioned nature of phenomena. These three types of suffering will be discussed in detail in chapter 5. We also wish that sentient beings be free of the causes of suffering, which are negative actions and mental afflictions. This is limitless compassion.

A sutra mentions that it would be very meritorious indeed if one could fill all the countless buddhafields with excellent items of offering to the buddhas, and do so every day, yet to practice loving-kindness toward all sentient beings, even for a short time, would be much more meritorious. This illustrates how beneficial it is to practice genuine, unconditional loving-kindness.

The benefit of practicing infinite compassion is also mentioned in this sutra. To attain buddhahood, you do not need to do many different practices; you only need one, which is the practice of great compassion. This is akin to extending an invitation to a king or a distinguished leader to your residence. When you invite a king, naturally, his entire retinue follows suit; there's no need for separate invitations. Similarly,

66 | THE FUNDAMENTAL PRACTICES

wherever there is great compassion, all the various practices will accompany it. It means that if one has great compassion, all other qualities will manifest, too.

It is normally the custom for authors of Dharma texts to pay homage at the beginning of their written work. Chandrakirti, the great Indian master from Nalanda, paid homage to great compassion instead of the buddhas and bodhisattvas. Chandrakirti said that all the hearers and solitary realizers are born from the buddhas, while the buddhas are born from the bodhisattvas, and the bodhisattvas are born from the three qualities, which are compassion, bodhichitta, and nondual wisdom. Of these three, great compassion is the root of the other two, bodhichitta and nondual wisdom. In other words, great compassion is the source of all ultimate qualities. Therefore, it is crucially important and powerful. Chandrakirti said that at the beginning, great compassion is like a seed; in the middle, like a sprout that grows due to fertilizer and water; and at the end, it is like a ripened crop. Great compassion is important to have at the beginning, in the middle, and at the end of the path to attaining buddhahood. Every Dharma practice in the Mahayana tradition should be sealed with compassion and bodhichitta, the enlightened mind.

BODHICHITTA

We develop bodhichitta based on positive thoughts of loving-kindness and compassion. Without loving-kindness and compassion, we cannot develop bodhichitta, without which we cannot become Mahayana Buddhists. As Sakya Pandita said in the *Treatise Distinguishing the Three Vows*, "All Mahayana practices and teachings are sealed by bodhichitta." There is no Mahayana practice that cannot be done as long as one has the awakening mind, bodhichitta. Therefore, we must cultivate bodhichitta. *Bodhi* is a Sanskrit term that means enlightenment or buddha. *Chitta* means ordinary mind—that is, not Buddha's mind. *Bodhi* refers to the result, buddhahood, to which one aspires; *chitta* refers to the one who generates the wish to reach buddhahood. So *bodhichitta* means the mind that wishes to attain buddhahood. In the Tibetan language we say, *jangchup sem*, which means the mind that wishes to attain buddhahood.

As a beginner, we should primarily focus on cultivating relative bodhichitta, which has two kinds: aspirational bodhichitta, generating the wish to attain buddhahood for the sake of all sentient beings, and engaged bodhichitta, engaging in Dharma practice in order to attain buddhahood. First, we need to develop aspirational bodhichitta. We develop this wish for bodhichitta first due to the magnitude of what it means to attain buddhahood. Space is limitless; similarly, sentient beings are limitless. Since we are born in samsara not just once but an infinite number of times, limitless numbers of sentient beings have been our parents and loved ones.

Our mental process has no detectable beginning; we have been born into samsara repeatedly from beginningless time. Each lifetime, we have different parents and loved ones; all sentient beings have been our loved ones in one lifetime or another. Just as we should repay the kindness of our loved ones now, we should repay the kindness our past loved ones. Our parents are dear to us because they gave us a precious human life. This is a great kindness. Even though some parents might not treat their children well, they are kind at least in the sense that they give their child a life to start with. Without this precious human birth, we could not meet a great teacher, receive the Buddha's teachings, and practice the Dharma. All these became possible because our parents gave us this human life.

At the moment, we are in samsara. Someone drowning in the ocean who cannot swim is unable to rescue anyone else who is also drowning. Similarly, as an ordinary person, we are drowning in samsara and unable to rescue our fellow sentient beings from drowning, too. Even powerful worldly divinities, hearers, solitary realizers, and bodhisattvas lack complete power to liberate all beings. Only a buddha has the ultimate power to liberate all beings from samsara and establish them in a state of liberation and enlightenment.

Therefore, in order to benefit all beings and fulfill their wishes, we sincerely aspire to attain buddhahood. To that end, we must engage in Dharma practice. Generally, this wish is called aspirational bodhichitta. If we develop such aspiration without receiving bodhisattva vows, then it is just a mere wish; it is not genuine aspirational bodhichitta. There is no aspirational bodhichitta without receiving bodhisattva vows. Similarly, there are "merely engaged" practices and engaged bodhichitta practices. "Merely engaged" means that one engages in virtuous deeds, such as the

68 | THE FUNDAMENTAL PRACTICES

practices of generosity, patience, and so forth, without having received bodhisattva vows. Engaging in Dharma practice having received bodhisattva vows is referred to as engaged bodhichitta.

Just wishing to go to another city is not enough to get there; we need to engage directly with a means to travel. Similarly, in order to attain buddhahood, having a mere wish is not enough. One also needs to embark on the path of liberation. Toward that end, having generated aspirational bodhichitta, one should cultivate engaged bodhichitta, which means engaging in practice, especially the preliminaries.

With all these in mind, we generate the right motivation—that is, to be engaged in Dharma practices or virtuous deeds for the sake of all sentient beings. Such motivation is what we should harbor in whatever practices we perform. When we have generated the thought of renunciation and right motivation, we can then proceed with refuge practice and other preliminary and main Dharma practices.

CHAPTER 5

THE FIRST COMMON NGÖNDRO: THE SHORTCOMINGS OF SAMSARA

Details of the common and the uncommon preliminaries vary according to different texts and traditions, such as the order of presentation of the common preliminaries, as we have discussed. The presentation that will be followed in this book is that which is found in the *Triple Vision* of the Lamdré tradition, where the order of the common preliminaries is (1) the shortcomings of samsara, (2) the difficulty of obtaining a precious human life, (3) death and impermanence, and (4) the law of karma.

Someone might think that the common preliminaries are for beginners. They might think that they can skip them to focus on the uncommon practices because those seem more interesting. This would be a big misunderstanding. Without a solid foundation in the common preliminaries, it will be difficult to practice Dharma genuinely and properly. This is because the common preliminaries help us to produce a strong thought of renunciation. Without that, we will never be genuine practitioners of the Dharma or followers of the path.

Ideally, it is better to approach the common preliminaries and then the uncommon preliminary practices in a gradual, sequential manner. It is difficult to master all four common practices in a short time, but we should try our best to practice them as much as possible. If we have at least a solid understanding, it will be a base from which to begin practicing the uncommon preliminaries.

What Is Suffering?

Buddha gave an immense number of teachings for the sake of liberating sentient beings from the ocean of samsara and leading them to ultimate buddhahood. However, if we are to practice the teachings properly to reach this great result, we need, first and foremost, to cultivate an attitude of renunciation toward the entirety of samsara. We develop this strong thought of renunciation by studying and contemplating the sufferings and the defects of samsara. Without a profound understanding of the sufferings of samsara, it will be impossible to have the genuine wish to transcend it or attain liberation.

As long as we remain in samsara as ordinary beings, we will experience suffering and be caught up in negative thoughts and actions. What's more, we have been suffering in samsara, controlled by defilements, since beginningless time. Naturally, then, generating the right positive thoughts will take a great deal of effort.

When Buddha Shakyamuni first turned the wheel of Dharma, he taught the four noble truths to five fortunate disciples in Deer Park in Sarnath, near what is now Varanasi, India. The first of the four noble truths is the truth of suffering. The other three noble truths are the truth of the origin of suffering, the truth of cessation, and the truth of the path. The truth of suffering is first because we must realize it first to become free from suffering. The four noble truths can be compared to the process a physician follows when curing an illness: First, the disease must be recognized. Only then can the right remedy be prescribed. In this case, the disease is suffering.

Moreover, recognizing the depth and the breadth of the suffering in samsara will help us broaden our perspective to be more aware of the suffering of others. Naturally, whenever we are suffering, we can find it easier to empathize with others who are suffering, too. And when we are aware of others' suffering, it is easier to cultivate unconditional loving-kindness and compassion for them. This is the basis for bodhichitta, which is itself the basis for becoming enlightened.

According to the Buddha's teachings, there are three kinds of suffering. They are the *suffering of suffering*, the *suffering of change*, and the *suffering of the conditioned nature of phenomena*.

The suffering of suffering

The suffering of suffering is easy to grasp, so there is no need to elaborate in depth. This is the suffering that is ordinarily recognized as suffering. It includes physical pain, but also anxiety, distress, and other mental pain. We are made up of aggregates, and on the basis of the aggregates, we experience suffering. Not all of the aggregates that appear are caused by negative actions and emotions. The Buddha's physical form, for example, is free from karma and afflictive emotions. However, our ordinary aggregates, caused by our karma and afflictive emotions, are the basis upon which we experience the suffering of birth, old age, sickness, and death, alongside other suffering such as not fulfilling our wishes, meeting unfavorable conditions, and so forth. Overall, the suffering of suffering consists of what one most likely associates first with the word *suffering*.

The suffering of change

The suffering of change refers to things that might ordinarily be happy. The Buddha teaches us that the happiness we experience in worldly pleasures is transient and is not *real* happiness, and ultimately leads to suffering. This is because mundane happiness will end, one way or another; also, mundane happiness always entails worry about loss. Consider food, for instance. When we eat something delicious, we feel pleasure, leading us to believe that consuming tasty food brings happiness. However, if this were true, we'd find more happiness in eating more. Yet, as we know, overeating brings discomfort and suffering instead. Therefore, the pleasure derived from delicious food is not genuine or lasting. Similarly, many other forms of worldly happiness follow this pattern of changing into something else over time. This is why such happiness is regarded as the suffering of change. All worldly happiness, including any of our current joy, is not true happiness. It stems from attachment and desire, which are negative emotions known as the three poisons: desire, anger, and ignorance. These poisons only perpetuate suffering and cannot bring about genuine happiness.

To give another example, imagine that a poor person suddenly moved into a luxurious home. In the beginning, they might feel great happiness.

72 | THE FUNDAMENTAL PRACTICES

But a luxurious home is not a cause of genuine happiness. If it were, then the longer the person stayed there, the happier they would be. This is not what happens. As time passes, their happiness wears off; they may find that the allure of staying in this house fades, or encounter situations where something within the house breaks—inevitable occurrences, as nothing lasts forever—leading to heartbreak. Alternatively, they may worry about the house being broken into, turning their apparent happiness into a source of fear. In essence, if residing in this luxurious house were a true and lasting source of happiness, their contentment would endure indefinitely, unaffected by external circumstances. However, this is not the reality, indicating that the house is not a genuine source of happiness.

Similarly, wealth and fame are not causes of happiness. We can easily see that there are extraordinarily rich people who are not the world's happiest people. All such people will find that they are not free from suffering, because although they may be rich or famous or live in luxurious homes, they still experience physical and mental suffering.

Mundane happiness is not genuine in the big picture. It is, at most, a series of temporary happinesses. As time passes, feelings change, and so we must go from happiness to suffering, to happiness, to suffering again. For this reason, we speak of the suffering of change.

The suffering of the conditioned nature of phenomena

All worldly beings have the inherent propensity to grasp at the five aggregates, which means all worldly beings experience suffering. Regardless of whether we encounter temporary pleasure, suffering, or a neutral state, we are continually establishing the groundwork for future suffering. This is because our current aggregates act as direct causes for our future aggregates, which will serve as the basis for future suffering. One's very existence in samsara entails suffering. This is the case regardless of what beings do or where they reside within samsara, be it in desire, form, or formless realms. This implies that all our present experiences contribute to the causes of sufferings that will arise later. Every element of our conditioned existence carries within it the potential for future suffering; hence this suffering is termed the conditioned nature of all phenomena.

THE FIRST COMMON NGÖNDRO: THE SHORTCOMINGS OF SAMSARA | 73

This is the most subtle form of suffering. Because other forms of suffering are more obvious, beings in samsara do not see the suffering of the conditioned nature of existence as a form of suffering. For example, many countries aim for development, a goal shared by nearly every nation and its citizens. However, achieving development often requires deforestation for building infrastructure, industrialization, and agricultural developments. These actions can have negative consequences, including environmental harms, the disruption of ecosystems, and contributions to global climate change. To give another example, winning the lottery may initially appear to be a fortunate event. However, acquiring wealth through the lottery might give rise to disharmony between the individual and their family. Such occurrences are not uncommon, and have been reported in newspapers. Other religions encourage a path of renouncing worldly life by realizing the first two sufferings, but to perceive the third one, and to renounce samsara because of it, is special to the Buddhist tradition.

THE SUFFERING OF THE SIX REALMS OF SAMSARA

The three types of suffering are correlated to the six realms of existence in samsara in a special way. The three lower realms—the hell realm, the hungry ghost realm, and the animal realm—correspond to the suffering of suffering. Of course, humans and other beings in samsara also experience the suffering of suffering, but it is especially severe for beings in the three lower realms.

The suffering of change is correlated to the three higher realms. The beings there are more aware of it than beings are in the three lower realms, so it is especially pronounced for them. The suffering of the conditioned nature of phenomena encompasses all states of existence in samsara.

THE SUFFERING OF SUFFERING IN THE THREE LOWER REALMS

When we reflect on the suffering of suffering in the three lower realms, the aim is to produce renunciation of samsara by evoking sadness. To produce this feeling, the teachings describe the truly terrible pain and the difficulties that beings undergo in these realms. As we familiarize

74 | THE FUNDAMENTAL PRACTICES

ourselves with these realms, it's important to recall that every being, including ourselves, has traversed these states numerous times throughout endless past lives.

The hell realm

There are three kinds of hells in the hell realm. These are the cold hells, the hot hells, and the neighboring and minor hells. Beings are born in these hells because of their negative karma, and their suffering is very intense. The teachings give detailed descriptions of the hells so that, through our study and meditation on the extraordinary suffering of the hell beings, we will feel sorrow, compassion, and the wish to renounce samsara.

The descriptions of the hells in the sutras and other teachings are quite vivid. For example, there are eight cold hells, and each one is twenty times colder than the one before. The first cold hell is called the Blister Hell. A hell being is born here miraculously, without parents, alone and on a vast, frozen plain. The plain is completely encircled by snowy mountains. Here, the hell being is tormented by piercing wind and snow, and there is not a single glimmer of light. The hell being's body is completely covered with blisters. This is why it is called the Blister Hell. Subsequent hells contain even worse things, all very terrible, that are experienced by beings who are born there.

Furthermore, the suffering experienced in the hells lasts for a very long time. To stay with our example of the Blister Hell, the teachings give a method for understanding the life span of a hell being there. Imagine that there is a large barrel filled with a huge quantity of sesame seeds. Once every hundred human years, one small seed is taken out of the barrel. The life span of the hell being in the Blister Hell lasts as long as it takes to empty that barrel full of seeds.

All eighteen hells will not be described here. However, you should know that although you cannot see them, they do exist. Not only are they described in the sutras, but there are also reports in the biographies of ancient masters who visited the hell realm and saw for themselves the suffering there.

The hungry ghost realm

The second lower realm is the realm of hungry ghosts. According to the sutras, there are thirty-six different kinds of hungry ghosts. They can also be classified into three: those with external obscurations, those with internal obscurations, and those with the obscuration of obscurations. This means, respectively, that they suffer from external sources, from internal pain, and in every way.

A ghost with external obscurations is born into a very desolate place stripped of vegetation or water—very much like a desert. There are many other ghosts there, all with similar karma. The mouth of the hungry ghost is the size of the eye of a needle, and his throat is as narrow as a hair from a horse's tail. His limbs are as thin as grass stalks, yet his belly is as huge as a mountain. He experiences such great hunger and thirst that he cannot rest even for a single moment. He drags his poor body about noisily like an old horse cart. He wanders constantly in search of food, even though he is in excruciating pain. Still, he cannot find even a grain of food or a drop of water. If he should, on a rare occasion, find a drop of mucus, pus, or blood to consume, then more powerful ghosts will immediately surround him, thrash him, and snatch it away.

The second kind of hungry ghost is the ghost with internal obscurations. Their bodies and circumstances are similar to the ghosts with external obscurations. Whenever they try to eat, because their mouths and throats are so tiny, it is very difficult for any food to pass through. When it finally does reach their enormously large belly, the craving, hunger, and thirst is only increased, causing more misery.

The third kind of hungry ghost has the obscuration of obscurations. Their situation is like the others. In this case, however, whatever food they manage to get into their stomachs will turn into fire, producing flames that emerge from their nostrils, mouth, and ears.

The hungry ghosts suffer in other ways, too. They must eat hot sand, and they fight and injure one another. They eat filthy things, such as the pus of their own infected goiters. Whenever they see a tree laden with fruit, they will dash toward it, but then it will completely wither when they reach it. If they see a river from afar, it will also completely dry up, so that they will find only sand and pebbles.

76 | THE FUNDAMENTAL PRACTICES

The cause of these ordeals is their defilements. In particular, their suffering results from the hoarding of material things in previous lives, such as grain or other foods, rather than offering to feed the hungry or make offerings to the buddhas and bodhisattvas.

The animal realm

The animal realm has three divisions. There are those who dwell in the ocean, those who dwell in the darkness between continents, and those who are scattered in the higher planes of existence. Of course, we have no immediate access to the hell realm or the hungry ghost realm, so we must rely on the sutras and the commentaries to understand them. In the case of the animal realm, however, we can see their suffering with our own eyes. Generally, all animals suffer due to ignorance, one of the three defilements. From the Buddhist perspective, this means that they are unable to know what is right and wrong, and so they are unable to think about their karma. The lifespan of an animal varies greatly from one kind to another. In the framework of Buddhist cosmology, some animals live for as long as an eon, while others live for a span as short as a moment.

First, regarding the animals that dwell in the ocean. Here, big creatures consume small ones, and very tiny ones bite the bigger ones. They live in a dirty environment without definite companions or homes, and they are perpetually saddled with the fear of meeting those who would kill them.

The second type of animal dwells in the darkness between the continents. According to Buddhist cosmology, there are four continents. Our Earth, known as Jambudvipa, is situated in the south. To the east lies Videha, to the west is Godaniya, and to the north is Uttarakuru. There are beings residing within the dark voids separating these continents, where visibility is completely obscured due to the profound darkness. Besides experiencing the typical suffering of oceanic life, as described in the previous category of animals, these creatures also endure significant hardship due to the surrounding darkness. Unable to discern even their own appendages, they ingest whatever appears in front of them, whether it is edible or not. Apart from this, there is nothing else to their existence.

Third are those animals who are scattered about in the regions of space where human beings and gods live. These are the ones we commonly see,

THE FIRST COMMON NGÖNDRO: THE SHORTCOMINGS OF SAMSARA | 77

such as mammals. They cannot afford to let down their guard even for a moment. They are always alert with constant fear of attack, whether from other animals or humans. They are slaughtered for their flesh, skin, bones, horns, and hair. Even domesticated animals are subject to being beaten and forced to work the whole day, and in many cases end up being eaten by their owners.

THE SUFFERING OF CHANGE IN THE THREE HIGHER REALMS

The three higher realms are the human realm, the demigod realm, and the god realm. These realms are especially touched by the suffering of change. We reflect on the pain and difficulties endured by beings in these realms to produce renunciation through the rejection of attachment, just as we reflected on the suffering of the three lower realms to produce renunciation by evoking sadness.

In the three higher realms, you might think that beings experience happiness. However, on careful examination, there is no true happiness in any of these realms. The fact is that what we normally consider to be happiness is only another form of suffering. As the Buddha taught, all compounded things are impermanent, and whatever is impermanent is subject to suffering.

The human realm

It is not difficult to see how the suffering of change affects those of us in the human realm. A family can be decimated in war, the rich can become penniless, the powerful can become powerless, friends can become enemies, and the healthy can become sick. Conditions change, sometimes quickly and sometimes slowly—but always and assuredly our life is subject to change. Nothing remains the same forever for us, and this change leads to suffering.

Among the beings in the higher realms, for humans in particular, no one is free from the four sufferings of birth, old age, sickness, and death. The suffering of birth is the root cause of all the other sufferings we experience, and it is also the result of the karma of our negative deeds. Although we commonly speak of birth as a beautiful thing, its nature is clearly suffering. Our texts say that when you were in the womb, it was like you were being suffocated by a bad odor. Whenever your mother ingested food, her stomach pressed down upon you. When she moved around, it felt to you like falling into a ravine. You felt the discomfort of coldness whenever she ate cold things and that of heat whenever she ate hot things. During birth itself, there was the suffering of being squeezed through the birth canal, resulting in the sensation of landing in a pit of thorns. Of course, you do not remember any of this now.

Next, there is the suffering of old age. Everyone knows the changes that old age can bring to a physical body. We become crooked and sickly. Our hair turns white and some might become bald. When you are old, it becomes difficult even to sit down with ease or comfort, and then it is difficult to stand up again. You lose your voice, your mind becomes senile, and you lose interest in all activities. You can no longer feel warmth anymore or savor the taste of food.

As an old person, you find that whatever you do seems to be wrong. Maybe you were brilliant and adulated before, but now all that is in the past. Your children criticize you. Your fortune begins to decline, and your words are not taken seriously.

When you are old and all your faculties are weakened, you suffer from many diseases, digestive disorders, and breathing difficulties, and death seems inevitable, even imminent. Even if there is no debilitating illness, the course of your life is tending toward death. Although most people wish to live a long life, a long life is in fact another form of suffering.

Next is the suffering of sickness. The pain and discomfort of sickness can be unbearable, involving harsh treatments such as surgeries. You lose your appetite, or else you cannot eat the things that you like and must eat things that you do not like. You suffer at night because you are unable to rest. You fear not being able to recover from your illness and fear losing your wealth from crippling medical bills.

Next, there is the suffering of death. Firstly, the uncertainty of when it will come brings suffering; you do not know when death will strike. It could be at any moment. Of course, everyone plans to live for a very long time, and few people give any conscious thought about suddenly dying, unexpectedly and without warning. But we all know that we

THE FIRST COMMON NGÖNDRO: THE SHORTCOMINGS OF SAMSARA | 79

can be struck suddenly by a severe illness or accident that leads to an untimely demise.

Buddhist texts tell us that sentient beings normally die as the result of the exhaustion of their life force, merit, or karma, or a combination of these. If only one of them is exhausted, then death can be averted through certain measures. For example, if one's life force is exhausted, then long-life rituals can help. If two are exhausted, then it is more difficult to prolong life, but not impossible. When all three are exhausted, the time of death has definitely arrived. At this point, nothing one does can prevent death—not rituals, practices, or medical treatments.

You may know that you are about to die soon, yet are unable to bear the thought of it. You are unable to find a way to avoid it. Very likely, you will be terrified by the messengers of Yama, the lord of death. You are also likely to recall your past wrongdoings; however, it is too late now to redress them. You are lying on your deathbed, surrounded by relatives for the last time, uttering your last words, sipping your last drop of water.

Maybe you have truckloads of money, but not even a single cent will go with you in death. You may be surrounded by your loved ones and your friends, but not a single person can accompany you. You will have to go to the next life alone, without knowing the destination, nor what it will be like or what will happen there.

Everything—your work and your plans—is half-finished. Now you must leave. Even your own body, which has been with you for all your life, must be abandoned. Your consciousness alone will depart, much like a strand of hair being removed from a block of butter, leaving everything behind. At that moment, though, the suffering can be terrifying.

Besides these four general sufferings in human life, there are others. For example, there is suffering caused by having wealth. First, in the process of accumulating wealth, there is no rest during the day or night. After acquiring it, there is the stress of having to protect it. Those with power can seize it, thieves can steal it, employees can embezzle it, and false friends can appropriate it through deception. Your kith and kin may be envious, even to the extent they become your enemies. There are those who will scheme to take over your wealth. Some people lose their lives trying to protect their wealth. In the end, you will certainly undergo the anguish of losing it. In the beginning, in the middle, and in the end, wealth is a source of suffering.

Of course, those without wealth suffer, too. They toil and grind, day and night, to scratch out a living. They may struggle to provide necessities for their families. Wealthy people look down on them. The rich suffer mentally, and the poor suffer both mentally and physically.

Other sufferings include the fear of meeting your enemies, the pain of separating from your loved ones, and the frustration of not being able to fulfill your wishes. There is suffering when it is difficult to please others who are important to us. Ordinary human life is full of suffering, some of which you may have already experienced.

The human realm is subject to the sufferings of the other realms, too. When you are experiencing extreme cold or heat, this is like the suffering of the hell realm. Having extreme hunger and thirst is like the suffering of the hungry ghost realm. Experiencing hard labor and exhaustion is like the suffering of the animal realm. Ferocious fighting and quarrels, like that of the demigod realm; changing from bad to good and from good to bad, like that of the heavenly realm.

The demigod realm

Next is the suffering of demigods. They are by nature jealous, constantly competing with the gods, but as their merit is never on par with the gods, they are always defeated. As a result, there is not a single moment when they are at ease. They are called demigods because their status is higher than human beings, but it is not as high as the gods. They are between the two. In battles with the gods, they are always defeated, receiving only injuries and death.

In the demigod realm there is a lake called All Appearance. Looking into the surface of the water, the female demigods can see all that is happening to the men on the battlefields. They can see their loved ones being injured or killed, and they experience inconsolable suffering from this. Finally, since the demigods are always engaged in negative deeds motivated by jealousy of the gods, most of them will fall into the three lower realms after death.

The god realm

Another way to divide the universe, besides into the six realms of samsara, is into three realms: the desire realm, the form realm, and the formless realm. The desire realm, or *kamadhatu* in Sanskrit, includes the three lower realms of samsara—hell beings, hungry ghosts, and animals—but also the human realm, the demigod realm, and the lower portion of the god realm. There are additional god realms in the realms of form and formless, which are considered higher god realms.

The gods who dwell in the lower portion of the god realm are called the desire-realm gods. There are six levels of such gods. Their physical appearance is remarkably beautiful, and they live long lives of great enjoyment and luxury in resplendent palaces. With such luxury, they are too distracted to spare any thoughts on practicing the Dharma. Nonetheless, due to their great merit, there is a big drum that resonates the four central Buddhist teachings, called the four seals. These are:

> All compounded phenomena are impermanent.
> All contaminated entities are suffering.
> All phenomena are selfless.
> Nirvana is peace.

These profound teachings sound out constantly, but the gods are so immersed in their extraordinary pleasures that they do not pay attention.

Although they live extraordinarily long lives, there are so many pleasant distractions that time passes very quickly. Then one day, the five signs of impending death appear. Their bodies, which were once exceptionally beautiful, suddenly turn ugly. Their minds become agitated so that they are unable to remain at ease. The perpetually fresh flower garlands that they wear fade. Their clothes, which were pristine before, are now soiled. They never perspired before, but now they do.

Besides these five main signs of death, these gods will first experience five near-death signs. Their bodies, which were once luminous, now appear dim. Previously, when they bathed, the water ran completely off their bodies, but now their skin remains damp. In the rustle of their clothes and the jangle of their ornaments, they hear unpleasant words

82 | THE FUNDAMENTAL PRACTICES

telling them things such as, "You are going to die soon." Previously, they never blinked their eyes, but now they do. Finally, their minds, which were very lucid, become dull.

When these signs appear, even their relatives and friends abandon them, afraid or unwilling to get too close. They only toss a single flower from a distance in farewell. Such things occur here in the human realm, too. In the early days of the AIDS epidemic, for example, many doctors, nurses, and even friends and relatives harbored similar hesitations to being near the dying.

The gods possess worldly clairvoyance—not perfect, but enough to know their next rebirth. Typically, because they have indulged only in enjoyments, they are destined to plummet into the lower realms. Therefore, when the time of death approaches, they suffer not only from physical pain but also mental agony, knowing what awaits them. In fact, this mental suffering is said to surpass any physical suffering in the hell realm.

The two higher god realms are the form and the formless realms. The gods in these realms are higher in status than those of the desire realm. During their existence, they do not experience any recognizable suffering because they have attained a high level of meditative concentration. Nevertheless, their long lives come to an end. Just as a bird, no matter how high it can fly, will eventually return to the earth, the gods will fall to the lower realms again upon the exhaustion of the good merit received from their previous pure virtues.

These gods have spent their entire lives in deep meditation, thinking that by being in this state they are liberated from samsara. This meditative state, though prolonged, is not permanent. Once their karmic energy of powerful meditational prowess is exhausted, they will rouse from their profound meditative absorption. The realization that they are still caught in samsara causes them to adopt the wrong view that there must be no such thing as liberation. This destroys all their virtues and results in rebirth in the lower realms.

The Suffering of the Conditioned Nature of Phenomena

The third suffering, as I said, is the most subtle. As with the first two, the point is to establish the resolve to seek liberation. This type of suffering arises from the inherent propensity for grasping at the five aggregates that are the basis of our existence. The five aggregates, sometimes called the five heaps, are form, sensation, perception, mental construction, and consciousness. The suffering of the conditioned nature of phenomena is inherent; it exists no matter what beings do or in what realm they reside within samsara. As was stated earlier, other religions teach renunciation, but to perceive the third type of suffering and to renounce samsara because of it is special to the Buddhist tradition.

In the *Triple Vision*, the third kind of suffering is explained through three topics: the suffering of ceaseless worldly activities, the suffering of never being satisfied with various forms of desire, and the suffering of never being wearied with birth and death.

As for the first, the suffering of ceaseless worldly activities, we can easily see that as soon as one project is complete, another one has already begun—and this goes on ceaselessly. For instance, upon completing one work assignment, meeting with your boss swiftly follows, and the same pattern applies to family activities, such as your children's school events or family gatherings you must attend, as well as social activities like a friend's birthday party or a trip you have to plan with your friends. You often find yourself occupied by these never-ending worldly activities. Regarding the second, the suffering of never being satisfied with various forms of desire, consider that you have had a countless number of births since beginningless time and have lived as all types of beings in samsara, one after another. You have relished all kinds of desire, and yet you are still not satiated. Regarding the third, the suffering of never being wearied of birth and death, consider that from the beginningless time until now, due to your karma and defilements, you have been born in every one of the six realms. In fact, there is not a single spot where you have not been born, and there is not a single other sentient being in whose womb you have not resided. And this continual cycling itself, never being weary of it, is a form of suffering.

Conclusion

Just as the nature of fire is hot, the nature of samsara is suffering. This is true whether one dwells in the lower realms or in the higher ones. Everything in samsara is only of the nature of suffering and a source of suffering. It is necessary to realize this and then conscientiously make an effort to get out of samsara. It is just like if your hair were on fire: you would instantly do everything possible to extinguish it.

As ordinary human beings, we must recognize that having attachment to things like money, clothes, property, or houses is just like having a taste for poisonous food. We feel happy to eat it because it gives us comfort, and we enjoy its taste. However, once it is digested, the poison causes pain and makes us sick. In just the same way, attachment to worldly things can produce joy and satisfaction, but these feelings and states will not remain. Attachment to worldly things is not a cause of happiness, only of suffering. We must recognize that mundane pleasures such as fame, power, and wealth are not real sources of happiness. This is the case even when we think we are enjoying them. If we can recognize the truth of suffering, then, even if we have such things as wealth or fame, we will not be seduced into pride or arrogance.

The only true way to overcome suffering is to develop renunciation for cyclic existence by recognizing its defects. If due to this realization you could generate a genuine and strong sense of renunciation, then whatever practice you do will become stable and effective. Otherwise, you might be enthusiastic and practice diligently, but only for a short while. Lacking firm renunciation, your diligence will not prevail. In order to achieve results in practice, it is absolutely necessary first to establish the firm foundation of renunciation.

CHAPTER 6

THE SECOND COMMON NGÖNDRO: A PRECIOUS HUMAN BIRTH

According to *Triple Vision*, the second common preliminary practice is reflecting on the preciousness of a human birth, which is so difficult to obtain with its leisures and endowments. When we understand how difficult it is to be reborn in samsara into a human body, we will do our best to use our life in the most meaningful way, without wasting this precious opportunity to practice Dharma. There are two important points to understand: first, the rarity of a precious human birth, and second, the great benefits of a precious human birth.

When we encounter something rare and precious in our everyday life, we treasure it. We treat it with great care and use it meaningfully, without wasting it. Our lives are precious like this; they are not only for earning a livelihood or experiencing comforts. If we use our precious human life only to earn a living, then we shall have wasted it. Animals also have to find food and shelter; some wander for miles and miles looking for food to feed their babies. If we live according to our material needs and wants, concerned above all with providing for ourselves or our families, we are not doing more than these animals. Life is not just about having a good time or taking part in mundane pleasures. Instead, we should use our life in the most positive way, which will help us obtain benefits in this and future lives. If we use this precious human life properly, we will attain real happiness.

In *The Way of the Bodhisattva*, the great master Shantideva said that this precious human life is like a boat, by which we can cross a great

86 | THE FUNDAMENTAL PRACTICES

ocean of suffering. It is not easy to obtain this precious human life again; therefore, do not waste this life while you have it, squandering it. With this precious human existence, we can gain happiness, liberation, and the awakened state for the sake of all sentient beings. Among the realms of samsara, the human realm is the best one in which we can practice Dharma. Even the gods do not have such an opportunity to practice profound teachings as we do. Hence, we should recognize the value of a precious human life and know how difficult it is to obtain it.

THE RARITY OF A PRECIOUS HUMAN BIRTH FROM FOUR POINTS OF VIEW

Although there are a considerable number of human beings on earth, nearly eight billion, understanding the various factors involved in being born a human from four points of view—cause, nature, examples, and quantity—reveals the rarity of a human birth. A "precious" human birth, in which one has the opportunity to practice Dharma, is even more scarce. In this section, we will explore these perspectives: the cause that necessitates virtues and good karma, the nature that involves eighteen favorable qualities, an example that illustrates the challenge of attaining human birth, and the limited number of humans compared to other beings in samsara.

From the point of view of its cause

In order to obtain a human life, we need to practice virtuous deeds. Unless we practice virtuous deeds and refrain from indulging in negative deeds, we cannot obtain a precious human life. Furthermore, there are very few people who are practicing virtue. As a consequence, obtaining a human life is also very rare. On the other side, it is very difficult to find someone who abstains from nonvirtuous deeds and has good discipline and good moral conduct.

From the point of view of nature

A precious human life is exceptionally rare in that it is by nature endowed with eighteen qualities. These eighteen qualities refer to being free from the eight unfavorable conditions and being endowed with the ten favorable conditions.

When we have a precious human life, we are free from the eight unfavorable conditions, which means the eight places where there is no opportunity to practice the Dharma. Four of these are nonhuman realms and four are within the human realm. We are free from the four unfavorable conditions that are in the nonhuman realms:

1. The hell realm. There is immense, unbearable suffering in the hell realm. Hell beings have no opportunity to practice the Dharma due to their intense, constant pain and anguish.
2. The hungry ghost realm. These beings have constant hunger and thirst, and because of this they too have no opportunity to practice Dharma.
3. The animal realm. Animals are very ignorant, in general. They do not know what is right and what is wrong. Even if the Dharma is explained to them, they cannot comprehend it. Therefore, animals have no opportunity to practice Dharma.
4. The god realm. It is said that the gods, even though they have long lives and the opportunity to practice Dharma, do not do so because they indulge in so much refined enjoyment that they do not bother. There is also a class of gods dwelling in the *rupdhatu*, the form realm, for whom, apart from the moments of their birth and death, all mental activities are ceased. They are in a type of meditation in which the mind is frozen in one state. If one is born there, there is, likewise, no opportunity to practice Dharma.

A precious human life is also free from the four unfavorable conditions that are possible in the human realm:

88 | THE FUNDAMENTAL PRACTICES

1. To be born a barbarian. People living in uncivilized lands do not have the opportunity to receive Dharma instructions or to learn what is right and wrong.

2. To hold wrong views. Even if one has the opportunity to receive Dharma instruction, the wrong views might be so deeply rooted that the mind is not really changed no matter how many times one hears the Dharma.

3. To be born in a time when a buddha has not appeared. Those times when a buddha appears are called "light eons," and the times when there is no buddha are called "dark eons." There are many dark eons but very few light ones. If a human is born in a dark eon, they will have no opportunity to hear the Dharma.

4. To have a significant learning disability or be unintelligent. Under such conditions, people may be unable to comprehend the Dharma even if they hear it.

Being free from these eight unfavorable conditions means that one has better opportunity to practice the Dharma. But to have a precious human life, one must also be endowed with the ten favorable conditions. There are five obtained from one's own side and five obtained externally.

The five favorable conditions that are obtained from one's own side are as follows:

1. One is born as a human being.

2. One is born in a central place, meaning a civilized place near the Dharma.

3. One is born with senses intact, making one able to receive teachings.

4. One has faith in the Dharma.

5. One has not committed any of the five heinous crimes: killing one's father, killing one's mother, killing an arhat, shedding the blood of a buddha's body, or creating a schism in the Sangha.

These must also be accompanied by the five favorable conditions obtained externally:

THE SECOND COMMON NGÖNDRO: A PRECIOUS HUMAN BIRTH | 89

1. A buddha has appeared in the world. Remember that it is extremely rare to live at a time when a buddha has appeared in the universe.

2. He has taught the Dharma. A buddha does not give teachings unless he sees that there are people ready to receive them. When the present Buddha Shakyamuni first attained enlightenment, he didn't teach right away. He said that although he had found the nectar-like teachings, there was no one around who could comprehend them. Then, Lord Brahma offered a golden wheel with a thousand spokes and requested Buddha to turn the wheel of Dharma.

3. The teachings have to be a living tradition. There are incredibly long gaps of time between when a buddha's teachings have died out and another buddha appears. In these periods, there is no opportunity for a human to hear the Dharma.

4. One must be born in a location where the living tradition is practiced. The opportunity to be born in a place where the Dharma is upheld is also scarce, as there are numerous heretics who reject the teachings of the Buddha.

5. One has the necessary means to support Dharma practice. Of course, one's means can be very simple, as when Milarepa had very little food to eat and survived on nettles.

In this way, we can see that a human life endowed with all eighteen qualities—free from the eight unfavorable conditions and endowed with the ten favorable ones—is quite precious in its rarity.

From the point of view of an example

Imagine that the entire universe is an ocean. There is a blind tortoise living in the ocean. Only once in every one hundred years, does he stick his head above the water. Floating on the surface of this vast ocean is a single golden yoke with one opening. It blows with the winds all over the vast ocean. Consider how rare it would be for the tortoise to stick his head above water and directly into that yoke—almost impossible. This example shows how difficult it is to obtain a precious human birth.

From the point of view of numbers

Although there are many human beings, when we compare our population with other animals, human beings are actually quite few in number. It is easy to count how many people are living in one country, but it is very difficult to count how many worms and insects exist even in a small place. For example, in summertime, we might see the corpse of a dead animal covered with worms. This indicates that there may be innumerable beings ready to enter from the bardo to the bodies of worms. There are many beings dwelling in the bardo who will not be reborn until the necessary causes and conditions arise. Many bardo beings are unable to obtain a body. The number is far greater than the number of human beings. As such, when we compare the numbers of bardo beings, human beings, and other beings, the number of human beings is quite small.

Due to our good deeds, fortune, and merit, we now have been endowed with a precious human birth. Furthermore, we have not only been born as humans, but we have also been endowed with the eighteen freedoms and endowments—something even more extraordinary. Having this opportunity, it would be an unfathomable shame to waste it on mundane pursuits.

The Great Benefit of a Precious Human Life

Not only is the precious human body hard to get, but once we get it, it is much more precious than a wish-fulfilling gem. If we have a wish-fulfilling gem and make an offering to it, it will grant our mundane wishes for food, clothes, and so on. However, it can only grant ordinary things useful in this life. It cannot bring us real happiness, a fortunate rebirth, or final liberation. If we make proper use of this precious life by adopting virtuous actions and abandoning nonvirtuous ones, we will experience happiness not only in this life, but in future lives as well. Eventually, we will attain liberation and the awakened state for the sake of all sentient beings. Once we have such results, we will not regress.

CHAPTER 7

THE THIRD COMMON NGÖNDRO: THE IMPERMANENCE OF LIFE

It is essential that we understand impermanence. This will help us eliminate attachments and see how meaningless it is to develop attachments to the phenomena of samsara. In a sutra, the Buddha says:

> Monks, who ponders impermanence worships the enlightened ones;
> who ponders impermanence is prophesized by the enlightened ones;
> who ponders impermanence is blessed by the enlightened ones.
> Monks, the footprint of an elephant is the best of footprints.
> The notion of impermanence is the best of notions.

So, knowledge of impermanence has great benefit and is clearly a worthwhile endeavor, extending beyond merely motivating us to engage in Dharma practice. Even from a mundane standpoint, recognizing the impermanent nature of life is invaluable. It prompts us to refrain from fixating on trivial matters and prevents us from investing time in unnecessary distress. Instead, we develop an inclination to cherish our relationships, possessions, and experiences. This awareness prompts us to be more appreciative and content, as it fosters a sense of gratitude for what we have. Embracing impermanence, we learn to savor every experience, relishing each sip of coffee or tea and every bite of food as if it were our last. Furthermore, adopting a positive outlook, we acknowledge that challenging times and adversities are transient—they, too, shall pass.

If we lack a strong practice based on understanding impermanence, we will find that we have strong attachments and heavy negative thoughts, including pride, arrogance, jealousy, anger, and so on. On the basis of these thoughts, we perform negative actions. If we had a strong practice based on impermanence, however, then we would be able to see very clearly that anger, attachment, and other negative thoughts are pointless. Remembering impermanence will reduce our negative thoughts and reduce our attachment and clinging to this life.

At the moment, we cling to our friends, family members, possessions, wealth, fame, power, and so on. We have all these attachments because we do not think about impermanence. We do not think about the inevitability of death or change. We must remember that we cannot bring fame, power, wealth, friends, or family with us into our next lives. We will have to leave all of these things behind us. Certainly, if we knew that we were going to die tomorrow, then we wouldn't feel the need to cling to these things anymore.

If someone knew they were going to die in an hour, that person would not be interested in buying a house or a car or some land. With only an hour to live, those things would be of no use and would not seem important anymore. Understanding that death is inevitable and that all things are impermanent will also diminish negative thoughts, such as anger. If two people knew they were going to die in an hour, there would be no point in fighting. Who wins a fight when both will die momentarily?

When we really know that something will not last for long, we are less likely to develop a strong attachment to it. We should think that this life is similar to such ephemeral things as dreams and bubbles. No one has a strong attachment to a bubble, no matter how beautiful it appears. Everyone knows that bubbles do not last. Similarly, in our dreams, all sorts of negative thoughts arise, but once we are awakened, those thoughts cease because we know that dreams are illusory and impermanent. Just like this, our present lives are impermanent and fleeting.

No one can live forever. Once born, we all will die. No one who is born into this world will not also die; no one can avoid death. It may be true right now to think, "This is my family, this is my car, this is my house, these are my things," and so on. But we should remind ourselves that it is true only temporarily—for the next few decades at most. It cannot be true forever, or for centuries to come. In a few decades, we shall be separated from all people and possessions, and there is nothing that we can bring with us to the next life. The only thing that goes with us to the next life is our karma. If our karma—be it good or bad—does not ripen in this life, it will stay with us and ripen in our future lives.

Instead of believing our thoughts of "this is my house" and so on, we should imagine "this is my temporary home, this is my temporary family, this is my temporary monastery." We should see everything as temporary. Life changes constantly, and so do our family members, homes, and material belongings. Our families, parents, homes, birthplaces, and so on are impermanent. Though our families and friends are impermanent, that does not mean that we do not love and care for them; rather, we understand that we must love them without clinging to the expectation of our relationship staying static, and must know that one day we will separate. Consequently, we cherish every moment spent together, understanding that we may not have the same opportunity again. Rather than engaging in conflicts, we treasure our relationships with them. Additionally, we do not know where we will take rebirth, since that depends on karma. With good karma, we are born in a good place. With bad karma, we are born in a bad place, like a desert or as a lower life form. This awareness motivates us to make the most of this precious human life by cultivating virtues and engaging in genuine Dharma practice to the fullest extent possible.

According to the *Triple Vision*, the topic of the impermanence of life is included in the teaching on the precious human life. However, elsewhere it is also reckoned as the third common preliminary. In the *Triple Vision*, it is further subdivided into three categories: the certainty of death, the uncertainty of the time of death, and Dharma practice as one's sole protector from now until buddhahood is reached.

The certainty of death

The Buddha taught that all compounded things are impermanent. There is not a single being born in samsara who will not die. Our lives are very fragile. Even inanimate objects can be dismantled and destroyed. Even solid mountains, which seem so permanent, can be destroyed by external factors such as powerful earthquakes or slow erosion. How much more so impermanent are these fragile living bodies, which break down, are easily harmed, and are eventually destroyed—be it by cremation, burial, or something else.

Year by year, day by day, minute by minute, moment by moment, we get closer and closer to death. Death confronts every living being—all who have been born. There is no escaping the Lord of Death. It does not matter whether we are rich or poor, powerful or not, educated or not, a good person or not.

Truly, we are like animals in a butcher's pen. It is certain that all will die, one after another. Stepping one step means drawing one step closer to the death; two steps means two steps closer to death, and so on. Moment by moment, we grow closer to our deaths. We are like fish caught in a net: all are going to die.

To demonstrate that the end of birth is death, even the great enlightened beings like Buddha Shakyamuni entered *mahaparinirvana*. Although Buddha Shakyamuni was free from birth and death—free from all suffering—he entered mahaparinirvana at Kushinagar as skillful means, to display impermanence for the eyes of common people.

The uncertainty of the time of death

As certain as death is, it is also uncertain when or how we will die. The time of death is not certain because one's lifespan itself is not fixed. People can die at any time and at any age. Some die in their mother's wombs, some at birth, some while young, and others while old. There are many factors or conditions, environmental and biological, that can destroy our dear lives. External factors include earthquakes, floods, fires, hurricanes, tornadoes, poison, the wrong medicine, accidents, sickness, and many other things. Meanwhile, there are very few favorable conditions that can prolong our time alive. Sometimes even conducive factors like food and medicine, which should protect our lives, become harmful—such as in the case of food poisoning, taking the wrong medicine, or overdosage.

Many people died in the COVID-19 pandemic. Some died young and some died old. Personally speaking, I knew a Sakya monk who caught the virus in the early days of the pandemic and unfortunately died. When I learned this, I saw that I had many years of chat messages with this monk still on my phone. The awareness of his sudden absence was strong at that time, looking at the messages and knowing that we could no longer chat as before.

The Lord of Death can take our lives at any time, and we cannot argue with him that we have not finished our projects or that we still have plans. Neither should we think that because we are young, we will not die soon. Young people die, too. We should not think that we are healthy, and because of this we will not die soon. The pandemic showed how quickly our health can change. We should not think that we will not die because we do not have enemies. There are many people without enemies who die from other factors. In the teachings, it says that no one can know which will come first: tomorrow or the next life.

Reflecting on the uncertainty of the time of your death should encourage you to practice the Dharma without any delay. Then, once you have begun, it will also help you to practice unceasingly and with great diligence. At the time of death, you will be prepared, and eventually you will gain realization.

Dharma practice is the only protector at the time of death

At the time of death, the only protector, refuge, and guide we have is our own Dharma practice. Fame, status, wealth, family, supporters, property, and so on cannot help us avoid the pain of dying and death. Taking all these into contemplation and reflection, we, therefore, must focus single-pointedly on our Dharma practice with great devotion and great faith, without further delay.

Ordinary people and those who have not done any good deeds experience great fear of death and strong regret at the end of life, as they have not used their time more meaningfully. They experience great mental suffering because they do not know how to handle their situation when the Lord of Death comes. Wealth, power, fame, family, possessions—

none of these things will help them. The only guide at the time of death will be one's Dharma practice.

It is important to have positive thoughts at the time of death. If we die with negative thoughts, like anger or attachment, they can harm us and prevent us from attaining higher rebirth in the next life. Even someone who has done a lot of Dharma practice can damage their future if they feel anger or attachment at the time of death. Similarly, someone who has not done many virtuous deeds in their life and has not practiced the Dharma, but who has positive thoughts or receives teachings or supplicates the guru at the time of death, will have a better chance of a higher rebirth and a brighter future in the next life.

Birth and death are interdependent—just like tall and short, high and low, right and left. Death is unavoidable once one has been born. The teaching on the four endings says that the end of accumulation is exhaustion, the end of birth is death, the end of meeting is separation, and the end of height is falling. By meditating on impermanence and death, we will come to see that there is more than this life alone. Our past lives have spanned countless billions of years, and our future lives will, too, unless we attain buddhahood.

Conclusion

Knowledge of impermanence has infinite benefits. If we have a genuine sense of impermanence, it will definitely reduce our negative emotions and prevent them from arising. However, knowing *about* impermanence and having an experiential understanding of it are not the same thing. Mere knowledge about impermanence without realizing it experientially will not have much benefit. Therefore, we need to feel and experience impermanence, instead of simply having knowledge about it. And if we continuously remember impermanence as we go about our daily lives, the effect is great and helps us control negative emotions.

The minds of great practitioners are very stable because they have realized impermanence. Merely external factors, like good or bad news, will not impact the stability of their minds or their Dharma practice. As ordinary human beings, we become excited when we hear very good news. We cannot calm our minds in such circumstances, and we cannot focus on our practice when we are excited by mundane things. In the same way, when we hear something very bad, we feel sad and anxious, and we have great mental suffering. Our minds are changeable and too much affected by worldly happiness and sadness.

I had a great teacher when I was at Sakya College named Khenchen Migmar Tsering, who was also the principal of Sakya College at that time. When he became sick with cancer, he was treated at the Rajiv Gandhi Cancer Institute in Delhi, India. All of his devoted students went there to see him, and when they saw him, they cried because they were very worried about him. But Khenchen Migmar himself did not cry. He was not worried. He thought that in his life he had done good things. He had listened to his gurus and served them well by managing Sakya College and other matters, like translation work, and had accomplished many other Dharma activities. It is rare to find a person who has performed virtue to such an extent that their mind is completely at rest at the time of death, rather than anxious or plagued by regret or doubt. How he faced death and lived his life was such an inspiration for me.

Understanding impermanence has other benefits. It is like a whip that makes a horse run faster and faster to its destination. It will help an inferior Dharma practitioner become a mediocre practitioner, a mediocre practitioner become an excellent practitioner, an excellent practitioner become a most excellent practitioner, and with this understanding, the most excellent practitioners will attain buddhahood.

Finally, realizing impermanence will help us realize emptiness. Impermanence and emptiness are connected. Impermanence means that phenomena are changing moment to moment, and because of this, we understand that they are not independently or inherently existent. Realizing impermanence will cause us gradually to realize emptiness, and realizing emptiness is truly the best way, the way that the great practitioners use, to handle good and bad situations properly.

CHAPTER 8

THE FOURTH COMMON NGÖNDRO: THE LAW OF KARMA

By contemplating the defects of samsara, we understand that all the negativity we experience in life is due to our past negative actions—that is, our nonvirtuous deeds. This brings us to the discussion of the law of karma, also known as the law of cause and effect.

The law of karma is one of the fundamental doctrines of the Buddha; he gave many teachings about it. Our beliefs and actions depend on the law of karma, because without the idea of karma, we could not practice properly. If we did not believe in karma, which in Sanskrit means "action," then we could not understand rebirth; and if we did not understand both karma and rebirth, then those who are dying, dead, or in the bardo[11] state, in addition to whoever is reborn, would not be considered sentient beings, because we would assume they did not exist. In simpler terms, believing in karma naturally leads to believing in rebirth. This belief strengthens our commitment to Dharma practice, making it more profound. Karma teaches us that positive actions lead to happiness, motivating us to engage in virtuous deeds and Dharma practice. Accepting rebirth also reinforces our understanding that all sentient beings were once our loved ones, inspiring us to cultivate boundless love and compassion for them. Without belief in rebirth, our practice may lack depth, as we may view life as too short to make a significant impact. Additionally, without belief in rebirth, our love and compassion may be conditional and biased—we tend to love those we like and ignore those we dislike. However, acknowledging that all beings, including those in the bardo state, were once dear to us, motivates us to cultivate genuine compassion for every being, whether visible or invisible to our naked eyes. This encourages us to extend compassion beyond personal preferences or biases. If we cannot comprehend the idea of "all sentient beings," then we cannot practice Mahayana refuge, loving-kindness, compassion, or bodhichitta, because all these are based on the idea of "all sentient beings." Any practice on the path is done for the sake of all sentient beings.

When we engage in an action, or *karma*, it is akin to planting a seed in soil. When the sown seed meets with all the necessary conditions, including fertile soil, water, sunlight, and suitable temperature, along with protection from threats like birds or human interference, the seed will germinate and eventually bear fruit. Actions cannot be undone; they endure until their consequences are fully experienced. However, karma can be considered incomplete if it lacks any of four essential factors. These factors—base, motivation, execution, and completion—determine the completeness of karma. For instance, scriptures often cite the act of killing to illustrate these factors.

1. Base: For the act of killing, the base refers to the object or victim being targeted for harm.

2. Motivation: The motivating factor involves the intention behind the action. If the individual intends to cause harm or kill, driven by negative emotions like anger or desire, the motivation is present. Conversely, if harm is caused unintentionally, such as accidentally stepping on an ant hidden in the bushes, the motivation for the act of killing is absent.

3. Execution: When the base and intention, motivated by negative thoughts or emotions, are present, the actual act follows. This act is executed either through bodily actions or speech. Examples of actions manifested by the body include killing and stealing, while lying and harsh speech are examples of actions manifested through speech.

4. Completion: When the action is fully executed through body or speech, accompanied by a sense of gratification, the act is complete. An example would be when a person kills with intention, and then upon completion experiences a sense of

THE FOURTH COMMON NGÖNDRO: THE LAW OF KARMA | 101

satisfaction, and thinks "Well, I did it," rather than feeling regret or remorse. This sense of gratification signifies the completion of the action.

If any of these four factors is missing, the karma becomes incomplete or weak, leading to a reduced impact on its effects. Nonetheless, it's important to note that weak karma can become stronger through repetition. Certain negative actions vary in severity; for example, idle talk is less severe than killing. However, consistently engaging in lesser negative actions over time accumulates a significant amount of strong negative karma.

Once karma is set in motion, it cannot be reversed. When the appropriate conditions align, its consequences will inevitably manifest. The ripening of karma will be inevitable if we don't confess and purify our negative actions. Negative karma that has not fully ripened can be purified through genuine and sincere acknowledgment of the misdeed, accompanied by deep remorse and a firm resolve to avoid repeating it. Failing to confess even the slightest misdeed can exacerbate its severity, with its negative effects intensifying over time. It's important to note that the intention to commit negative actions with the belief that they can be purified later only serves to perpetuate negative karma, rather than purifying it. The Buddha said when a king dies, his wealth, family members, followers, and kingdom will not follow him to the next life. Rather, wherever he goes, his own actions, or karma, be they good or bad, will follow him and ripen for him alone; they will not ripen for other sentient beings or inanimate things.

In all Buddhist traditions the law of karma is essential. The Buddha's teachings are entirely based upon it. Karma derives from one's past lives, present life, and future lives together, not only one's present life alone. The law of karma is fair to all sentient beings without any discrimination. There is no special treatment for anyone. There is no special law of karma just for rich, famous, or powerful people. It is the same set of karmic laws for everyone. Ordinary beings have no choice but to obey the law of karma.

Take me for example. In this moment, in the Sakyapa community, I hold a high position and have the high title of "His Holiness." But it does not mean I am above the law of karma. I still have to follow the law of karma. If I do something wrong, I have to experience suffering caused by my own actions. Whether one is poor or rich, ordinary or high ranking, no matter who we are, we are all the same in the view of karma. We cannot cheat the law of karma. We can deceive fellow human beings through our behaviors or through our self-expression, and we can hide our bad actions from other human beings, but we cannot hide from the law of karma. For instance, if one takes poison, no matter where one takes it, in front of others or secretly, the consequence will be the same—one will suffer. Similarly, whether we disclose our negative actions or keep them secret, a bad action is always a bad action, and will be the cause of suffering. The best-case scenario is always to respect and follow the law of karma according to the Buddha's teachings. Therefore, we should try to abandon nonvirtuous deeds.

The Buddha stated that all our experiences stem from our own karma. Our experiences typically fall into two types of projections: illusory appearance and karmic appearance. Illusory appearance implies that what we perceive lacks inherent existence; however, we still perceive subjects and objects as dualities, such as "happy and sad" or "like and dislike," trapping us in this dualistic view. Karmic appearance refers to phenomena that arise as a result of individual karma, leading to diverse experiences such as varying lifespans, wealth, companionship, and other circumstances. So, whether we are happy or not, whether we are reborn into better or worse circumstances, is all based on the law of karma. Regardless of how powerful, great, rich, or famous we are at present, in this world we are subject to karma. We all need to understand karma and have a sense of conviction about it.

The law of karma relates especially to rebirth. Without accepting rebirth, we cannot accept the law of karma completely. Because karma will ripen in more than one lifetime, it applies to future lives in addition to our present one. So to accept the law of karma completely, one must also accept rebirth.

KARMA AND REBIRTH

Our conviction in rebirth should be based on logical reasoning, not on blind faith. The logical reasons we use are predicated on causal relation-

THE FOURTH COMMON NGÖNDRO: THE LAW OF KARMA | 103

ships. In a Buddhist text on the topic of *pramana*, or valid cognition, it says that the main cause of the present moment of consciousness is the previous moment of consciousness. Although the present moment of consciousness can have other conditions, such as other beings or inanimate objects, its main cause is its own previous consciousness. Other inanimate objects or other beings cannot be the main cause of the present moment of consciousness. If something exists in relative truth, then it is not necessary to perceive it directly, because it is a safe assumption. Although we cannot perceive karma directly, we can accept it based on logical reasons connected to the effects of karma that we can perceive directly.

I heard once that a scholar was asked, "How can you prove there is a next life when you cannot see it?" I think this happened in the 1950s. The scholar replied, "How can you believe there is tomorrow? You cannot see tomorrow today." The other person laughed. Although we cannot see tomorrow, we believe there is a tomorrow after today. Similarly, despite the fact that we cannot see the next life, we believe it to be there.

Belief means we do not need to see the matter we believe in now. We cannot see tomorrow today, but we believe there is a tomorrow after today. We can prove there is a next life because of the principal cause of the first moment of consciousness in a future life is a previous moment of consciousness.

Consciousness is an unbroken continuum that never breaks and always continues. Although it is not an identical consciousness that persists over time, it is a single continuum. It is just like a waterfall. A waterfall on a steep mountain can remain for years, but it is not the same water from year to year, or even from moment to moment. The water changes each moment, but the continuity of the waterfall remains. Likewise, our consciousness changes from moment to moment, but the continuity of consciousness persists. For that reason, we believe in rebirth, and based on this, we can accept the law of karma completely.

Anyone can engage in whatever actions they wish. Yet by positive acts, one reaps good results; by negative acts, one reaps bad results. We are free to choose how to act, but once something is done, we do not have any freedom to choose the result of the action. For example, once something negative is done, we cannot choose to attain happiness or other good results by it. By doing bad things, one has no choice but to experience suffering as a result. Once a rice seed is planted in a field, it will only grow rice. No other grains will grow from that seed, no matter how much we may hope they will. Similarly, we have no right to choose happiness as a result of having done negative actions.

Whether we practice virtue or not depends on us. Once an action is done, the result follows choicelessly. We all have the potential to attain liberation and the awakened state if we engage in virtuous deeds and practice Dharma. We all have buddha nature, which means we all have consciousness. The nature of consciousness is beginninglessly pure, whereas all negative thoughts are temporary and superficial. They are not the nature of mind or consciousness. This is true in terms of relative truth. Overall, all the apparent phenomena that arise from our perceptions and the workings of our mind are the illusions of confusion, representing relative truth. The core of our consciousness, which naturally illuminates our experiences, and the underlying truth that this consciousness is empty of the illusions we create—these are considered ultimate truth. For this reason, we all have the ability and potential to attain liberation, but whether we succeed or not depends on the individual. If you sow a seed in a dry box, although this seed has the potential to grow into a plant, it will only grow when has the right conditions—the right soil, moisture, fertilizer, and light. Likewise, we all have the potential to reach awakening, but whether we get to buddhahood depends on our choices. If we have the right method and apply it, then we will reap the desired results: liberation and full awakening. So, it is important for all of us to follow the law of karma and practice virtue.

The way the Buddha guides us is by showing us the path, which means showing the difference between right and wrong. Whether we can benefit from the Buddha's teaching or not depends on us. If we practice the teachings, then we benefit; if we only listen without practice, then we do not benefit.

Whether we gain the right result depends on our methods, practice, and motivation. To achieve any good results, we have to make an effort. In a school where there are adequate teachers, textbooks, and facilities, whether or not a student learns a great deal does not depend on teachers or resources alone, but mostly on the student. If a student has no interest, no diligence, and does not pay attention, then no matter how skilled the teacher happens to be, the student will not learn anything. If both the teacher and student make a collaborative effort, then the student can learn. Likewise, though the Buddha has done a lot for us, whether we can get the help from the Buddha comes down to each of us individually. The Buddha has undertaken so many noble activities for our sake, but whether we can benefit depends on us—our interest, motivation, action, study, meditation, and practice.

The Buddha once stated that he had shown his disciples the methods that lead to liberation, but liberation depended on them, so they should exert themselves. If we follow the Buddha's teachings properly, we can embark on the path, progress on it, and eventually gain liberation. This is how the Buddha helps us and guides us.

It says in the teachings that the Buddha would not wash away others' negative karma, remove suffering by a laying-on of hands, or transfer his ultimate realization to others. But the Buddha showed us the nature of reality, and through this he liberates us from suffering.

The Buddha also stated that one is one's own savior and protector, one is one's own enemy. This means if one personally adopts positive acts and abandons negative acts, then one's own good deeds are protectors. Our worst enemy does not exist externally; rather, it is our own mind. Our negative thoughts are our enemies and demons. The "four maras," or demons, are the demons of afflictive emotions, such as our own aggression, greed, jealousy, and so on. They destroy our happiness and block positive outcomes. Our worst enemy is the one who causes us the greatest suffering—that is, the afflictive emotions that take us to the three lower realms, where we have to experience inconceivable and inexpressible suffering, to which human suffering is incomparable.

We must understand the necessity of practicing virtue, to help ourselves and others. As long as we do good things, we are able to help ourselves and others.

TYPES OF KARMA

Since *karma*, in fact, literally means "actions" or "deeds," there are various kinds of karma. In general, there are three kinds of karma: negative,

106 | THE FUNDAMENTAL PRACTICES

positive, and neutral. There are additionally three steps involved when we study the law of karma: first, we need to know the types of karma; second, we need to contemplate the results of these different types of karma; and third, we must make great effort to avoid negative deeds, engage more in positive deeds, and transform neutral deeds into positive deeds.

Negative karma

Nonvirtuous or unwholesome deeds are actions that have been motivated by the three poisons: anger, ignorance, and desire. There are ten nonvirtuous deeds, which can be further divided into deeds committed with body, speech, and mind. Three nonvirtuous deeds are committed physically: (1) killing, either doing so oneself or asking others to slaughter or kill any living being; (2) stealing, again either doing so oneself or asking others to do so, whether a precious thing or an insignificant thing; and (3) sexual misconduct, which entails activities apart from one's life partner or those done at an improper time, in an improper place, or by improper passages. The next four nonvirtuous deeds are committed through acts of speech: (4) telling lies in a nonvirtuous way—that is, not for virtuous reasons, such as lying to a hunter about the whereabouts of deer in order to save the lives of the innocent animals, which in fact, is considered a virtuous deed; (5) creating schisms or creating disharmony between individuals or groups; (6) using harsh words; and (7) making idle talk that has no benefit and that will create more harm. Finally, three nonvirtuous deeds are committed by the mind: (8) having greed; (9) harboring feelings of hatred, wishing someone to experience misfortune; and (10) having wrong views, such as not believing the law of karma.

There are three consequences for committing nonvirtuous deeds. The first consequence, which is determined by motivation and the amount of nonvirtuous action committed, is to be reborn in the lower realms. If the negative deed is committed with anger, such as killing out of anger, one is more likely to fall down to the hell realms. If a negative deed is committed out of greed, such as killing animals for their meat, one will most likely fall into the hungry ghost realms. If a negative deed is committed out of ignorance, such as killing animals for fun, then one is likely to be reborn in the animal realm. Further, if one performs the ten nonvirtuous deeds to a great extent, one will be born in hell realms; if performed to a middling extent, its consequence is to be reborn in a hungry ghost realm; if committed to a small extent, one will be reborn in the animal realm. It is important to note that one's negative karma will grow more if the negative deeds have been committed many times.

The second consequence is a result similar to its cause, which also has two different parts: the experience similar to its cause and the action similar to its cause. For example, by killing, one will have an unhealthy life and short lifespan because one has shortened the lifespan of another being—since one has created pain for them, one will thus have pain. Likewise, if one steals, one will experience poverty; by telling lies, one will not hear the truth; and so forth. These consequences are examples of an experience similar to its cause. If one has committed negative deeds, an intrinsic habit of similar negative action will form; thus, in future lives, one will enjoy committing such negative actions again. For example, if one kills many animals, in one's next life, one will commit killing again and again. This is an example of a consequence that is an action similar to its cause.

The third consequence of committing the ten nonvirtuous deeds is that negative karma will ripen as the environment of the world where one is going to be reborn. For example, by committing the nonvirtuous act of killing, one will be born in very unhappy places, where there are extreme weather conditions and natural disasters, and so on. This consequence is known as the prevailing result.

Positive karma

There are three steps to understanding virtuous deeds: to identify the ten virtuous deeds, to reflect on the results of the ten virtuous deeds, and to engage in virtuous deeds as much as possible. The ten virtuous deeds are the opposite of the ten nonvirtuous deeds: (1) to abstain from killing, (2) to abstain from stealing, (3) to abstain from sexual misconduct, (4) to renounce telling lies in a nonvirtuous way, (5) to give up creating schisms, (6) to abandon using harsh words, (7) to abstain from idle talk,

108 | THE FUNDAMENTAL PRACTICES

(8) to renounce covetousness, (9) to abandon harboring thoughts of hatred for others, and (10) to cease having wrong views.

Regarding the results, there are three consequences to performing the ten virtuous deeds. First, as a result of virtuous actions, one will take birth in the higher realms. By performing virtuous deeds to a great extent, one will be born in the god realm; by virtuous deeds done to a middling extent, one will be born in the demigod realms; and by virtuous deeds done to a small extent, one will be born in the human realm. Some might question this, since a human birth is deemed the most precious, why is it the result of virtuous deeds done only to a small extent? In this context, the results of virtuous deeds are determined by the quantity of virtues performed in past lifetimes. Yet, among all the six realms, a precious human birth with its leisures and endowments still provides the best and most conducive conditions for Dharma practice.

The second consequence is the result similar to its cause, which is twofold: an experience similar to its cause, and an action similar to its cause. When one abstains from killing, one will have a long and healthy life; when one abstains from stealing, one will have a wealthy life. These are examples of a result that is an experience similar to its cause. In regard to a result that is an action similar to its cause, if one abstained from negative deeds, an intrinsic habit of not committing negative deeds forms in future lives. For instance, when one abstains from killing, one will not indulge in killing in next life.

The third consequence of performing virtues is related to the outer environment: one will be born in beautiful places with no natural disasters. Such a consequence is the prevailing result of performing virtuous actions.

Having learned about the positive outcomes of practicing virtuous actions and the negative consequences of engaging in nonvirtuous actions, it is imperative that we strive to cultivate as many virtuous behaviors as possible and completely abandon nonvirtuous deeds, no matter how small they may seem. Why? Because we all seek happiness and wish to avoid suffering. Knowing this, why would we willingly act against our own well-being, especially now that we are aware of the consequences? Practicing virtues is not an impossible mission; we can start right here, right now, in our daily lives. Every action we undertake with our body, speech, and mind has the potential to be virtuous, free from ignorance, desire, and greed. Additionally, many actions we perform in our daily lives may seem neither virtuous nor nonvirtuous—neutral. In the following discussion, I will elaborate on how we can transform these neutral actions into virtuous acts.

Neutral karma

There are again three steps to understanding neutral or indifferent deeds: to identify the neutral deeds, to reflect on the results of neutral deeds, then endeavoring to transform neutral deeds to virtuous deeds. Neutral karma refers to deeds that are neither virtuous nor nonvirtuous, such as walking, sitting, sleeping, and so on. These actions are far better than nonvirtuous deeds because they do not produce any suffering, yet they do not produce any positive results, such as happiness, either; they are kind of useless. Neutral deeds can be transformed to virtuous or nonvirtuous deeds, depending on our motivation. Such transformation is possible because, according to the Paramitayana and Vajrayana traditions, whether an action is deemed virtuous or nonvirtuous depends on one's motivation.

Transforming neutral deeds into positive deeds

When we see a stick on the floor, the stick is not helping or harming anyone, but it has the potential to help or harm someone, depending on how it is used. If it is used as a walking stick, the neutral stick has become a helpful stick. If the same stick is used by someone to beat someone else, then it has become a harmful stick. When it is just lying on the floor, it is neutral. It is how a person uses the stick that transforms its neutral quality to a helpful or harmful one. While neutral, the stick is like our neutral activities, such as eating and sleeping. Neutral deeds can be converted into helpful or harmful deeds depending on our own motivation.

Normally, we assume that we need to have a good rest so that we can do more Dharma study and practice the next day. If we exercise, then it will help and sustain our body, making our body healthy so that we can do more Dharma activities with more physical and mental power. These are examples of how neutral activities can turn positive, for the Dharma. The main thing is to have the right motivation: thoughts of renunciation, loving-kindness, and compassion.

A sutra mentions how to convert ordinary activities into positive deeds. For example, whether we are alone or with our family at home, we can pray that all beings may be able to gain liberation. When we are sitting, we can pray that all beings may be able to sit on the vajra seat on which they will attain buddhahood. When we go to sleep, we can pray that all beings may attain the *dharmakaya*.[12] When we wake up, we can pray that all beings may attain the *rupakaya*.[13] When we put on clothes, we can think we are wearing the "clothes of modesty"—that is, of abstinence from doing anything nonvirtuous. While bathing, we can imagine that we are washing away afflictive emotions. When eating, we can imagine that we are eating the food of *samadhi*,[14] or concentration. When leaving home, we can think, "May I be liberated from the samsara." When embarking on a trip, we can think, "May we gain the noble path, such as the path of seeing," or the first stage to realization. When meeting people, we can imagine we are meeting the Buddha. While doing regular tasks, we can imagine, "May this complete two purposes: for myself and for others." When going to a town, we can think, "May we enter the city of liberation." When we get there, we can think, "May we reach the stage of buddhahood." These are just some examples mentioned by the Buddha himself in the sutras.

So, by changing our motivation and intentions, we should try to convert neutral actions into positive ones. If we are careless, neutral actions can become nonvirtuous. For example, we could wish for a good sleep so that tomorrow we could better destroy our enemies—with that intention, sleep becomes nonvirtuous. Even neutral actions such as eating or sleeping become nonvirtuous if done with the wrong intention. Since we have this opportunity to convert our actions, we should use it, and transform our lives in a positive way.

CONCLUSION OF THE FOUR COMMON PRELIMINARIES

This concludes the topic of the common preliminary teachings: the defects of samsara, the rarity of a precious human life, the impermanence of life, and the law of karma. Ideally, whenever we practice the Dharma, we should remember these common preliminaries. They greatly impact our minds, enabling us to deal with nonvirtuous thoughts, develop positive thoughts, and practice virtue. If we contemplate these four topics within the context of our main daily practice, our meditation will be effective, because it will have a positive impact on the mind.

CHAPTER 9
THE FIRST UNCOMMON NGÖNDRO: REFUGE

Before we engage more deeply with the first uncommon ngöndro, it is important to understand the context of the set of uncommon preliminary practices. The five uncommon ngöndro, or uncommon preliminary practices, are practices of refuge, bodhichitta, Vajrasattva, mandala offering, and guru yoga.

The first uncommon preliminary practice is refuge. Refuge is preliminary to all Buddhist paths and is the root of all Dharma. Refuge vows are the basis of all Buddhist vows, and are what distinguish Buddhists from non-Buddhists. Taking refuge is also part of pratimoksha vows.

The second uncommon preliminary is bodhichitta. With the bodhichitta vow, we elevate our practice to the level of Mahayana, the Great Vehicle. Bodhichitta is what differentiates the Mahayana from the Shravakayana, or Hearer Vehicle.

The third uncommon preliminary is Vajrasattva meditation and mantra recitation, which purifies obscurations, negative karma, and obstacles on the path. It can also restore the minor faults of the Mantrayana and enhance the Mantrayana vow.

The fourth uncommon preliminary is mandala offering, which is a method for accumulating merit on the path.

The fifth uncommon preliminary is guru yoga, which assists us in gaining personal experience and realization of the path in a short time, and helps hold the root and lineage gurus' blessings in one's mind.

The Importance of Refuge within Buddhism

To become a Buddhist, it is not enough just to have faith in the Buddha and his teachings. Even though we have faith, if we do not take refuge, then we are not genuine Buddhists. Without taking the refuge vow, even a person with unshakable faith in the Buddha and his teachings would not really be considered "Buddhist" in name. Being born in a Buddhist family does not necessarily make you a Buddhist, either. Neither does studying Buddha's teachings, or just believing in rebirth and the law of karma. Just having altruistic thoughts, wishing to help others, does not make us a real Buddhist. To become a Buddhist, we must take refuge and we must receive the refuge vow from a qualified teacher. Only then are we really considered Buddhist.

The Triple Gem

The Triple Gem is called *könchok sum* in Tibetan, with *sum* meaning "three." *Kön* means "rare," and *chok* means "supreme." So, the literal translation of *könchok* means "rare and supreme," but metaphorically, *könchok* means "precious gem," because gems are rare. Precious gems like diamonds are more valuable than gold, silver, or other gems. That is why a precious jewel like a diamond might be called *könchok*, rare and excellent.

Diamonds are just an example. In the Buddhist context, *könchok sum* refers to the Buddha, Dharma and Sangha, the Triple Gem. Why are these "rare and precious"? Because those who have accumulated merit can meet the Triple Gem, whereas those who lack sufficient merit will not. Without any merit, finding the Triple Gem is impossible. To encounter the Triple Gem is rare, but it is also better than finding a powerful god or another powerful being. Therefore, the Triple Gem is the rarest and best place for us to take refuge from samsara and is termed *könchok*, "rare and supreme."

The Benefits of Taking and Practicing Refuge

Traditionally, there are several benefits to taking refuge and practicing

THE FIRST UNCOMMON NGÖNDRO: REFUGE | 115

it consistently after the refuge ceremony. It's crucial to understand that taking refuge isn't merely about the formal ritual; it entails seeking mental refuge in the Triple Gem. Contemplating and practicing refuge can purify our karmic obscurations. One cannot be harmed by the negative actions of humans and nonhumans. It can also reduce our physical and mental suffering. In other words, refuge eliminates unfavorable conditions. By taking refuge, one gains a new "name." No longer an ordinary person, one is now a "Buddhist," and from that time onward, one belongs to the Buddhist clan.

By taking refuge one becomes worthy of veneration by humans and gods. One will be protected by divinities or *dharmapalas*, the divine beings who protect the Dharma. One will have confidence that one will never be separated from the Triple Gem in any future lives.

Refuge is the root of all Dharma practices. Therefore, taking refuge in the Triple Gem has great benefit, and ultimately one will become a buddha through the practice of refuge. But to be able to conceive a genuine vow of refuge, we first need to have the right causes and conditions. That is, we need to know the reason for taking refuge and then take refuge genuinely. That is essential.

Different Types of Refuge Vows

Let it be noted that not all refuge vows are genuine. There are two types of refuge vows: pure and impure. Impure refuge vows are those taken without the attitude of renunciation, or those taken with a mundane intention. When it is taken with the hope of only benefiting oneself, especially for accomplishing a worldly purpose for this present lifetime, the refuge vow cannot be considered a Mahayana vow or even a genuine Buddhist refuge vow.

There are two types of impure refuge vows. The first type of impure refuge vow is taken without a wish to receive it. For example, one might be forced to take refuge by one's own teachers or loved ones in order to avoid punishment, to make them happy, or not to disappoint them. The second type of impure refuge vow aims for worldly results like fame, wealth, power, and so on. Such refuge lacks the attitude of renunciation, so it is not genuine.

Refuge should be taken with the thought of renunciation, as well as the pratimoksha vows. Pratimoksha vows, or individual liberation vows, form the bedrock of Buddhism, primarily emphasizing disciplined physical behavior and refraining from harming others. *Prati* means "oneself" or "an individual," and *moksha* means "liberation from samsara." There are seven or sometimes eight types of pratimoksha vows, applicable to both lay practitioners and monastics. In the Tibetan Buddhist tradition, lay pratimoksha vows encompass the five precepts: abstaining from killing, stealing, false speech, sexual misconduct, and using intoxicants. Generally, during the refuge ceremony, a practitioner may choose to adopt all five precepts, none of them, or a combination thereof. Male and female lay practitioners who opt for all five precepts are referred to as *upasaka* and *upasika*, respectively. However, for those embarking on the Vajrayana practices, regardless of the specific vows one takes, cultivating the thought of renunciation is considered fundamental when taking refuge. It is also worth mentioning that afterward, one should keep the rules, which include the general rules—observing the five precepts—and the specific rules.

Without the attitude of renunciation, one is not aligned with the sense of pratimoksha. Without renunciation, one cannot be liberated from samsara. Unless you wish to go somewhere, you will not make an effort, so without that motivation you will not reach your particular destination. Similarly, without a wish for liberation, one makes no effort and therefore will not be liberated. The great Sakya master Gorampa Sönam Sengé said, "To receive any pratimoksha vows, one must have renunciation." This means we need to abandon any harmful thoughts and aspire for liberation and enlightenment.

So, we need to know what refuge vows are, and how to distinguish genuine refuge vows from false ones. Then, having clearly understood that distinction, we should take the genuine refuge vow with renunciation. Without renunciation, we do not take refuge vows in a genuine way, which means we fail to take any Buddhist vows at all. Thus, cultivating the thought of renunciation from samsara is vital.

Generally speaking, there are two kinds of refuge a person might seek out: worldly, mundane refuge, and beyond-worldly, supramundane refuge. In order to fulfill mundane wishes, people take refuge in mundane deities, or deities who are beings still bound in samsara, such as Brahma and Shiva; here, both the intention of the practitioner and the object of refuge are mundane. Moreover, some go for refuge in ordinary beings, as opposed to mundane divinities, just because they seem more capable than us on a particular matter. So, we might go to such-and-such person for refuge, for whatever mundane ordinary matters. This is also considered mundane refuge, being based on mundane intentions and mundane objects.

If one goes for refuge in the Triple Gem with mundane objectives, such as wealth, power, longevity, work, or other ordinary desires, then that refuge is still a mundane refuge. The intention is mundane even though the object of refuge is not. It will not cause oneself or others to be liberated from samsara.

There are two types of supramundane refuge: common refuge and uncommon refuge. Common refuge refers to refuge in both the Shravakayana, or Hearer Vehicle, and Pratyekabuddhayana,[15] or Solitary Realizer Vehicle, and also to Paramitayana refuge, which occurs in the context of the general Mahayana tradition. Uncommon refuge, on the other hand, refers to refuge in the Vajrayana tradition.

Refuge in the Shravakayana and Pratyekabuddhayana traditions

Although Shravakayana practitioners take refuge in the Triple Gem, they primarily take refuge in the Sangha, because their ultimate goal is to achieve liberation as a shravakabuddha, who is part of the Sangha. According to the Mahayana, because a *shravakabuddha* is not a complete buddha, they are still considered part of the Sangha, and therefore their main object of refuge is the Sangha. Pratyekabuddhayana practitioners, those aiming to be solitary realizers, primarily take refuge in the Dharma.

Refuge in the Mahayana tradition

Mahayana practitioners, such as us, primarily take refuge in the Buddha because our ultimate goal is to attain perfect buddhahood for the benefit of all sentient beings.

118 | THE FUNDAMENTAL PRACTICES

In the Tibetan language, *kyab dro* means "go for refuge." The avenues for taking refuge are with our body, speech, and mind; of these three, mind is the main avenue for taking refuge. This means we should be taking refuge mentally, not just by way of physical prostrations, showing respect, or verbally reciting refuge prayers hundreds of thousands of times. Although these are also beneficial, they are much more beneficial with the full participation of the mind. In other words, we should take refuge with the right motivation and proper visualization.

Reasons for Taking Refuge

To take refuge, it is important to have the right reason or cause to do so. Simply because other people are doing so is not a genuine reason. According to the teachings, there are three reasons for taking refuge in the Triple Gem: fear, faith, and compassion.

The three fears

Practicing refuge well depends on contemplating the appropriate reasons for taking refuge. Every result depends on causes and conditions. If there is no appropriate cause, then there is no suitable result. In order to practice refuge properly, we need an appropriate reason to do so. The first reason is fear, which is actually threefold: the fear of suffering in samsara, the fear of self-cherishing thoughts, and the fear of deluded clinging to ordinary phenomena.

The first type of fear, fear of suffering in samsara, is the common Buddhist reason for taking refuge, and the common reason for taking Buddhist vows. "Common" in this case means that it is common to Shravakayana and Pratyekabuddhayana practitioners, as well as to Mahayana practitioners—all have the same fear when they take refuge. Any Buddhist wanting to seek refuge will have this fear. Without this fear as a motivation, one cannot receive any genuine Buddhist refuge vows.

Why do we need to have such fear? As you know, the nature of samsara is suffering. As ordinary beings, as long as we remain in samsara, we are caught up in negative actions and afflictive emotions. In order to overcome suffering, we must be liberated, and to achieve liberation we must first fear the suffering of samsara. Due to such fear, we will make an effort to overcome suffering. For instance, if we are ill, we fear increased pain and discomfort. Because of that fear, we might go to the hospital and consult doctors to make sure our illnesses will be treated. Likewise, having experienced enormous suffering in the past, we fear more such suffering in the future. To avoid it we take refuge in the Triple Gem.

The second kind of fear is the fear of self-cherishing thoughts. This is an uncommon reason for taking refuge, meaning it is the Mahayana reason for taking refuge but not the Hinayana reason for taking refuge. Self-cherishing thoughts are the root of all the suffering because suffering is caused by negative actions, which are themselves cause by the three types of poisonous thoughts, or afflictive emotions. All negative actions are motivated by those three basic afflictions—that is, ignorance, attachment, and anger—and the root of these afflictions is self-cherishing. When we do not recognize the true nature of all phenomena, we cling to a "self" out of ignorance. Thus self-cherishing thought is none other than ignorance.

Strong or afflicted fixation on ourselves arises with this basic confusion, beginning as some kind of perception of "self" and "other." On the basis of that, we experience increased attachment to ourselves and anger or hatred toward others. So, it is due to self-cherishing thoughts that the two poisons of attachment and anger develop. The three afflictions then lead to many other negative emotions, such as pride, jealousy, stinginess, and so on. The root of these afflictions, this self-cherishing, is not outside us but within our own mind.

When there is an actual source of suffering, fear is legitimate. For example, the mere sight of a poisonous snake in one's bedroom ought to incite fear. Even if we've never before been attacked by a snake, the presence of a snake produces fear in us because we know it could be a cause of pain and suffering. Due to fear or not wanting to suffer from the attack of the snake, the moment we see a snake we instantly want to escape—we want to take refuge in a safer place. The fact of the snake being a potential cause of suffering is what compels us to do so, not any perceived movement by the snake to attack. Similarly, self-cherishing thoughts have already caused so much pain and suffering in the past and

120 | THE FUNDAMENTAL PRACTICES

will continue to cause more pain and suffering in the future; we should therefore be fearful of this cause of suffering, and out of such fear, take refuge in the Triple Gem. This is the second type of fear, which is the uncommon Mahayana cause of refuge.

The third fear is the uncommon Vajrayana-oriented reason for taking refuge, which is fear of deluded clinging to ordinary phenomena. In Vajrayana, all appearances are considered pure. However, clinging to ordinary appearances, sounds, and thoughts poses the main obstacle on the Vajrayana path. This fear serves as a motivating factor for Vajrayana practitioners to seek refuge. If you are a Vajrayana practitioner, you should have these three fears and take refuge. If you have not yet received any Vajrayana empowerments, as a Mahayana practitioner you should take refuge in the Triple Gem incited by the first two fears.

The three types of faith

The second primary cause of taking refuge is faith, which is itself three-fold: clear faith, eager faith, and confident faith. All these three types of faith are required to take refuge.

The first of these, clear faith, is being impressed by the infinite and ultimate qualities of the Buddha. For example, if an entrepreneur sees great profit potential in a particular business, they will invest in that business with excitement and joy, even if they have to make great sacrifices and assume great risk along the way. Likewise, having seen the infinite qualities and great results attained by the buddhas, one feels immense joy and is amazed at such qualities, one's mind becomes clear and relieved, and one is comforted.

The second type of faith is eager faith, or passionate faith, which means not only being impressed and amazed by the infinite qualities of the Buddha, and feeling joy and excitement for them, but really wishing to attain the ultimate state, buddhahood, for the sake of all sentient beings.

The third type of faith required for refuge in the Triple Gem is confident faith. We cannot actually fathom all the infinite qualities of the Buddha, but if our faith is sincere, free of any hesitation or doubt about those infinite qualities, then that would be confident faith. In other words, one has no doubt regarding the infinite qualities of the Buddha.

We really believe such things are possible. Without belief, one cannot develop confidence. Practicing with doubt and hesitation makes it difficult to succeed greatly when undertaking practice. So, we must have confident faith in the Triple Gem, free of any doubt or hesitation.

The three faiths are crucial to the practice of refuge and to Buddhadharma in general. For genuine, unshakable faith, we need strong belief, but that cannot mean blind belief, without grounds or reasons. We should have strong conviction and belief in the Triple Gem based on logical evidence. When we claim that the Buddha is the ultimate excellent being, we say so not because we are Buddhists, but because there are logical reasons for saying so.

How would we establish the Buddha's greatness? The Buddha has given precious and profound teachings, which are true and genuine. No matter how much we examine them, we cannot prove these teachings are wrong. Because the Buddha has given precious and profound teachings, which are true and genuine, we cannot prove these teachings are wrong, no matter how much we examine them. For that reason, we can establish the Buddha's greatness with reference to his teachings. The more we examine and investigate the teachings, the more conviction and belief we have in the Triple Gem. Even if someone criticizes our faith, it will not have any influence and impact on our belief system—that is to say, we will not doubt our own faith. We would not then criticize our own faith or change our faith.

The actual method to develop genuine and unshakable faith is to know the reasons why the Buddha, Dharma, and Sangha are so great. If we examine them and try to understand their qualities, we will definitely have genuine reasons to believe in the Triple Gem.

Compassion

The third cause for taking refuge in the Triple Gem is compassion, the sincere wish for all sentient beings to be free from suffering and the cause of suffering. Examining and reflecting on the shortcomings of samsara, where all sentient beings of the six realms are suffering as the consequence of their nonvirtuous deeds, one wishes to remove their suffering. While cultivating the sincere wish to alleviate suffering and its causes for

122 | THE FUNDAMENTAL PRACTICES

all beings is undoubtedly positive, mere compassionate thoughts alone cannot liberate all beings from samsara. Therefore, driven by our compassion, our genuine desire to liberate beings, including the ones in the bardo, from suffering leads us to the realization that buddhahood is the ultimate means for achieving this goal. A buddha possesses the highest power, the ultimate ability to liberate all beings. Motivated by our compassion, we aspire to attain buddhahood, and to embark on this path, we must first take refuge.

OBJECTS OF REFUGE

Having reflected on the causes for taking refuge, we need to identify the objects of refuge, which are the Buddha, Dharma, and Sangha.

The Buddha

According to the Mahayana tradition, Buddha Shakyamuni, similar to any buddha, has three *kayas*, or bodies. These are the *dharmakaya*, or truth body; *sambhogakaya*, or enjoyment body, a form body that appears only to bodhisattvas; and *nirmanakaya*, or emanation body, which is a form body visible to sentient beings. Sometimes we say there are two kayas, which refers to the dharmakaya and *rupakaya*, or form body, of which there are two types: sambhogakaya and nirmanakaya. Therefore, to say there are three kayas or two kayas means the same thing.

To elaborate on these further, *dharmakaya* means "ultimate wisdom," or "the wisdom that has twofold purity." The first purity is the natural purity that all sentient beings have. The second purity refers to the purity that is free from all obscurations—that is, the purity that manifests when one overcomes all the obscurations. With this twofold purity, one possesses the ultimate wisdom.

The sambhogakaya is comprised of five certainties. First is the certainty of form or body, meaning a sambhogakaya buddha is always adorned by the thirty-two major signs and eighty minor qualities. Secondly, a sambhogakaya buddha has the certainty of teaching the Dharma, and always gives Mahayana teachings. Third is certainty of place, meaning a sambhogakaya buddha always dwells in the Akanishta realm, not in other places. The fourth is certainty of time, which means a sambhoga-kaya buddha will always remain and will never enter into mahaparinir-vana. The last is the certainty of followers, meaning that a sambhogakaya buddha's followers are noble bodhisattvas who have already attained the irreversible state, or reached the tenth bhumi. Those having these five certainties are known as sambhogakaya buddhas.

A nirmanakaya is a physical manifestation, or emanation, of sambho-gakaya. Wherever, however, and whenever a particular form is needed, a buddha will manifest as that form. Buddha Shakyamuni is regarded as a supreme nirmanakaya form. There are other types of nirmanakaya forms, such as the buddhas who manifest as great bodhisattvas, practitioners, Dharma kings, and so forth. Sometimes a nirmanakaya may manifest as an inanimate object, like a bridge or boat that brings tremendous benefit to help beings in whatever way is needed.

These are the three kayas of a buddha. Buddhas are perfectly enlight-ened beings, who have abandoned all faults and obscurations, who came to possess all ultimate, enlightened qualities.

The Dharma

The Dharma is the second object of refuge. Here, *Dharma*, capitalized, refers to the Buddhadharma, the teachings of the Buddha. According to the Mahayana tradition, the expression *Buddhadharma* is shorthand for the Mahayana teachings, or Mahayana Dharma. According to the great fifth-century master Vasubandhu, the Sanskrit word *dharma* has ten distinct meanings, such as "phenomena," "path," "teachings," "nirvana," and so on. Its meaning depends on context. These various meanings require studying commentaries or listening to teachers' explanations; comprehending all the distinctions requires more than referring to a dictionary. A dictionary might indicate a certain meaning, but the text in which the term appears might use the word in a different sense than the dictionary definition, in relation to a different context. A word can even have hidden meanings. So, we should not automatically assume a word's literal meaning is the intended one. Instead, we should look for the hidden meaning of words. This is an important point as one studies the Buddhadharma.

124 | THE FUNDAMENTAL PRACTICES

There are two types of Buddhadharma: teachings and realizations. Teachings here means primarily the Buddha's actual spoken teachings, which have been collected in written form in the Kangyur, a series of 108 volumes of the Buddha's discourses that have been preserved in Tibetan translation. All the authentic teachings taught by the Buddha's followers from India, Tibet, or elsewhere are collected in Tibetan translation in the volumes of the Tengyur.

The second type of Buddhadharma, realization, is obtained by realizing the teachings, which means one understands the true nature of phenomena just as it is. To obtain such realization, with a basis of moral conduct, first one should listen to Dharma teachings. Through the wisdom that arises from listening, one can understand the meaning of teachings and then, via the wisdom of contemplation, one can fully ascertain the sense of the teaching. The wisdom that arises from contemplation will clear away all doubts. The wisdom of meditation applies one's understanding in practice. With the wisdom that arises from meditation, one can gain experience, spiritual qualities, and realization. And this kind of inner realization is Dharma.

The main Dharma is our own realization, because the Buddhadharma is a method that transforms ordinary beings into buddhas and ordinary thoughts into ultimate wisdom. Buddhadharma is a method to remove all suffering and gain ultimate happiness and unlimited qualities. With realization, one can tame a wild mind. Just hearing and understanding the Dharma will not help us subdue negative thoughts and emotions. What makes a great impact on the mind, transforming and eliminating mental afflictions, is our own realization; that is the most crucial method. Therefore, mere acquisition of knowledge and understanding is not the final goal in studying the Dharma. The final goal is to attain buddhahood, and to achieve that, we need to gain realization. To gain realization, we need to listen, contemplate, and meditate on the Dharma.

We should follow the path and teachings step by step. As Vasubandhu said in the *Treasury of Abhidharma* (*Abhidharmakosha*), "Based on the pure moral conduct, one should listen to, contemplate, and meditate on the Dharma." This structure is the general structure that applies to all Buddhist traditions, including the Shravakayana tradition. Therefore, the main Dharma practice is to keep our vows. In order to keep our com-

THE FIRST UNCOMMON NGÖNDRO: REFUGE | 125

mitment, we need mindfulness and alertness. Gaining more realization can also definitely help us enhance our vows and improve our qualities.

In short, there are two types of Dharma: the teaching and realization. We should maintain emphasis on gaining realization, but to do that we have to depend on the teachings.

The Sangha

Generally speaking, the Sangha comprises the followers of the Buddha. Sangha does not necessarily mean celibate monks and nuns; lay followers are also Sangha members. There are two main types of Sangha: celibate Sangha and lay Sangha. But really, all Buddhists are considered Sangha; anyone with refuge vows is considered Sangha. There are various levels within the Sangha, just as there are different levels on the Buddhist paths. In the Mahayana tradition, there are five stages or paths toward buddhahood: the paths of accumulation, application, seeing, meditation, and no more learning. When one embarks on the Mahayana path by taking the bodhichitta or bodhisattva vow and generating relative bodhichitta (see chapter 10), it is considered the path of accumulation. The first two paths—accumulation and application—are referred to as ordinary bodhisattva levels. Those who dwell on the path of accumulation are called Sangha, as are those who dwell on the path of application.

Those who are dwelling on these two paths are known as ordinary Sangha, since they have not eliminated afflictive emotions and are still in samsara. According to Mahayana tradition, once their afflictive emotions have been eliminated, they immediately enter the third path. That is the path of seeing, where they become noble bodhisattvas and gain liberation from samsara. This means practitioners in the path of seeing have eliminated the afflictive emotions completely. Next comes the path of meditation, the fourth path of the Mahayana, wherein the wisdom previously cultivated—fully perceiving emptiness—is refined through persistent mental training. Therefore, the third path and fourth path are known as noble paths or noble bodhisattva levels. Upon the complete elimination of both obscurations of defilements and obscurations to knowledge, further training becomes unnecessary, marking the

126 | THE FUNDAMENTAL PRACTICES

attainment of the path of no more learning. When we taking refuge, we take refuge in the noble Sangha—those who reached liberation, such as Manjushri, Avalokiteshvara, and Vajrapani.

PROPER REFUGE PRACTICE

After considering the reasons for taking refuge and recognizing the objects of refuge, how do we actually take refuge? The uncommon preliminary practice of taking refuge is based on the uncommon Vajrayana refuge practice, which according to the Sakya tradition requires previous empowerment in any of the two-day major empowerments. However, since this book is intended for general readers who may not have received such empowerments, I will explain this topic in accordance with the common Mahayana refuge practice, where our refuge object is Buddha Shakyamuni. This can be practiced without receiving any prior empowerment or initiation.

How to properly practice refuge

Imagine that in front of you, in the space above, there is a jewel throne held by two lions at each of the four directions, for a total of eight lions. Imagine that on that throne there is a lotus; on that lotus there is a full moon disc; and on that moon disc is Buddha Shakyamuni. All these appear three-dimensional and made of light, not like a human body made of flesh, bones, and blood. Nor is it like a statue made of solid material, such as copper, bronze, or stone. It is also unlike a mural or a thangka painting, which are two-dimensional. So, you should visualize a three-dimensional form, yet it is not solid. It is transparent, very clear and most vivid, but cannot be touched because it is made of light, like a rainbow. We can see the colors of a rainbow very clearly, yet we cannot touch the rainbow with our own hand, because it is of the nature of light, and is not something solid. That is how you should visualize the Buddha's form. Behind the Buddha, visualize the Buddha's realization or infinite qualities in the form of a well-decorated pile of Dharma books. These are surrounded by the noble bodhisattvas, like Manjushri and others. The place where you visualize the refuge field and the place where you are sitting are all visualized as a pure realm, where the whole ground is lapis lazuli with gold veins in it. It is simply not an ordinary place. This is how we visualize the field of refuge, or object of refuge, to whom you are going to seek refuge.

Consider this: When you visualize this form, understand that it embodies all the buddhas from every direction and across all time—past, present, and future. If you take refuge in this visualization with a clear perception that it truly represents the Buddha, you'll receive blessings equivalent to those bestowed by the actual Buddha. Furthermore, if you perceive this visualization as encompassing all buddhas, you'll essentially be taking refuge in every buddha throughout space and time.

However, if you perceive this image merely as a representation of the Buddha, it won't convey the blessings of the genuine Buddha; rather, it will only carry the blessings associated with an image, such as that of a statue. There's a significant disparity between these two types of blessings. If you seek to deeply impact your mind through your practice, you should regard this visualization as the authentic embodiment of the Buddha's luminous nature, and recognize it as the synthesis of all buddhas. By doing so, your practice will accrue immense merit, attract greater blessings, and yield more profound results. It's crucial to grasp this concept fully.

When you say, "I take refuge in the Buddha," focus on Buddha Shakyamuni, golden in color with three Dharma robes. Reflect that the Buddha is the one who shows us the path. When you say, "I take refuge in the Dharma," focus on the pile of Dharma books and imagine those are the real spiritual path or Dharma path. When you say, "I take refuge in the Sangha," focus on the surrounding noble Sangha members, and imagine these are your spiritual companions.

In this manner, with your hands folded in prayer, recite the four lines of the refuge verse as many times as possible:

> *Together with all sentient beings, equal to the bounds of space,*
> *from this time forth until the essence of enlightenment is*
> *reached:*

> *I go for refuge to the glorious, holy gurus.*
> *I go for refuge to the blessed perfect buddhas.*

I go for refuge to the holy Dharma.
I go for refuge to the noble Sangha.

As I mentioned before, all Dharma practices are mainly mental practices. Taking refuge should also be practiced by way of the mind, using visualization. Mainly we take refuge in Buddha Shakyamuni. Because the Buddha has all the ultimate qualities required of an object of ultimate refuge, the Buddha is an infallible object of refuge. For example, when we face a problem that we are unable to solve in our mundane life, we will seek help from others—when water is leaking in our home, we contact a plumber to fix it. In a way, we are "seeking refuge" from them in mundane matters.

In whom should we "seek refuge"?

Such a person in whom we should seek refuge should have three qualities. First of all, they know how to fix our problem. Secondly, they are willing to help us solve the problem. And thirdly, they have the power to solve the problem.

A person might be very knowledgeable and have a wish to help us, yet lack the power; as a result, they will not be able to help us. A comparable analogy is a disabled mother who sees her precious child carried away by a strong current. Due to being disabled, she does not have the power to swim and rescue her child even though she knows how to rescue the child and strongly wishes to do so.

The Buddha has these three ultimate qualities: knowledge, willingness, and power. First, the Buddha is omniscient and possesses all knowledge and methods necessary to guide and liberate us. Second, the Buddha possesses limitless, ultimate compassion for all sentient beings, without exception. The Buddha has unique and extraordinary compassion toward all sentient beings, as though all were his only child. Third, the Buddha has the ultimate power to liberate all beings from suffering. Just by radiating one beam of light from his body or teaching one time, he can liberate countless beings. Thus, the Buddha has the ultimate power. With this said, the Buddha is the one who will help us solve our problems and overcome our suffering if we seek refuge in the Buddha and uphold the precepts properly. Furthermore, when taking refuge, we need the proper motivating reason for refuge, and then to perform the actual refuge practice with great concentration and proper visualization. If the mind is distracted, no matter how many times one recites the refuge prayers, it will not yield great results. We have to do the refuge practice mainly through the mind—that is, with visualization. Otherwise, even an animal like a parrot would be able to recite prayers. The fact is, without doing the visualization, they cannot comprehend the meaning, and therefore would not accumulate great merit. We as human beings, especially those who have this precious human life with its endowments, have more power and ability to practice properly. We should utilize this potential to practice refuge properly.

We are going for refuge not for our own sake, but for the sake of all sentient beings. Since this is refuge in the Mahayana context, we must have a great purpose in mind, which is to serve all sentient beings. When we say "serve" all sentient beings, it just means to benefit them, but saying "I benefit" reinforces the sense of doing something good for someone less fortunate or less important than ourselves. If we instead say, "I serve," our choice of words helps control our pride, and puts us in the humblest position relative to sentient beings. This helps our practice.

Geshé Langri Thangpa's *Eight Verses of Mind Training* says, "We should perceive ourselves as the lowest of all sentient beings." We should do this in order to tame the mind, particularly to subdue our pride and arrogance. It is taught in the Vinaya that arrogance stains and damages the precepts of body and speech, even if they have been kept pure and intact.

Whenever we serve other beings or undertake any virtuous deeds, we should do so without pride, arrogance, or any negative thoughts. We do not show off our virtuous deeds. Virtuous deeds are meant to accumulate merit, not to be a performance. We do not require the attention or acknowledgment of others when we do virtuous deeds. If we show off or publicize our virtues or practice, our virtues will be weakened due to our vanity. The proper motive for Mahayana practice is service to all sentient beings. We do not practice the Dharma to preserve the Dharma. We do not practice the Dharma just to serve a certain group of people, to care for our loved ones, or to look out for ourselves. We practice the Dharma to better serve all sentient beings, without discrimination.

This genuine sense of purpose is naturally allied with positive thoughts like infinite loving-kindness, infinite compassion, and bodhichitta. But lacking that sense of purpose, it is impossible to take Mahayana refuge or to practice loving-kindness, compassion, or bodhichitta. Genuine motivation overcomes our biased assumptions. For now, being ordinary humans, we like some people and dislike others. But such thoughts obstruct our Dharma practice; they are contrary to it because Dharma practice is for the benefit of all beings. If we like some beings but do not like others, then how are we going to generate infinite loving-kindness and compassion for all?

Instead of studying Dharma books, sometimes we should take a moment of self-reflection to consider our thoughts and actions. We should look and see whether we have criticized anyone, entertained any jealous thoughts, been angry, or shown disrespect to anyone today. As ordinary human beings, we often engage in negative actions unintentionally because we do not examine our actions or observe our minds constantly. So, we should cultivate mindfulness and alertness, observe our conduct, and reconsider actions before doing anything. We should ask ourselves, "Who benefits from criticizing others with negative thoughts?" No one benefits. Rather, expressing criticism easily becomes negative conduct, producing suffering for oneself and others, without any good result. Therefore, we need to consider and examine every thought and action.

It's important to feel regret and remorse without developing shame. This helps us acknowledge the mistake and commit to not repeating it, without feeling negatively about ourselves. If we have done something good, then we should feel joy, but without becoming proud or arrogant. We should just rejoice in our positive actions. In this way, then, one can become a better person. This means we are aligning our actions with the Dharma teachings. They should have such a connection. If there is no connection between the Dharma knowledge that we gain and our actions, then it will not help us; nor will it help us to make a great impact on our mind.

Without this impact on our mind, without changing our attitude, we cannot subdue our wild mind. This wild mind definitely must become subdued. If we put effort into it, if we have the right method and the right remedy, then we certainly can subdue this wild mind, which is full of negative thoughts and afflictive emotions. For example, a good trainer can train a totally wild elephant. If someone can train a wild elephant, then why cannot we train our wild minds? There is no reason we cannot do so. It is definitely possible for us to tame our wild minds, and it is something that really needs doing.

Without taming the mind, changing our attitude, or making some impact on our mind, we cannot improve. Physical and verbal virtuous actions alone will not help us gain realizations. To gain realizations, we first need a change of attitude. We need a more peaceful mind. Negative thoughts disturb a peaceful mind, and what's more, they also can disturb others. If we use harsh words or criticize others due to afflictive emotions, when the person we've criticized hears about what we have said, it will produce hurt feelings and emotional distress.

And we also will experience suffering as a result of our verbal negative actions. There is no doubt about it. Criticizing others with mundane attitudes or in a state of afflictive emotion does cause suffering for oneself and others. The same goes for other negative motives and actions, such as jealousy, ill will, and others. The point is to do our best to tame the wild mind and our negative thoughts. That is most important.

To tame the mind, we should respect and serve others. We should make use of the causal interdependence that we have learned about from the Dharma, in terms of our conduct or practice. In this regard, there are many kinds of cause-and-effect relationship links. For instance, listening is a cause; it is though listening we that we gain knowledge of the Dharma, which is the result. Furthermore, Dharma knowledge is a cause; putting it into action is a result of the knowledge gained. Then, putting knowledge into action is a cause; its result is gaining realization or personal experience.

We can implement all of these causal relationships; making use of these and others definitely will make you a better person. After all, isn't Dharma practice supposed to do just that? Dharma practice should make for a peaceful mind, remove our negative thoughts, and eliminate harmful actions toward family members, neighbors, or other sentient beings.

132 | THE FUNDAMENTAL PRACTICES

Practicing Dharma is necessary for peace and a better world—not only this world, but in the service of all sentient beings from every realm.

THE FOUR SPECIAL QUALITIES OF MAHAYANA REFUGE

Mahayana refuge has four special qualities. The first special quality is the motivating cause for taking refuge. Every tradition of Buddhist refuge has a motivation or determinant cause, but the special motivating cause in Mahayana is great compassion. In other Buddhist traditions there is refuge, but great compassion is not considered a causal motivation for taking refuge. That is to say, fear of cyclic existence and faith in the Triple Gem are motivational causes for taking refuge there, but traditions outside Mahayana do not invoke great compassion as a reason for taking refuge. Therefore, from the point of view of the causal motivation, great compassion is the characteristic feature of motivation to take Mahayana refuge.

The second special quality is that the duration of refuge in the Mahayana tradition is understood to be from now until we each realize buddhahood. That is, we take refuge not just until this life ends, but until we ourselves attain buddhahood for the sake of all beings. The third special quality concerns the purpose of taking refuge. In the Mahayana tradition, we take refuge for the sake of all the sentient beings, not only to fulfill our own needs. And then fourth special quality concerns the object of refuge. According to the Mahayana tradition, the Buddha is the principal refuge. So, the four special qualities concern causal motivation, duration, purpose, and object of refuge. With these four then our refuge practice becomes a Mahayana practice.

ATTENTION IN MAHAYANA REFUGE PRACTICE

When we take refuge in the Buddha, Dharma, and Sangha, we visualize these three objects of refuge, and we need to focus clearly and maintain attention. When we recite refuge prayers, even though we are counting the number of times we accumulate the prayers, we should think less about the number of refuge prayers we recite and focus more on the quality of our refuge prayer recitations. So, we can remind ourselves, "If

I recite the prayer one time with the visualization, that has more merit and benefit than reciting it hundreds of times without the visualization, or in a state of distraction."

In *The Way of the Bodhisattva*, the great master Shantideva says, "Even if practiced for a long time, all recitations and austerities accomplished with a mind distracted elsewhere are pointless."[16] No matter how many recitations you complete, if they are done with a distracted mind, such action is not greatly beneficial. To accumulate the most benefit from recitation, we must do the proper visualization. Without that we cannot get the greatest benefit from reciting refuge prayers. Not only refuge prayers, but whatever we recite should ideally be done with an understanding of the meaning of the visualization.

THE PRECEPTS OF REFUGE

It is said that taking the genuine refuge vow with the thought of renunciation has great benefit. In a sutra, the Buddha says, "If the benefit of taking refuge took material form, the whole of space could not contain it." This means taking a proper refuge vow has inconceivable benefit or limitless benefit. But after we take the refuge vow, we have to keep it. And to keep the vow we must know the rules, or rather, the *precepts* of refuge. Without knowing the precepts, we cannot keep the vow in a proper way.

There are two types of precepts: general precepts and specific precepts.

General precepts

There are many general precepts to follow once we have taken the refuge vow. There may be variations in the naming and explanation of the general precepts, depending on different teachers or texts. What's important is the core message of not abandoning the Triple Gem, but continuously cultivating genuine devotion and faith in it through various aspects and practices in our daily lives. Here, I will elaborate on a couple of them: relying on a qualified spiritual master, practicing in accordance with the Dharma, listening to the genuine Dharma, never abandoning the Triple Gem, always remembering the buddhas, and making offerings to the Triple Gem.

134 | THE FUNDAMENTAL PRACTICES

First, we need to rely on a qualified spiritual master, and we need to listen to the Dharma teachings from that qualified master. We need to abandon the friends who influence us to commit more and more negative actions. We can say that such friends are negative friends; we should abandon them and rely on positive friends or on Dharma friends, those who can help, influence, and encourage us to do more and more positive deeds and Dharma practice. Our environment, neighborhood, those with whom we associate—these also can be impactful. If we do not have a very strong mind or strong practice, then the people we associate with can really influence us in a great way. If our neighbors or friends are negative, then they can influence us to commit more and more negative actions. If people nearby are kind and spiritual, they can really influence us to do more Dharma practice and more virtuous deeds.

To "abandon" nonvirtuous friends does not mean that we totally ignore them while we are supposed to be practicing loving-kindness and compassion. Rather, there are a couple of different things to do, depending on the situation. In the first case, we guide nonvirtuous friends and convert them into virtuous friends by offering advice and other skillful approaches that help them positively transform their mentality and conduct, so they eventually abandon nonvirtue on their own accord and turn to virtuous actions. In the second case, if they do not respond to skillful means or listen to advice, then we must avoid physical and verbal contact with them, but on the inside, in our minds and from the depth of our hearts, we should always practice loving-kindness and compassion toward them and all sentient beings, without exception. In both these cases, all-inclusive loving-kindness and compassion are essential.

But, simply put, we must rely on a qualified spiritual master, and to do so means we listen to their teachings and follow through with them. This means we give up negative friends and rely on spiritual friends, and we share the Buddha's message or introduce others to a qualified master. All these are indicative of one's own reliance on a spiritual master.

Second, we must listen to the genuine Dharma, that which is based on authentic sources and on the Buddha's teachings. If there happens to be a Buddhist teacher who criticizes the Buddha or the great masters, like Nagarjuna for example, we can truly and objectively state that this person has misunderstood or is not teaching genuine, pure Dharma.

We must follow genuine Dharma. The Dharma is not something created by my own or another teacher's thoughts, though in the course of giving a Dharma teaching, we can be creative in how we portray the actual meaning of the Dharma as it applies to the modern-day world. We may present it creatively, but we cannot change the meaning creatively. That is fundamental. If we change the meaning, then the connection between the teachings and their real source is cut—a teaching can no longer link back to the Buddha's own words. We can use contemporary examples and avoid using archaic examples, and we can find innovative ways to present a teaching by using modern technology or social media. But we cannot innovate the meaning of the teaching or the actual teaching as it must be represented. So, listening to teachings necessarily implies listening to genuine, accurate, and authentic teachings.

Virtuous deeds are part of Dharma practice—for example, we share the message of the Buddha with anyone who has the interest. This is not to convert anybody from another religion to Buddhism; only, sometimes, people have a clear wish to practice, but do not know how. They may not have received teachings and personal guidance, and so for such a person we should do whatever we can to guide them by giving the right teachings or by introducing them to the right teachers—that is, to genuine qualified masters.

Third, we must practice according to the Buddhadharma. The great Sakya Pandita said that our conduct must accord with Vinaya, our meditation must accord with sutra, our exposition must accord with Abhidharma, and our mantra must accord with genuine teachings of the tantras. So, what sort of conduct would be required of us? We need to act in accord with our vows; our mediation should accord with the Buddha's discourses; our teaching should accord with the great masters of the past; and our Vajrayana practice should accord with the authentic instructional texts.

Fourth, we should never abandon the Triple Gem, even in the most mundane circumstances. Generally speaking, when we take refuge in the Buddha, Dharma, and Sangha, we should understand that it is through them we experience any real joy or ease in samsara. Whenever we feel joyful and happy, we should think that these are due to the blessings of the Triple Gem. In addition, whenever we face problems, such as illness, we should rely wholeheartedly on the Triple Gem, placing ourselves under the protection of Triple Gem. So, in this way, the Triple Gem is our protector, guide, and refuge.

Although we still need to consult doctors and take medicine when we are sick, at the same time, we also need to take refuge and think that all these medical treatments and facilities are due to the blessings of the Triple Gem. We should never abandon the Triple Gem; we need unshakable, unconditional faith. Whether we're happy or sad, we should always generate faith in them. Even if someone were to criticize the Triple Gem, it would never change our minds, and our sincere faith would continue. If we have this unshakable, unconditional faith, it cannot be changed or disturbed by any circumstances.

Fifth, we should always remember the buddhas and make offerings to the Triple Gem. When we eat, we offer our food to the Triple Gem first. Wherever our journey takes us, whether walking, facing a particular direction, or traveling, let us follow the Triple Gem by remembering the Buddha of that direction. In the east, let us recall Buddha Akshobhya; in the south, Buddha Ratnasambhava; in the west, Buddha Amitabha; in the north, Buddha Amoghasiddhi; and at the center, Buddha Vairochana. If we find it challenging to practice in this manner, let us at the very least remember the Buddha wherever we go and in whatever we do. In these ways and more, we always take refuge in the Triple Gem.

The specific refuge precepts for the Buddha, Dharma, and Sangha

In addition to our general precepts for taking refuge, there are specific precepts explaining what we should and should not do in regard to the three objects of refuge: the Buddha, Dharma, and Sangha. After taking refuge in the Buddha, we are not allowed to take refuge in any mundane god. We can make offerings to them, such as *tormas*—ritual cakes usually hand-molded from butter and roasted barley flour—but we cannot take refuge in mundane gods. Additionally, we should always respect any kind of Buddha image. Some statues or paintings are not very well made or well painted. But however it looks, well made or not, we should always respect it, because it is still a representation of the Buddha. We should not place them on the floor—we should not step over statues or keep them under our bed. Neither should we put these images in dirty places. We should always pay respect to any kind of buddha image. So, these are the specific precepts of taking refuge in the Buddha.

The second specific precept for taking refuge is in regard to the Dharma. After taking refuge in the Dharma, we are not to harm any sentient beings intentionally. We should never harm or kill even the tiniest insects. We should also not practice any non-Buddhist religion. We should pay respect to Dharma books or anything that has words of the Dharma written on it—even if it is only one verse of Dharma, we should show it respect. We should not step over any paper that has words of the Dharma written on it, and should not place it on the floor. We should always store these higher up than other things. We should not view Dharma books the same way as any ordinary, mundane books. We have the tendency to put such books on the floor, under a mattress, or in the restroom. Dharma books are different from mundane books or magazines, so we should not treat them the same way.

We do not bring them in the restroom, for example, because printed Dharma words or Dharma books should be perceived as an actual buddha. Buddha's teachings are precious and profound, therefore we maintain the utmost respect for the Dharma teaching or Dharma words by keeping them in clean, respectful places. It is disrespectful to Dharma materials for us to step over them or store them under the bed or with our own clothes—for instance, to pack our socks above a Dharma book in our travel bag. So, even when packing, we try to put Dharma books and papers in a higher place, not under our own clothes and so forth. This is all to say that we should have respect for the Dharma, and also should not think of a Dharma object as an ordinary object.

Furthermore, we should not sell Dharma objects or Dharma books with the aim just to make money for ourselves. To do so just for profit and for our own livelihood is against the precepts of refuge, especially the precept of taking refuge in the Dharma. So, we should pay respect to the Dharma at all times.

Third, after taking refuge in the Sangha, we should not make non-Buddhists our spiritual companions. Of course, we will still have contact with and associate with non-Buddhists, but we should not take up

138 | THE FUNDAMENTAL PRACTICES

practices in a non-Buddhist community, and should not discuss profound Dharma teachings with non-Buddhists, who may be apt to misunderstand them. Even if someone is Buddhist, they may lack great faith and criticize these profound teachings, so we have to be careful about what teachings are discussed and what topics should be avoided.

Some people present themselves as Buddhists, but inwardly do not keep their samayas—the Vajrayana commitments taken when receiving empowerment—or other vows. If someone criticizes their own gurus or the Dharma teachings they have received, then we should be wary of associating too closely with them; they lack proper respect. If we reassociate with such individuals, it provides them with yet another opportunity to broadcast their criticism or show disrespect. At that point, we may lose our faith if it is not strong enough, or we might change our minds with respect to how we take refuge. Therefore, we must be careful with apostate individuals.

We should pay respect to celibate monks and nuns. We should refrain from criticizing them, because expressing such criticism of that person in the presence of your own friends, for example, will not help that person, even if they are at fault. Instead of helping, it would just lead us to engage in more and more negative actions.

Discussing the faults of other people is rather pointless, since it will not improve someone else's behavior. If we genuinely want someone to change, then we should meet that person face to face and, with strong intention and right motivation, speak directly: "You should not do this or that." That is not criticism, but an attempt to correct someone's behavior. This gives us the opportunity to point out someone's faults or misdeeds, where saying as much to them personally can help them to correct or to change. If, however, we convey the same information elsewhere, not in front of that person but in private among friends, broadcasting lots of negative information about the person, that will not help. It is simply a negative action through one's speech, which is a cause of suffering for oneself and one's friends. It is not virtuous, it is not meritorious, and it is the cause of suffering.

After taking refuge in the Buddha, Dharma, and Sangha, we pay them respect, and we develop sincere faith and devotion. It is one thing to say, "I like the Buddha," but to say, "I have faith in the Buddha" is something else altogether. Faith in the Buddha is much more than just liking the Buddha. We can like anyone—our friends, family members, neighbors, and so on—but ordinarily we do not have faith in them the same way we do the Triple Gem. Faith in the context of taking refuge means relating to the Buddha as the genuine protector, as our unique refuge and guide in samsara. With faith, we surrender ourselves wholeheartedly to the Buddha from the moment we receive the refuge vow until we reach buddhahood. No matter what situation we face in life, we should always believe in the Buddha, pray to the Buddha, rely on the Buddha, and have strong devotion to the Buddha. These are expressions of faith. Normally these matters do not concern us in the context of family relationships, friendships, and so on. However much we adore our friends or family members, that is not the same as faith, which we should develop sincerely in the Buddha.

The Benefits of Upholding the Refuge Vow

As mentioned before, the benefits of taking refuge are limitless. That is to say, in taking refuge vows and being motivated by renunciation in accordance with the pratimoksha vows, the actual assumption of refuge vows has limitless benefits. Taking refuge is the foundation of all Dharma practice. Incidentally, Dharma practice and virtuous deeds are not always paired. Non-Buddhists also commit to doing virtuous acts, such as refraining from killing or stealing, helping others, giving food to the hungry, and so on, but such conduct is not Dharma practice since they lack refuge vows. With the refuge vows, whatever virtuous conduct we undertake is within the sphere of Dharma practice. So, to practice Dharma, refuge vows are indispensable as the basis of engaging in various Dharma practices.

Moreover, taking proper refuge vows plants the seed of attaining liberation and the enlightened state for the sake of all sentient beings. If you have taken refuge vows and keep them, which means not engaging in negative acts, then you engage in more virtuous deeds and more Dharma practice. Refuge multiplies our virtue, since we will engage in more and more virtuous conduct and Dharma practice as long as we abide by the refuge vows.

140 | THE FUNDAMENTAL PRACTICES

Refuge vows are not physical, but mental or spiritual in nature. Refuge vows extend beyond this lifetime until we attain buddhahood, because our alaya, or storehouse, consciousness persists through future lifetimes. One could say that what we commonly perceive as consciousness is alaya consciousness. Alaya consciousness never stops; it remains uninterrupted even when we faint, sleep, or die. The refuge vows can never be separated from our alaya consciousness. In that sense, the vows can persist across lifetimes; they are inseparable from, which is not say they are equivalent to, alaya consciousness.

Because refuge vows are mental vows, no one else can damage them, not even our worst enemy. An enemy can harm one's physical body, but they cannot harm one's mental state or sense of commitment outright. If we are not strong psychologically, when an enemy harms us physically, it is that much easier to upset our mental state and disrupt our vows. We might do something malicious toward that person, like express anger or hatred. We can imagine that if someone harmed our guru, for example, we would want to protect them and would express anger. But it is taught that anger is always negative and nonvirtuous; for this reason, anger cannot be a motivation for serving Buddhadharma or the guru.

There are cases when anger and wrathful conduct are sometimes displayed out of compassion and right motivation. These become virtuous conduct, since they are mere displays of wrath and anger, not ordinary impulsive behavior. That is because a disturbed angry mind will damage our vows. If someone criticizes or attacks our guru, our refuge vows are not damaged, but reacting with anger and hatred damages our refuge vows. Again, the primary cause of damage to our refuge vows is our own mind, through afflicted emotions of anger, pride, and so forth.

Similarly, even though we should do everything to protect monasteries and holy objects, if we are angry with those who destroy them, we too are in the wrong. Since our negative emotions always have the potential to damage our refuge and bodhichitta vows, we must preserve our mental state, which is the actual meaning of taking the refuge vow. In *The Way of the Bodhisattva*, the great master Shantideva said that if you wish to keep the precepts, then with great effort, you need to protect your own mind. Otherwise, you can't keep the precepts. With vows, the principal factor is the mind. Therefore, to keep vows one must guard the mind from negative thoughts.

The great Sakya master Sachen Kunga Nyingpo said that if conceptual thoughts are controlled by wisdom, there is no samsara; if wisdom is under the control of conceptual thoughts, there is no nirvana. When conceptual thoughts are more powerful, liberation is impossible, and one stays in samsara. When wisdom is much greater, we can defeat these thoughts and attain liberation. When we protect our minds from negative thoughts, we become free of all fears and mundane problems.

Noble beings, like bodhisattvas, are beyond mental afflictions; traditional sources even say that they will not be attacked if they encounter dangerous animals, such as tigers or lions. Because noble beings have no karma to precipitate an attack by a wild animal, those animals behave peacefully in their presence. Similarly, while Buddha Shakyamuni was meditating under the Bodhi Tree, demons and maras tried to disturb him with showers of weapons, but the Buddha was free from the effects of karma that would be needed in order to be struck by weapons. Due to having cultivated loving-kindness, compassion, and wisdom, the shower of weapons was transformed into a rain of flowers. Able to withstand the demon army's great offensive, the Buddha was intact. Because an enlightened being's mind is free of obscurations, no attack can hurt them.

Once our minds are protected from negative thoughts, it is easy to maintain physical and verbal conduct that is free from negative actions; body and speech follow the mind, not the other way around. If the mind has desire or negative intention, body and speech follow naturally. In understanding that refuge vows and spiritual commitments are primarily related to the mind, we recognize the need to guard ourselves against negativities. In particular, harming another being is the direct opposite of taking refuge in the Dharma. Once we take refuge in the Dharma, we should refrain from harming any sentient being, no matter whether they are our own family, friends, enemies, or anyone or anything else.

It is important to be familiar with these and other precepts and do our best to keep them. If we can manage that, naturally we will refrain from wrongdoing and our virtues will increase.

142 | THE FUNDAMENTAL PRACTICES

Without receiving refuge vows, we cannot receive any other Buddhist vows; it is the basis for all Buddhist vows and a preliminary of all Buddhist paths. This is a great benefit of taking the vow. By receiving genuine refuge vows, we enter the Buddhist path generally, and specifically, the path of accumulation. At that very moment we become genuine Buddhists and become a member of the Buddha's clan. The distinction of Buddhist versus non-Buddhist depends on whether one has taken refuge vows. Taking refuge in the right way and for the right reasons is essential for all Buddhists.

By keeping refuge vows, we will be happy in the here and now, will be reborn in elevated circumstances, and will eventually attain liberation. In this lifetime we will not be isolated from the Triple Gem. In short, all favorable conditions will assemble, if we keep the refuge vows well.

The final benefit of taking refuge vows is the ultimate attainment of buddhahood for the sake of all beings. Specifically, the ultimate benefit of taking refuge in the Buddha is that one becomes a buddha, and the ultimate benefit of taking refuge in the Dharma is that one will turn the Dharma wheel without any interruption, and the ultimate benefit of taking refuge in the Sangha is that one will have genuine disciples. Buddhahood and a retinue of fortunate disciples are the results of one's conduct on the path of learning. Others will receive benefit from our refuge vows because we will influence them toward greater virtue and away from negativity.

Simply put, if the benefit of taking refuge had physical form, the whole of space would be too small to contain it. Such is its great benefit. To affect the greatest possible benefit, we must practice refuge with proper visualization, correct motivation, and genuine dedication at the end.

In order to receive this benefit, it may be helpful to note that in general, creating powerful positive karma requires a successfully completed action. If an action is not complete, then our efforts lack power and are not of benefit. A complete action has three phases: a preparatory phase, a main phase, and a concluding phase. The preparatory or preliminary phase in our context is generating thoughts of renunciation toward samsara, and then understanding the meaning of refuge, such as the motivating cause and the field of object of refuge, the manner of taking refuge, the purpose and duration of taking refuge, and the precepts of refuge. After all these preparations, we can take refuge.

Taking refuge vows is then the main phase. It is followed by the concluding phase, which occurs when we feel as though we have really received the refuge vows, and also there are reminders to the effect—that, for example, we are bound to attain temporary and ultimate benefits, but we also need to keep the precepts. In fact, once you feel you have actually received the refuge vows, the act of doing so is already complete; but if you follow the precepts as well, it becomes even more complete. The basis to enter the doorway to the Buddhist path is to take genuine refuge with the Triple Gem. One is strongly encouraged to also uphold the precepts as well, since its good outcome is even more certain.

It is important to know the precepts, otherwise one cannot keep the vows. Even in ordinary activities, such as competitive sports, first one learns the rules; without knowing them, we cannot become skilled in that field. Similarly, to become a good refuge practitioner, first we learn the precepts, then follow them to become great refuge practitioners—at which point we attain all the benefits, of course.

After Refuge Practice

Ideally, after completing the common or uncommon refuge practice, we should recite a short prayer focusing on the four immeasurables: loving-kindness, compassion, joy, and equanimity as we cultivate these positive thoughts within our minds. Once we have embarked on the path of Dharma, the next step is to cultivate altruistic thoughts toward all sentient beings. We commonly express these aspirations for all beings through the following prayer:

> May all beings have happiness and the cause of happiness.
> May they be free from suffering and the cause of suffering.
> May they never be parted from sorrowless joy.
> May they dwell in equanimity, free from attachment and
> aversion to those near and far.

While reciting this prayer, it is beneficial to visualize and concentrate on the words, allowing positive thoughts to arise in your mind. You may recite these four lines once or as many times as you wish. If you have the time, it is also encouraged to spend some time contemplating these four. This practice will aid you in cultivating them naturally as you continue to engage in them.

Loving-kindness

The essence of limitless loving-kindness lies in our aspiration for boundless sentient beings to experience happiness and the causes of happiness. Happiness stems from engaging in virtuous deeds, so our wish is for all beings to attain happiness through the practice of virtuous actions.

When our love is selective, directed toward some beings while harboring hatred toward others, our mind becomes divided, which hinders the boundless nature of loving-kindness. To truly cultivate limitless loving-kindness, we must extend this wish to all beings without exception.

Discrimination among sentient beings is another obstacle. When we speak of "all beings," this refers to every sentient being as the object of our loving-kindness. If we wish happiness for a specific number of individuals, our loving-kindness remains limited to those individuals. It is crucial to extend our loving-kindness universally, encompassing all beings without exception. In practicing loving-kindness, we focus on the commonalities among sentient beings rather than their differences. Regardless of our backgrounds or beliefs, we all share the desire for happiness and the wish to overcome suffering.

To comprehend the vastness of "all sentient beings," consider the global human population of nearly eight billion individuals. Therefore, "all sentient beings" encompasses every person from every country and religion, as well as nonbelievers. Extending loving-kindness to all sentient beings encompasses not only humans, but also animals and beings across the six realms of existence. Although we may not physically reach every corner of the universe to perform positive actions, our minds can extend the wish for happiness to all beings universally.

When we wish for the happiness of all beings, we wish for their genuine happiness, distinct from transient worldly pleasures. True happiness arises from liberation from suffering and is sustained by virtuous actions.

To create a more peaceful and harmonious world, we must cultivate positive minds through loving-kindness. Peace and harmony emerge from love, whereas hate and anger only breed discord and suffering. Wars and conflicts throughout history serve as stark reminders that hate and violence yield no lasting happiness. Even in familial relationships, love and respect foster happiness, while quarreling only brings misery.

Starting with our families, we can gradually extend loving-kindness to friends, neighbors, and eventually all beings without exception. Through this practice, we foster friendships, promote harmony, and navigate life's challenges with ease.

Ultimately, the practice of loving-kindness entails wishing for the happiness of all beings and their engagement in positive actions. When we wish others happiness, we also wish for them to cultivate positive qualities, like loving-kindness, thereby eliminating the possibility of harm and fostering a world filled with compassion and goodwill.

Compassion

The second of the four immeasurables is limitless compassion. Loving-kindness and compassion are akin to two facets of the same essence. They share a unified nature, analogous to two sides of a single coin. Limitless compassion entails wishing for others to be liberated from suffering and its underlying causes, which primarily stem from wrongful actions. Cultivating such limitless compassion is a commendable endeavor. As we engage in contemplation on boundless compassion, we reflect on the three types of suffering experienced by all sentient beings in samsara, as discussed in chapter 5.

In Buddhist teachings, it is asserted that possessing boundless compassion engenders the acquisition of all other virtuous qualities effortlessly. Just as inviting an emperor ensures the attendance of their entire retinue without issuing separate invitations, genuine compassion attracts all other positive traits. When we nurture authentic or boundless compassion, other virtues naturally manifest without requiring additional effort.

Joy

The practice of limitless joy entails wishing that no being will ever be separated from the happiness that is devoid of suffering, known as "sorrowless joy." However, our worldly happiness is fleeting. With a human lifespan typically shorter than a century, and marked by both joy and suffering, the scale often tips toward more suffering than happiness.

Even if one were to live a century, the span of genuine happiness might be minimal, sometimes resulting from one's unethical actions. Worldly happiness, often transient and dependent on changing conditions, fails to qualify as genuine happiness. Whether examining its nature, duration, or causality, worldly happiness falls short of offering lasting fulfillment.

Equanimity

The fourth immeasurable is equanimity, which involves genuinely desiring that all sentient beings maintain a state of impartiality, devoid of aversion or attachment toward those who are distant or close. "Near and far" refers to individuals who are either physically distant or close in proximity. Equanimity entails refraining from both aversion toward distant individuals and attachment to those nearby. Any presence of these emotions signifies a departure from equanimity, which constrains the mind rather than allowing it to embrace boundless qualities.

It is important to strive to maintain these four immeasurable thoughts consistently in your mind. Everyone has the capacity to engage in these four limitless meditations. While it may not be feasible for ordinary individuals or beginners to sustain them constantly, we should endeavor to do so. With continued practice, we can gradually extend the duration of maintaining these thoughts and eventually attain the ability to uphold them at all times.

Chapter 10

The Second Uncommon Ngöndro: Bodhichitta

The second of the uncommon preliminary practices is cultivating bodhichitta. As we've discussed, *bodhi* means "awakening," the ultimate result of buddhahood, while *chitta* means "mind." Here, "mind" does not refer to the enlightened mind of a buddha; in this case, it means our ordinary mind. Hence, bodhichitta is the mind of an ordinary being that generates the wish to attain buddhahood for the sake of all sentient beings. In ngöndro practice, we recite the bodhichitta prayer that mentions both aspirational and engaged bodhichitta: "For the sake of all sentient beings I will attain perfect enlightenment. For this purpose, I will practice this profound path."

Generally speaking, there are two kinds of bodhichitta: conventional, or relative, bodhichitta, and absolute, or ultimate, bodhichitta. Relative bodhichitta signifies an aspiration, which is undertaken as a vow that one can obtain from a teacher through a formal ritual, often known as receiving the bodhichitta vow. Within the relative bodhichitta, there are two further divisions: aspirational bodhichitta and engaged bodhichitta. Relative bodhichitta also has three aspects: the person who generates bodhichitta, the actual generation of bodhichitta, and the object of bodhichitta. Ultimate bodhichitta, however, is nothing other than the wisdom of realizing the ultimate truth directly. Ultimate bodhichitta refers to the wisdom of realizing the true nature of all phenomena directly. You cannot receive ultimate bodhichitta from anyone; it must

148 | THE FUNDAMENTAL PRACTICES

stem from your own practice of relative bodhichitta. Through gradual practice and meditation, ultimate bodhichitta will develop within you.

As a beginner, we must emphasize relative bodhichitta more. When we're climbing stairs, we need to place our foot on the first step before stepping on the second. Likewise, before realizing ultimate bodhichitta, first we need to cultivate relative bodhichitta, since without it, we cannot have ultimate bodhichitta. In a definitive sense, ultimate bodhichitta is an exclusive quality of noble bodhisattvas, or those who have reached the path of seeing, the first bhumi, and beyond. As ordinary human beings, we first focus on developing aspirational bodhichitta while aspiring to develop ultimate bodhichitta. When we have strong relative bodhichitta, eventually we can genuinely conceive ultimate bodhichitta.

Once we have formally received the bodhichitta vows from a qualified teacher, we generate the sincere wish to attain buddhahood for the sake of all the sentient beings; this is aspirational bodhichitta. If we generate such an aspiration before receiving the bodhichitta vows, while positive, that is not aspirational bodhichitta. We cannot have bodhichitta before becoming a bodhisattva or before receiving bodhichitta vows. If we could develop aspirational bodhichitta before receiving the bodhichitta vows, then it would mean that before we entered the Mahayana path, we would already have bodhichitta, which is impossible.

We must take bodhichitta vows formally with a qualified teacher to develop bodhichitta. Before receiving the bodhichitta vows we can certainly have faith in the Buddha and admiration for the Buddha's qualities. We may even generate an aspiration to attain buddhahood for the sake of all sentient beings. But such a wish is not the same as actual aspirational bodhichitta; instead, it is regarded as a mere wish.

Engaged bodhichitta is twofold: merely engaged bodhichitta and engaged bodhichitta. Before we've received the engaged bodhichitta vows, if we undertake virtuous deeds to reach buddhahood for the sake of all beings, such engagement is referred to as "mere" engagement. However, engagement in virtuous deeds after receiving the vows is engaged bodhichitta. Shantideva's *Way of the Bodhisattva* compares these two to wanting to go somewhere and then actually getting there.

There are two possibilities when you want to go somewhere: you can wish to go somewhere before embarking on the journey or you can start wishing to go there after you have already departed. Since aspirational and engaged bodhichitta occur simultaneously when you take the vows, the method of aspirational bodhichitta is like generating a wish once the journey is already underway.

A mere wish alone cannot convey us to a destination. We must start out on an actual journey, putting one foot in front of the other. A mere wish is similar to just fantasizing about a journey to Bodh Gaya without taking tangible steps to save money and arrange the trip. Similarly, once aspirational bodhichitta is conceived, we must start a journey on the path to buddhahood—that is, practice the Dharma.

With this understanding, we turn our attention to the development of the two types of bodhichitta. Bodhichitta is based on loving-kindness, compassion, and the willingness to serve all beings without distinction. Without a sincere wish to benefit all beings, it is not possible to develop aspirational bodhichitta.

The Benefits of Practicing Bodhichitta

There is great benefit to bodhichitta because it is the fundamental teaching for the Mahayana and Vajrayana paths. The great master Shantideva says in *The Way of the Bodhisattva* that bodhichitta is the supreme medicine that cures the maladies of all sentient beings. Bodhichitta is like a moon that removes all darkness of confusion. Bodhichitta is like a sun that illuminates all. Bodhichitta is the essence of the Dharma, like, for example, the essence of milk is butter. Bodhichitta is the essence of the Dharma, especially according to the Mahayana teachings. The great master Sakya Pandita, in his text called *Treatise Distinguishing the Three Vows*, says that in the teachings of the Paramitayana, or Perfection Vehicle, there is no Dharma without bodhichitta. In other words, without bodhichitta, we cannot practice any Mahayana teachings.

Bodhichitta brings great benefit. As with taking refuge vows, receiving vows of bodhichitta means one receives a new "name," this time that of "Mahayana Buddhist," superseding one's previous name, that of "ordinary Buddhist." By taking these vows, one becomes worthy of veneration and respect from gods and human beings. Bodhichitta is like a

150 | THE FUNDAMENTAL PRACTICES

philosopher's stone, or an elixir that transforms base metals to gold, in that it transforms ordinary thoughts into the ultimate wisdom that is buddhahood. It turns ordinary humans into buddhas. Bodhichitta is the essence of the Buddhadharma. As Shantideva says, when you churn milk, you get the essence of milk, which is butter; similarly, the essence of all the Dharma is bodhichitta. Practices and virtuous actions without bodhichitta are not the direct cause for attaining buddhahood. Though they might be an indirect cause, they are not the direct cause, since without bodhichitta, we are not even Mahayana Buddhists.

Bodhichitta is the most excellent friend, virtue, and Dharma practice. Based on it, one can approach other excellent Dharma practices. No virtue excels the virtue of bodhichitta. Thus, it is meritorious to have bodhichitta.

BODHISATTVAS

Sometimes a practitioner might think, "I am a Mahayana Buddhist, but I am not a bodhisattva." They believe that bodhisattvas are these very high beings, and that a Mahayana Buddhist is lower than bodhisattva. People might think that they could never be a bodhisattva themselves. But in reality, you cannot become a Mahayana Buddhist without becoming a bodhisattva. You might hear someone praise their teacher, saying, "The guru is great—a real bodhisattva." But that is not real praise, because every Mahayana Buddhist is a bodhisattva. If someone wants to praise their guru according to the Vajrayana, one should aim to think of them much higher than a bodhisattva.

As soon as we develop genuine bodhichitta, and after we receive the bodhichitta vow, we gain the title of "bodhisattva." At that moment we actually enter the Mahayana path, specifically the path of accumulation. These happen simultaneously. After receiving the bodhichitta vows, one becomes the object of veneration by demons and gods.

Bodhisattva and *Mahayana Buddhist* actually mean the same thing, because becoming a Mahayana Buddhist requires the bodhichitta vows. We need to have bodhichitta in mind; without it, we cannot become Mahayana Buddhists. A bodhisattva is a person with bodhichitta. So the terms *Mahayana Buddhist* and *bodhisattva* have the same meaning.

There are various levels among bodhisattvas, however. For instance, we refer to Manjushri as the bodhisattva of wisdom and Avalokiteshvara as the bodhisattva of compassion; their realization is much, much higher than ours. If you are a Mahayana Buddhist, you are definitely a bodhisattva—but that does not necessarily mean one on the same level as Manjushri, Avalokiteshvara, or others, because among bodhisattvas there are many different levels. Bodhisattvas on the path of accumulation and bodhisattvas on the path of application are ordinary beings who are within samsara. Within the path of accumulation, there are different levels of bodhisattvas. There are also noble bodhisattvas, who have already gained liberation from samsara, on the first bhumi to the tenth bhumi, according to the Paramitayana tradition.

THE PROPER WAY TO PRACTICE BODHICHITTA

When we recite the other preliminary practices, such as refuge, Vajrasattva, mandala offering, or guru yoga, it is good to incorporate recitation of the prayer of loving-kindness and compassion at the same time, as many times as possible: "May all beings have happiness and the causes of happiness. May all beings be free from suffering and its causes."

Having recited the refuge prayer and these two lines many times, we can proceed to reciting the bodhichitta prayer that describes aspirational and engaged bodhichitta. If you recite loving-kindness and compassion prayers with visualization, it can really improve your loving-kindness and compassion, make great impact on your mind, and become a strong cause to develop bodhichitta. Your bodhichitta practice will also improve. Whether we have a good bodhichitta practice or not depends on the strength of its cause, and the cause of developing bodhichitta is great compassion.

So why do we have to cultivate aspirational bodhichitta? And why do we have to serve all sentient beings? There are several reasons. First of all, we ourselves wish to achieve happiness and avoid suffering, and so does every living being, so we all have common objectives. It is wrong to focus only on our own well-being and ignore everyone else. If someone in one's family were living very comfortably while the rest were poor, then, if that person is warm-hearted and kind, they will not feel so happy or enjoy

152 | THE FUNDAMENTAL PRACTICES

life as much because everyone else is suffering. Someone in that position would strive to solve the family's problems and provide help. In the same way, since all beings have common concerns, it is not right if we only focus on our own interests.

Secondly, as Shantideva says in *The Way of the Bodhisattva,* "Helping others is the cause of your own happiness; wishing for your own happiness is the cause of your suffering." So, we ought to emphasize the well-being of others, for that way we make both ourselves and others happy, and we can give everyone what they want.

A third reason we should aim to help others is that we have taken rebirth in samsara countless times. Every time we are born, we have different parents. So, just as we should feel a moral obligation to return the kindness of our parents of this lifetime for giving us this precious human life and for raising us, we likewise should return the same kindness of our parents and loved ones from past lives.

As Mahayana Buddhists, the most important reason for us is to help others. Having bodhichitta vows means promising to help all sentient beings, liberate them from samsara, and guide them to the states of temporary and ultimate happiness. When we make such a promise, we should act accordingly and not break it.

In our everyday lives, those who fail to uphold their promises are not regarded as virtuous individuals; a person of integrity remains faithful to their word, striving to honor every commitment they make. Similarly, failing to honor the promises made during the reception of bodhichitta vows is deemed inappropriate. For instance, if we extend invitations to guests in our home, it is incumbent upon us to treat them with warmth and hospitality when they arrive; failing to do so is deemed unacceptable. Likewise, during the reception of bodhichitta vows, we extend an invitation to all sentient beings, pledging to aid them in achieving both temporary and ultimate happiness. Failing to keep this promise is likewise deemed inappropriate.

To keep our promises, we must help and serve all beings. The best way to serve them is by attaining buddhahood, because buddhas have the ultimate power and unlimited qualities that liberate all beings from three forms of suffering. So, based on the pure, limitless loving-kindness and compassion, we develop aspirational bodhichitta. Whether we develop genuine aspirational bodhichitta depends on whether we develop genuine loving-kindness and compassion, because those are the causes of bodhichitta.

Just as bodhichitta has these causes, attaining buddhahood also has its own causes. Causes, paths, and practices lead one to attain buddhahood. It is not realized with mistaken causes, mistaken paths, or through non-Buddhist practices. We cannot reach buddhahood with incomplete causes and incomplete paths—that is, by the paths of hearers and solitary realizers exclusively. In order to attain buddhahood, we require correct and complete causes and paths. This means practicing Mahayana teachings and engaging in the Mahayana paths—what is referred to as engaged bodhichitta. We engage in certain behaviors to attain buddhahood for the sake of all sentient beings.

Sentient beings are quintessential to the bodhisattva's path. To become buddhas we relate to two resources, or fields: the field of sentient beings and the field of buddhas. This is illustrated in Shantideva's *Way of the Bodhisattva*. Without both sentient beings and buddhas, it is impossible to attain buddhahood. Without sentient beings, it is impossible to practice all the Mahayana teachings, because without including all sentient beings we cannot really practice the fundamental practices and virtues of Mahayana, such as refuge, infinite loving-kindness, infinite compassion, bodhichitta, patience, material generosity, and so on. Moreover, without sentient beings we cannot maintain moral conduct, since helping others depends on the very existence of beings. So, without sentient beings it is not possible to be a Mahayana Buddhist or to practice in the Mahayana tradition. We must consider all sentient beings in order to attain buddhahood.

Without the field of buddhas as the object of refuge we would have no refuge, nor any Dharma teachings to listen to, contemplate, or meditate on. To attain buddhahood requires both fields of sentient beings and buddhas. So, whenever we encounter living beings, we ought to remember they are the key to our liberation and ultimate buddhahood. Keeping that idea in mind reminds us to be more respectful of others and to cherish all sentient beings.

Some people do not respect or find value in others, so they might harm or kill living beings, thereby bringing enormous suffering to others for their own satisfaction. To do so shows some people have lost any sense of value in or respect for living beings. If we respect and value sentient beings, we will regard them in a positive and altruistic-minded way. So, it is crucial to always consider the welfare of sentient beings in our actions.

"Sentient beings" refers to all beings in the six realms of samsara, including bardo beings—not just all the Buddhists among us. Considering the welfare of all beings compels us to develop unbiased loving-kindness and compassion. It naturally inspires us to develop bodhichitta, since bodhichitta is similarly based on unbiased principles. If we are attached to ideas and assumptions based arbitrarily on distinctions of race, religion, gender, culture, and so on, it will be impossible for us to develop bodhichitta. Our loving-kindness, compassion, and bodhichitta are based on unbiased and inclusive propositions. To consider sentient beings without bias is essential. On that basis we can develop loving-kindness, compassion, and bodhichitta the Mahayana way.

To maintain our precepts, we must have respect for the guru and not give up serving sentient beings. It is also helpful to gain a clear understanding of the four aspects of precepts: faults, faultlessness, apparent faults, and apparent faultlessness. "Faults" refer to actions that violate the precepts, such as killing and stealing, while "faultlessness" refers to the absence of these faults, indicating one's adherence to ethical conduct. Both faults and faultlessness are easily recognizable. Apparent faults are whatever looks like a fault but is not one. For example, a parent, out of deep concern for their child's safety, may be compelled to take strict measures, such as scolding or other disciplinary actions, when the child repeatedly refuses to heed warnings and engages in potentially harmful behavior, like playing with matches or fire. Despite the appearance of fault in their actions, the parent's motivation is solely to protect the child from danger. In appearance the parent's act was negative, but their deed was virtuous because of pure motivation. Such a deed would be called an apparent fault. However, it is crucial that we are completely honest with ourselves, carefully examining our motivations before undertaking any action. If we outwardly profess one motive while harboring another internally, we are only deceiving ourselves. Merely claiming that our motivation is pure, when it is not, does not make it so.

Apparent faultlessness is what outwardly seems virtuous but is actually negative. For instance, if we prostrate with the motivation of showing off how devoted we are or the number of prostrations we have done instead of out of humility or genuine respect, it may look like a virtuous act, but actually it is not.

We should strive to understand these four aspects of precepts— abandoning faults and apparent faultlessness, while adopting faultlessness and apparent faults—as guidelines to cultivate self-awareness and mindfulness in observing all the precepts of bodhichitta.

Attaining buddhahood is a far-reaching plan. Ordinarily the idea of undertaking a project that will last one or two decades would seems like a big undertaking. From the perspective of the Dharma, once we have taken refuge and bodhichitta vows, our project is attaining buddhahood, which lasts much longer than a few decades—in fact, countless eons, according to the Perfection of Wisdom scriptures.

Thus, attaining buddhahood is not easy, but we should not feel discouraged; rather, we should be optimistic. Once we have taken bodhichitta vows, we should not forsake our vows. The great master Shantideva said in *The Way of the Bodhisattva*: "If insects strive at Dharma, they too can reach buddhahood. If even they reach buddhahood, people knowing right from wrong have still a better chance." For this reason, we need not be discouraged.

Out of fear of suffering in samsara, we should never discard bodhichitta, but make the effort to preserve it in our self-reflective process so that we refrain from negative actions. And just as young children need teachers, each of us needs a teacher. As long as we have gross mental affliction, we need a teacher for guidance. We must listen to the advice given by our guru and develop mindfulness and vigilance in our daily lives so that we might examine how our conduct accords with the Dharma.

Bodhichitta makes you a better person, someone with the motivation to remove the suffering of all beings. Having cultivated genuine bodhichitta, we can fulfill the wishes of all beings and lead them to temporary and ultimate happiness. Therefore, cultivating bodhichitta is vital. Bodhichitta is like a wish-fulfilling tree, since with bodhichitta one can accumulate great merit and obtain all enlightened qualities. Bodhichitta is like a great ship's captain who leads sentient beings across the ocean of samsara.

156 | THE FUNDAMENTAL PRACTICES

In the sutras and *shastras*—the commentaries and treatises on the words of the Buddha—the Buddha and the great masters all expound on the importance of developing bodhichitta. Bodhichitta is the essence of the Mahayana teachings; there is no Mahayana practice without it. Endowed with bodhichitta, we have the skillful means to handle worldly challenges and problems, whereas those lacking bodhichitta often fail to deal with them. For instance, in the face of death, great practitioners who hang onto bodhichitta more fiercely than to their own lives will have no fear. Without Dharma practice, most people would have a great fear of death. Regardless of the situation, great practitioners maintain composure. Whereas worldly beings might be carried away by any situation, being overjoyed by favorable conditions or disappointed by unfavorable ones, Dharma practice makes one's mind strong and stable. Such stability and strength of mind is paramount; based on that, one can attain realization of the truth of reality and reach buddhahood.

Prerequisites for Practicing Bodhichitta

There are common and uncommon, or exceptional, bodhichitta practices. Relative bodhichitta practices are essential for nurturing genuine, limitless love and compassion toward both ourselves and others. However, our self-grasping makes it challenging to cultivate genuine love. Often, our affection for others comes with strings attached, expecting reciprocity in return. These expectations and attachments lead to dissatisfaction and suffering. There are two relative bodhichitta practices: equalizing oneself and others, where we recognize the equal importance of others' happiness and freedom from suffering, and exchanging oneself and others, which involves meditating on taking on others' suffering and giving them happiness. While equalizing oneself and others is considered a common practice, exchanging oneself and others is exceptional due to its transformative nature, which involves prioritizing others over ourselves, although it is more challenging to implement. Also, one could say that relative bodhichitta as a whole is common practice, while ultimate bodhichitta, resting in the fundamental state of consciousness, is the exceptional practice.

Furthermore, one could say that bodhichitta practice in Mahayana generally, which is not sealed by the Mantrayana vows, is common bodhichitta, whereas bodhichitta practice in Vajrayana, which is sealed by the Mantrayana vows, is the exceptional one. Generally speaking, an exceptional bodhichitta practice refers to an extraordinary method and wisdom that accelerates the generation of bodhichitta, thereby bringing us closer to buddhahood. In each case, however, exceptional bodhichitta cannot be practiced by everyone due to individual capacity.

We have said that proper refuge vows, being part of the pratimoksha vows, are the basis of all Buddhist vows. So, first and foremost, one must receive proper refuge vows from a qualified guru and then, based on that, one must receive the bodhichitta vows. After receiving the bodhichitta vows, one engages in bodhichitta practice.

We can receive the bodhichitta vow during an initiation or empowerment. On the first day of a two-day major empowerment, we repeat the words of the seven-limb prayer after the guru with full visualization. If we repeat this after the guru with full visualization, then we receive the refuge vow and bodhichitta vow on the first day of empowerment. In the authorization empowerment—*jenang* in Tibetan—as well, we should repeat the seven-limb prayer after the guru. If we repeat this after the guru with full visualization, then we also receive the refuge and bodhichitta vows during the seven-limb prayer recitation at the initiation.

There are also special ceremonies that can be done to transmit the bodhichitta vow. There are two main traditions for receiving the bodhichitta vows: one according to the Chittamatra, or Mind Only, philosophical school, and the other according to the Madhyamaka, or Middle Way, school. Within the Madhyamaka school, there are different kinds of bodhichitta vow ceremonies. In particular, there is a Vajrayana tradition for receiving the bodhichitta vow ceremony that is based on the Madhyamaka tradition. For instance, during the Lamdré teaching, after receiving the teaching and transmission of the *Triple Vision*, one needs to receive the bodhichitta vow. That ceremony is from a special Vajrayana tradition based on Madhyamaka tradition, which is referred to as the special two-lineage bodhichitta vow ceremony. "Two-lineage" means it comes down from both Naropa and Mahasiddha Virupa. These two traditions are combined together in this elaborate bodhichitta vow ceremony conducted during the Lamdré teaching.

CHAPTER 11
THE THIRD UNCOMMON NGÖNDRO: VAJRASATTVA PRACTICE

All of the suffering that we experience in samsara is produced by our negative karma and obscurations. Our negative karma is the obstacle to our progress on the spiritual path. We need to accumulate merit, because that accumulation enables us to progress on the path, but in order to do that, we must purify our negative karma and obscurations. In sutra and tantra many methods for purifying karma and obscurations are explained. But among them, the very best method is the Vajrasattva practice, if it is done with the full four powers, the correct visualization, and with concentration. Vajrasattva, a sambhogakaya buddha, is revered in tantric meditation as a means to cleanse one's karma. This practice, rooted in Mahayana principles aimed at benefiting all sentient beings, is undertaken with the bodhichitta aspiration to swiftly attain buddhahood and serve others. Ultimately, Vajrasattva represents the primordial purity of mind beyond conceptualization. The purification ritual involving Vajrasattva is integral to the ngöndro, the foundational practices of Vajrayana Buddhism.

Vajrasattva practice consists of the correct visualization of the deity and recitation of the hundred-syllable mantra associated with Vajrasattva. In addition to being part of a formal ngöndro practice, this mantra also appears as a part of the preliminary recitations in the daily sadhanas for major deities. In the Sakya tradition, one must have received an empowerment in the *anuttarayogatantra*, the highest yoga of the four classes of tantra, before practicing Vajrasattva, along with a

160 | THE FUNDAMENTAL PRACTICES

special transmission that is similar to a reading transmission. I will say more about this in the concluding section of this chapter on the prerequisites to the practice of Vajrasattva. Because in the Sakya tradition we consider Vajrasattva to be a Mantrayana practice, we also do not discuss the details of the visualization or the mantra unless one has received the empowerment, even though people may have heard or read about these things somewhere else.

The practice of Vajrasattva can bestow great benefits. In general, all negative karma or nonvirtuous actions can be purified with proper Dharma practice. It is said that nonvirtue inherently lacks positive attributes. However, it can still be purified through appropriate practices. So, while nonvirtue itself may lack qualities that are inherently good, the ability to purify it is considered a positive attribute in its own right. The practice of Vajrasattva purifies the ten nonvirtues, including the five heinous crimes. It also purifies the broken samayas and vows of the pratimoksha, bodhichitta, and Mantrayana vows. All these faults can be purified. In the sutras, there are many stories of people who committed very serious crimes and later purified their karma from these deeds. For example, Angulimala killed 999 people and cut one finger from each victim to make a *mala*, or rosary, of fingers. He planned on collecting one thousand fingers, so he was looking for one more victim to complete his necklace. But before he could kill the thousandth person, he met the Buddha, who guided him to the right path. Angulimala purified all his grave misdeeds, including the killing of 999 individuals, through genuine purification practices. After transforming his life by becoming a monk and embarking on a retreat in Shravasti, he received various teachings and was driven by profound remorse and unwavering faith in the Buddha and his teachings. As a result, he effectively cleansed himself of the negative karma associated with his past actions and later attained arhatship. Such is the power of Buddhist purification rituals.

THE FOUR POWERS

To purify our negative actions effectively, we utilize the four powers, which are essential elements in the practice of confession: the power of support, the power of regret, the power of antidote, and the power of resolve. Integrating these four powers into the Vajrasattva practice enhances the efficacy of the purification process. It's crucial to grasp that confession isn't about fostering guilt, as guilt serves no constructive purpose and does not aid in our improvement. Rather, the essence of purification and confession lies in self-reflection, acknowledging our misdeeds, and committing to refrain from repeating them.

The power of support

The first of the four powers, the power of support, means we must have a support or situation in which to confess any negative actions we have done. After having done refuge and bodhichitta practices, we then practice Vajrasattva. Based on those previous vows and practices, we visualize the guru as Vajrasattva on a seat on our head. That Vajrasattva—or together with the mother consort if it is Vajrasattva Heruka—is the power of support, being the sacred space or witness toward whom one confesses one's negative deeds and obscurations.

The power of regret

Out of ignorance, we have done many negative things; out of disrespect or negligence, we have committed nonvirtuous deeds from beginningless time until now. We should confess with strong regret whatever negative actions we have committed. We should feel regret because all those actions include those done in the past whose karma has not yet ripened. This is like the strong regret we feel when we have taken poison by mistake, knowing it will bring physical pain and danger to our own precious life. But our regret for having done negative actions in the past should be even more intense than what we would feel after taking poison by accident.

We should confess all negative deeds we can remember, as well as those we cannot remember or committed unknowingly from beginningless time until now. In our self-examination we should not hide from ourselves, but confess everything negative, all deeds and obscurations. We can disclose everything. If we do not disclose every item one by one,

162 | THE FUNDAMENTAL PRACTICES

then we can just state or imagine that we are confessing all the negative deeds we have done. In fact, it is impossible to declare every misdeed out loud, one at a time, but it is with such an intention that we feel strong regret. Through the power of support and confessing with strong regret in the presence of our guru in the form of Vajrasattva, our negative deeds can be purified.

The power of antidote

In order to purify one's negative deeds and downfalls, one must rely on an antidote. As the great master from Nalanda, Shantideva, says in *The Way of the Bodhisattva*, even though one fears sickness, one should rely on a doctor's advice and medicine to cure the sickness. Similarly, one should follow the guru's advice and rely on an antidote that overcomes negative deeds, downfalls, and so forth. For example, the antidote for anger is cultivating patience, compassion, and loving-kindness. So, one adopts and uses antidotes, while also making a fervent promise to avoid the same mistakes again. One needs a strong unshakable sense of commitment such that one would never repeat previous nonvirtuous deeds.

In our ngöndro practice, or as part of the sadhana practices of the deities for which you have received initiation or empowerment, we should recite the hundred-syllable mantra of Vajrasattva, or of Heruka Vajrasattva if one is initiated, at least twenty-one times with the seven visualizations. These visualizations are mentioned in the Hevajra and Vajrayogini practices and elsewhere. Among the seven visualizations, three are common and four are uncommon. Generally speaking, Vajrasattva is an uncommon Vajrayana practice, so I will not go into detail here. Suffice it to say that these visualizations and the mantra recitation are part of the power of antidote.

The power of resolve

Having the right motivation and by using the first three powers, one is fully convinced and actually believes one's negative deeds and downfalls are purified. Here in this practice, "belief" means complete conviction and total certainty. If one has done Vajrasattva practice with proper visualization and sincere regret, at this point one can be convinced that one's negative deeds and downfalls are all purified—our negative karma is resolved.

There are alternative explanations of the four powers. In other texts, instead of the power of resolve, the power of the antidote is mentioned as the fourth power.

SAMAYA

Samaya—a commitment taken when receiving empowerment to awakening—concerns the rules and precepts of the Mantrayana vow. There are many different samayas, depending on which empowerments and initiations one receives and from which tantras they originate. For example, if one receives an empowerment from the *kriyatantra*, or action tantra class of teachings, then one must keep the samayas of the kriyatantra tradition. If one receives an empowerment from the *charyatantra*, or performance tantra class, then one must keep the samayas from that tradition. Normally, when we receive a major empowerment, it is in the *anuttarayogatantra*, or highest yoga tantra class, such as the Hevajra empowerment; then one must keep the samayas of the anuttarayogatantra tradition. If one receives major empowerments from all four classes of tantra, then one should keep samayas from all these four tantras; Mantrayana vows also can be classified as Mantrayana vows from the kriyatantra tradition, charyatantra tradition, yogatantra tradition, and the anuttarayogatantra tradition. Sometimes even if students receive the same type of empowerment from the same teacher in the same location, it does not necessarily mean that each student shares the exact set of samaya. It can be very individualized and customized. So, we need to keep all the rules of all these Mantrayana vows. All Mantrayana vows are based on refuge and bodhichitta vows. The fourteen root vows of the Mantrayana are universally recognized precepts across all Vajrayana schools in Tibet. Regardless of the specific tantric empowerment one receives, it is essential to adhere to these vows. They consist of refraining from the following: disrespecting the guru, transgressing the words of the buddhas, insulting one's Dharma siblings, abandoning love for sentient beings, abandoning bodhichitta, criticizing the teachings of the

164 | THE FUNDAMENTAL PRACTICES

sutras and tantras, revealing Vajrayana teachings to those who have not yet received them, mistreating one's body, abandoning the view of emptiness, keeping bad company, failing to reflect on the view of emptiness, upsetting those who have faith in the Dharma, failing to observe the Mantrayana vows, and denigrating women.

PREREQUISITES FOR VAJRASATTVA PRACTICE

In general, Vajrayana practice requires the refuge and bodhichitta vows as the basis upon which one may receive the major empowerments of the Vajrayana tradition. With those, one receives the Mantrayana vow, which is the vow from that time onward to keep one's samaya and precepts, and to follow rules of the three vows—the refuge, bodhichitta, and Mantrayana vows. Then one can do the Vajrayana practice. This applies to all the other preliminary practices of the Vajrayana tradition.

In particular, after receiving the Hevajra empowerment, for example, one must receive the Vajrasattva oral transmission for the Vajrasattva practice in the set of ngöndro practices that accord to the Hevajra tradition. That is not only a reading transmission, nor is it a jenang or initiation—it is a special transmission between a reading transmission and a jenang, called a *gyelung* in Tibetan. In other words, you need to receive the Vajrasattva gyelung in order to practice Vajrasattva according to the Hevajra tradition as your ngöndro practice.

In brief, if one is doing the Vajrasattva practice of the Sakya tradition, first one must receive the major empowerment of the highest yoga tantra of the Sakya tradition, and then one must receive the Vajrasattva gyelung. Then one can engage in the Vajrasattva practice of the Sakya tradition.

CHAPTER 12
THE FOURTH UNCOMMON NGÖNDRO: MANDALA OFFERING

In order to attain perfect buddhahood, we must realize the true nature of the mind. To realize the real nature of the mind directly, we must accumulate merit and wisdom. Without accumulating these two, we cannot realize the genuine view of emptiness. "Emptiness" does not mean literally empty, but rather, the actual nature of things, which is free from all extremes. In other words, without the perfection of merit and wisdom, we cannot reach the first bhumi—that is, the first stage of the bodhisattva path, which is the path of seeing. Once we achieve the path of seeing through directly realizing the genuine nature of mind, we are able to move forward on the bodhisattva path and eventually attain perfect buddhahood.

To realize the genuine nature of the mind we have to rely on the accumulation of merit especially. For example, suppose there are two high-rise buildings, one to the east and the other in close proximity to the north. To see the roof of the eastern building, first we must climb up on the roof of the northern building, since that is the vantage point from which we can see the other roof. Similarly, to realize emptiness, we must accumulate merit—for example, by practicing loving-kindness and compassion for all sentient beings, generating bodhichitta, circumambulating holy places, making offerings, or offering prostrations to teachers and the Triple Gem.

Once we have accumulated merit it is easier to accumulate wisdom. By completing the accumulation of merit, one can attain the rupakaya—that is, the sambhogakaya and nirmanakaya of a buddha. By completing

166 | THE FUNDAMENTAL PRACTICES

the accumulation of wisdom, one attains the dharmakaya. Therefore, without accumulating these two completely, we will not be able to attain the two kayas, or bodies, which is perfect buddhahood. To perfect the two accumulations is essential.

MANDALA OFFERING: AN EXCELLENT METHOD FOR MERIT ACCUMULATION

Although there are many methods to accumulate merit, the most excellent method is to practice mandala offering. To make other types of offerings, such as to offer butter lamps, tormas, incense, and so on, first we have to purchase or gather those materials. This requires spending money, and in the process of acquiring money, oftentimes negative deeds are committed, such as deceiving others directly or indirectly. Thus, our physical offerings can become tainted by negative deeds.

When we actually make the offering, we might feel stingy, in which case the offering would be tainted by stinginess. After offering something we might feel pride and arrogance, or we might use social media to show off the offerings that we made. Moreover, if we do something virtuous hoping to gain something in return—whether that's fame, power, praise, happiness, or even merit—then it is not a genuine offering. In such instances, material offerings become tainted by our negative intentions or actions at the beginning, at the actual time of offering, and in the end. When an offering is made with worldly intentions, through negative deeds, or with afflictive emotions, the offering becomes tainted. It is difficult to accumulate merit and wisdom, especially through tainted offerings.

In contrast, if a material offering is completely devoid of any stains—from the beginning, during the actual offering process, and at the end—then of course great benefits will be received.

Mandala offering is taught to be an excellent form of offering because it is done mentally, and hence is not tainted in the same ways as physical offerings may be. Although the mandala plates and offering objects need to be acquired, they are not significant compared to other kinds of material offerings, and hence there is less likelihood that the offering will give rise to defilements like stinginess and pride at the beginning, middle, or end of the mandala practice.

Dharma practices are not for show. They are for us to benefit others and to accumulate merit and wisdom—to plant the seed to gain liberation and ultimately the state of enlightenment. If we continue our practice properly with the right motivation, the seeds of liberation and buddhahood will grow and eventually we will be able to reap their harvest. Hence, it is important to have a pure mind. One might be physically and verbally practicing the Dharma exactly as explained in the authentic teachings, yet if one's motivation is impure and incorrect, one's practice is still not genuine and authentic.

Although the mandala offering practice is performed by our physical body and speech, it is primarily practiced mentally. It is important to keep this in mind. At the time of a mandala offering, first and foremost, we must have the right motivation, especially thinking that for the sake of all sentient beings, we wish to attain buddhahood. To achieve this goal, we are performing the mandala offering practice.

Physically we hold the mandala plate with our left hand, verbally we recite the mandala offering prayer, while mentally we focus on the visualization. We then place heaps of offerings on the plate; one can make the seven-heap offering or the thirty-seven-heap offering adorned with many other valuable objects. Keep in mind that these are not the actual offerings—mentally, we are actually offering our body, wealth, and the virtues of the three times in the form of Mount Meru, the four continents, and the eight subcontinents to the offering object, which is our guru in the form of the deity. These pure realms possess the ten auspicious worldly necessities, such as earth for horses, earth for fields, wood for a house, wood for fuel, water for drinking, water for fields, stone for a house, stone for grinding meal, grass near the house, and grass in paddocks. All the sentient beings dwelling there also possess the eighteen freedoms and endowments, which are prerequisites for Dharma practice (as described in chapter 6) and the seven qualities of the higher realms—this is, lineage of family, physical beauty, wealth, wisdom, power, being devoid of illness, and possessing a long life—and the four great conditions—that is, dwelling in a suitable place, relying upon the holy ones, having applied oneself to Dharma practice in previous lives, and having accumulated merit.

We can visualize the offering object in an elaborate or a simplified form. When we make an offering, we should not think that we are just making one set of seven or thirty-seven heaps of offerings; instead, we visualize that these heaps of offerings are multiplied millions and billions of times. In this way, inconceivable merit and unbelievable benefit will be granted.

With the right motivation—to benefit all sentient beings who are as countless as space through this mandala offering—we make offerings to the guru, deities, and bodhisattvas. In actuality, this merit field does not require our offerings, yet we need to make offerings to accumulate merit for countless sentient beings. Thinking that we are doing this practice to accumulate merit for ourselves, or our own purposes, is not right. Whatever we do, we should do it based on the thought of wishing others to be happy, which is known as the altruistic thought.

We request the merit field of the guru, deities, and bodhisattvas to accept these offerings with great compassion and bless us to purify our two obscurations: of mental affliction and of knowledge. Both obscurations are negative thoughts, but they are different kinds of negative thoughts. According to one of Maitreya's texts, it is said that stinginess and other defilements are obscurations of mental afflictions, whereas the conceptual clinging to the three spheres—that is, to the person who does the action (the subject), the action itself (the act), and the person to whom one is doing the action (the object)—is the obscuration of knowledge.

When we reach the first bhumi, we have eliminated the obscuration of mental afflictions completely. After obtaining the first bhumi, the obscuration of knowledge is still there, however. In the first bhumi, the wisdom that realizes the real nature of phenomena is smaller than one's obscuration of knowledge. As we progress on the path, this wisdom increases while the obscuration of knowledge decreases. Finally, when the smallest remnant of the obscuration of knowledge is also eliminated, a noble bodhisattva becomes a buddha.

After making mandala offerings mentally to the merit field, we request the field of merit to bless all sentient beings, including ourselves, in order to purify the two obscurations and complete the accumulations of wisdom and merit.

The six perfections, or paramitas, comprise the training of a bodhi-

THE FOURTH UNCOMMON NGÖNDRO: MANDALA OFFERING | 169

sattva, which is bodhichitta in action—these are the perfections of generosity, discipline, patience, diligence, meditative concentration, and wisdom. But it is through practicing the first three of these perfections that merit is accumulated. The accumulation of wisdom occurs through practicing the last two perfections: meditative concentration and wisdom. The fourth perfection—the perfection of diligence—belongs to both merit and wisdom accumulations. This is one of the ways to identify whether you are accumulating wisdom or merit within the six perfections, but there are also other ways to classify them.

When making offerings, it is important for us to have the correct understanding that all appearances are the projection of our own mind; they are not separate from our mind. If all phenomena were not the projection of one's own mind, then it would be impossible for us to make such vast offerings. Having gained the understanding that all appearances are the projection of our mind, we can make any offerings, or as many offerings, as we can imagine. For instance, we can make an offering by visualizing that the whole of space is filled with offering substances. There is no barrier to our imagination in terms of the objects of our offering. Mentally, we can visualize them as big as we want or as numerous as we want. In fact, these terms "big" and "small" or "vast" and "narrow" are created by our thoughts. They do not exist inherently in reality. The object of the offering, which is the merit field; the actual offering, which is the mandala; and the intention of the offering, which is loving-kindness, compassion, and bodhichitta—these three are none other than the alaya consciousness, which has three characteristics: clarity, emptiness, and nonduality. These three spheres are the projections of our own mind. With such understanding, when we make offerings then we can accumulate great merit in a very short period of time.

What's more, these offering objects also do not have an inherent existence. We should think that all the offerings of objects are like a rainbow. We can visualize them clearly, yet they are not in solid form, not something we can touch with our hands, just like rainbow. When we see a rainbow, we can see the different colors clearly, yet instead of being solid the rainbow is just natural light.

We should also understand these offering objects are impermanent. If something does not change, it means that kind of object is permanent. But there is not a compounded thing that is not changing; therefore, they are all are impermanent. The first of the four Dharma seals states, "All compounded things are impermanent." It is essential to know all compounded things are impermanent, especially in the case of making an offering. We should have the understanding that the objects of offerings, the offerings themselves, and the offerors are not permanent either.

The Outer Setup for the Mandala Offering

During the mandala practice, we need two outer mandalas to accompany our visualization: the propitiation mandala and the offering mandala.

Propitiation mandala setup

To set up a propitiation mandala, first set the shrine on a square table or on another elevated place. Place the propitiation mandala on a stand in the middle. Then place five heaps of rice onto the propitiation mandala. (See figure 1 for a sample illustration of this propitiation mandala.)

The center heap represents your root guru in the form of the deity, surrounded by the lineage gurus, in a clockwise direction beginning at the front. Here, the "front" refers to the front of your root guru in the form of the deity, which is at the center of the propitiation of the mandala facing you—not our front.

The front heap represents the deities of the four classes of tantras.

The right heap—that is, the one to the right side of the center heap—represents Buddha Shakyamuni and all buddhas in sambhogakaya and nirmanakaya forms.

The back heap—that is, the one to the back of the center heap—represents the Dharma. The "Dharma" here is in fact the realizations of your guru and the buddhas, symbolized by well-decorated stacks of Dharma texts in the traditional Tibetan *pecha* format, which are loose-leaf books that typically feature wooden, cardboard, or similarly sturdy materials for their top and bottom cover plates. They are commonly encased in cloth for safeguarding. King Trisong Detsen sent scholars

THE FOURTH UNCOMMON NGÖNDRO: MANDALA OFFERING | 171

Fig. 1. A sample propitiation mandala with offerings.

to India, where they crafted the Tibetan script still utilized today. This alphabet was designed expressly for the propagation of Buddhist teachings, endowing it with a sacred status. Consequently, Dharma texts preserve these revered characters, embodying the essence of the teachings through their consonants and vowels.

The left heap—to the left of the center heap—represents the noble Sangha, such as Manjushri, Avalokiteshvara, Vajrapani, and so on. They are surrounded by *viras*, *dakinis*, *dharmapalas*, wealth deities, and so on.

We should not view these as rice heaps; rather, we perceive these in the forms of the objects they represent, such as our root guru and lineage gurus in the form of the deity, and the four heaps of the four directions in the forms of the deity, Buddha, Dharma, and Sangha.

Next, set the offerings in a clockwise direction surrounding the mandala plate, beginning with water for drinking, water for washing, flowers, incense, a lamp, scented water, food, and music.

172 | THE FUNDAMENTAL PRACTICES

The offering mandala

In addition to the propitiation mandala, an offering mandala plate and the material things that we put on the offering mandala plate as heaps will be required. The types of mandala plates and offering materials we use depend on our means.

In general, the superior mandala plates are made of gold, silver, or other precious metals. The mediocre mandalas are made of brass or copper. The inferior mandala plates are made of stone or wood. Regardless of what type of plate you use, its surface should be very smooth.

There is no specific size requirement if your mandala plate is made of gold or silver. However, according to Gatön Ngawang Lekpa Rinpoche, it is recommended that the plate of such material should not be smaller than six inches. If your mandala plate is made of other materials, like copper or stone, the distance between its eastern edge and its western edge or its southern edge and its northern edge should be at least fifteen inches long, or twenty-four finger-spans in size.

On occasions when we do not have a mandala plate when we are doing a mandala offering recitation, such as while attending empowerments, according to the Sakya tradition, we do not use any mudras instead. In this circumstance, we can fold our hands for the duration of the mandala offering recitation.

The offering materials

Offering materials can be categorized as superior, mediocre, and inferior. Superior materials are pearls, turquoise, and other precious gems. Mediocre materials are medicinal herbs, such as the three types of myrobalan: yellow (*arura*), beleric (*barura*), and emblic (*kyurura*). Inferior materials are rice and grains. Whatever offering we make, we should ensure it is clean before it is offered; it must not have dust or be stained by dirt.

Very simple practitioners who do not have anything to offer may use white pebbles that are clean and uncontaminated. There are amazing stories in ancient time about very simple Indian yogis. These yogis resided in the cemeteries and offered mandalas using white pebbles; eventually they gained realization and went to the Khechari Realm, the celestial pure realm of Vajrayogini, without abandoning their own bodies.

To make your offering objects for the offering mandala better, you can change them for fresh ones after every session or each day. The more often we change them, the more merit we will accumulate. Take note that the offerings for the propitiation mandala are not required to be changed frequently.

Grains used for the mandala offering should not be used later as our own food. Rather, we can give them to the hungry or to birds or other animals.

Does Counting Matter?

There are several versions of mandala offering prayers, such as the thirty-seven-heap mandala composed by Drogön Chögyal Phakpa, and the seven-heap mandala offering (see appendix 2 for more details on these). A short mandala offering verse was composed by the great Sakya Pandita, while another short mandala offering verse was composed by Atisha. You can choose any of these to practice. Although it is good to practice the thirty-heap mandala offering, it requires a longer duration to complete one hundred thousand times. Instead, you can alternate your practice between the seven-heap and the thirty-seven-heap mandala offerings. For every round of the mala, or 110 times, that the seven-heap mandala offering is made, one thiry-seven-heap mandala offering can be made. You may also recite the shorter mandala verse by Sakya Pandita or Atisha in place of the seven-heap mandala. However, regardless of which mandala prayer we recite, it is beneficial to occasionally perform the elaborate thirty-seven-heap mandala offering with proper visualization. This practice is esteemed, as indicated by Chögyal Phakpa, who, through the power of the thirty-seven-heap mandala offering, attained unparalleled spiritual and worldly wealth. Therefore, if performed with the right motivation and proper visualization, it can swiftly perfect the accumulation of merit and wisdom. As the Forty-First Gongma Trichen Rinpoche often advises us, the quality of our ngöndro practice is more important than the quantity. Therefore, we should focus on the quality

174 | THE FUNDAMENTAL PRACTICES

more than numbers as we accumulate one hundred thousand mandala offerings as part of our preliminary practices.

If our mandala offering practice is of high quality, signs of genuine mandala practice will be obtained. For instance, we would have stronger faith and purer perception than before, have better dreams, and our renunciation and bodhichitta would be enhanced.

THE ACTUAL MANDALA OFFERING PRACTICE

Before beginning the mandala offering practice, you should sit on a comfortable seat in a meditation posture, then begin by contemplating the four thoughts that turn the mind to the Dharma, the four common preliminaries. Then recite the refuge prayers, generate bodhichitta, and if possible, perform some Vajrasattva mantra recitation. Then perform the mandala offering practice according to the text you have adopted.

When making these offerings, we should imagine that we are actually offering thirty-seven objects with other precious objects; we can also visualize multiplying them to a countless amount. Through such skillful means, we can accumulate great merit quickly and reach buddhahood faster.

All ngöndro practices depend on visualization. If you have good visualization, thinking that in front of you there is a real merit field, there are real buddhas and bodhisattvas, and offer to them, it is exactly the same as making offerings to actual buddhas and bodhisattvas in front of you. If you have good visualization, then it is no different from offering to the real buddhas; both will have the same amount of merit. This shows how important it is to do proper visualization. Without proper visualization, or when visualization is done with a distracted mind, one accumulates much less merit.

There is a story from ancient times that says there were once two children playing with sand when they saw the Buddha on alms rounds, but they did not have any food to offer. Given they were too short to reach the Buddha's begging bowl, one child knelt down while the other one climbed on his back and offered sand in the begging bowl. As a result of their merit, in their next lives, the one who put the sand in the bowl became a king, while the one who knelt down became a minister.

THE FOURTH UNCOMMON NGÖNDRO: MANDALA OFFERING | 175

This illustrates that if you have a pure intention, even if you are offering something of insignificant value, you can still accumulate great merit. Conversely, if your intention is impure, then even though you offer the most precious, valuable, and expensive objects in the world, you will not earn great merit. Whether you earn great merit or not does not depend on what you offer. Making offerings with more expensive objects does not mean you will gain more merit. It all depends on your intention. If your intention is not right, if your intention is to show off or make yourself more famous, you will not gain great merit even if you offer the most expensive object to the buddhas. Thus, the amount of merit accumulated depends on one's motivation. This is important for us to know and apply in our daily lives.

INCORPORATING GURU YOGA SUPPLICATION IN THE MANDALA OFFERING

Although this is mandala practice, after every mala round of recitation, one can recite the one-verse guru yoga supplication:

> The precious guru of unequaled kindness, the embodiment
>   of all objects of refuge,
> to the immensely kind master of Dharma, I pray:
> looking with all-encompassing compassion,
> may you bless me in this life, the next, and the bardo state.

When mandala offering is associated with guru yoga in this manner, our practice becomes more powerful and meritorious.

Moreover, we should supplicate to the guru wholeheartedly, from the depth of our hearts, with strong and unshakable faith and devotion. This sincere approach can profoundly impact the transformation of our mind. This strong devotion comes with signs, like hairs standing on our skin, tears coming out from our eyes, and so forth. Until these signs appear, we should continue to practice. These signs indicate that we have done the practice successfully.

Generally speaking, whichever practice we do, the fruition should be becoming a better person as a result of this practice. If we are the same

176 | THE FUNDAMENTAL PRACTICES

person with the same number of negative thoughts, without a greater number of positive thoughts, then it means we are doing our practice in a superficial way. Whereas having done genuine practice, we would definitely see transformative changes, eventually eliminating all the negative thoughts and attaining the ultimate qualities.

CHAPTER 13
THE FIFTH UNCOMMON NGÖNDRO: GURU YOGA

Generally speaking, the root of all knowledge and qualities depends on the teacher, especially in Vajrayana practice. Due to our own karma and obscurations, we do not have the fortune to see the Buddha directly with our own eyes. We do not have the fortune to receive the teachings from the Buddha directly. This means we also do not have the chance to practice Buddhadharma by receiving these teachings from the Buddha. At this time, then, it is through our guru that we are able to listen to the Buddha's authentic teachings and to practice; the Buddha's blessings reach us through our own guru. For us, the guru is the most kind and precious person because we are able to receive and practice the teachings through the guru. It is through the guru that we will gain liberation and eventually the highest realization, which is none other than the enlightenment state. According to the Vajrayana tradition, the guru is the epitome of all objects of refuge—Buddha, Dharma, and Sangha—so we should imagine the guru as such. We should imagine that the guru and buddhas are the same; the guru has the same quality as the buddhas. In other words, the guru is an actual buddha. The guru is omniscient.

In guru yoga, the fifth uncommon preliminary practice, one imagines the guru as the epitome of all refuges. To reach buddhahood, we must realize the true nature of the mind. The true nature of the mind cannot be realized through scriptures, studies, contemplations, reasoning, examples, or any other means. Despite diligent searching, the mind remains elusive, devoid of color, shape, or form. It defies ordinary expression or illustration. It cannot be located within the body, its organs, or the external world; it transcends all physical boundaries. The primary method to realize the nature of the mind is guru devotion, as well as accumulating merit as a support. But again, the main necessity is strong, unshakable guru devotion. With that assumption, we supplicate the guru, and through this we receive blessings. The guru's blessing is essential; to receive the guru's blessing is to receive the blessings of all objects of refuge. By receiving a powerful blessing, within a short period of time one can better understand the teachings and gain temporary and then ultimate realization, which is none other than final buddhahood. It is said that in the past, Sakya Pandita practiced guru yoga and then, in the eyes of ordinary people, gained great realization. In reality Sakya Pandita was Manjushri personified, but in the eyes of ordinary people he was known to practice guru yoga. Before he entered mahaparinirvana, Sakya Pandita put his hands on Drogön Chögyal Phakpa's head and told him that in the future, if someone practices guru yoga, they will gain realization. Throughout the history of the Sakya lineage there are many great masters who gained realization through guru yoga practice. Therefore, guru yoga is an important practice, as through it one can gain many blessings in a very short time.

In general, it is believed that superior practitioners can attain buddhahood solely through the practice of guru yoga. For mediocre practitioners, guru yoga serves as an excellent means to progress along the path. For those of inferior ability, guru yoga is an ideal preliminary practice, as it helps to purify obstacles and receive blessings, facilitating a deeper immersion into the path of Dharma. This foundation enables practitioners to progress to more advanced practices, and ultimately leads to enlightenment. Bear in mind that Dharma practices can be integrated into our daily lives at any moment and in any place. Similarly, we can maintain devotion to our guru outside of formal sessions, incorporating it into our everyday activities consistently. Chapter 2 offers valuable insights on integrating guru devotion into daily interactions, extending beyond formal spiritual practices. It provides practical guidance on nurturing a profound connection with one's guru in various aspects of everyday life.

The Benefits of Guru Yoga

It is said in the tantras and *Fifty Verses on Guru Devotion* by Ashvaghosha that paying respect to the guru is like making offerings to all buddhas and bodhisattvas, who are equal in number to as many atoms as there are in all the sand on earth. In this way, then, making offerings to the guru or practicing guru yoga is more meritorious than making offerings to numberless buddhas and bodhisattvas. All the domains for merit accumulation equate to the Triple Gem, and the Triple Gem is epitomized by the guru. Hence, the guru's body is the Sangha, the guru's voice is the Dharma, and the guru's wisdom is the nature of the Buddha.

Prerequisites for Guru Yoga

The prerequisites for the uncommon guru yoga practices vary depending on the type of practice. This is in the context of the uncommon guru yoga practices, according to the Sakya order. For general guru yoga practice, one must have received refuge and bodhichitta vows, as well as Mantrayana vows through any major highest yoga tantra empowerment.

If one's guru yoga practice is based on Hevajra, then one must have received refuge and bodhichitta vows, as well as Mantrayana vows through the Hevajra cause empowerment.

If one has received any of the major highest yoga tantra empowerments, one can use the ngöndro text titled *The Excellent Path of the Two Accumulations*.[17] If one has not received the Lamdré teaching, one should skip the Lamdré lineage guru prayer in this text. If one has only received the common Lamdré lineage, then one should just recite the common Lamdré lineage guru prayer, but not the uncommon Lamdré lineage guru prayer. If, however, one has received the uncommon Lamdré teaching, then one can recite the uncommon Lamdré lineage guru prayer that is found in this text.

CHAPTER 14
DEDICATION

In any Dharma practice, three things are indispensable: proper motivation at the beginning, proper visualization as our focus in the middle, and proper dedication at the conclusion of practice. This applies to all preliminary practices, as well.

WHY VIRTUE IS DEDICATED

If we dedicate the virtues gained from our Dharma practices properly, our virtuous practice is much more powerful and meritorious. Sealing our virtuous practice with the right kind of dedication makes our merit less vulnerable to destruction by our afflictive emotions or negative thoughts, such as anger. The practice of dedication is the right antidote to eliminate suffering and the causes of suffering.

We should seal each session of ngöndro practice immediately with proper dedication, even if we are doing more than one session of practice each day. If negative thoughts arise in between sessions without having sealed the previous session of practice with a proper dedication, the virtue just accumulated is easily destroyed by just a moment of negative thought.

How Dedication Works

So how does the system of dedication function? We may worry that our personal cake of virtue has fewer slices left after we dedicate virtue to others. But that is not how dedication works. In fact, when we dedicate our virtuous deeds and merit, our merit not only does not decrease, but the opposite occurs. It increases. A teacher shares knowledge with students, but that does not make the teacher more and more ignorant as they keep sharing knowledge. Conversely, the more teachers share by teaching others, the more they gain personally in experience and knowledge. Similarly, dedicating all our virtuous deeds and merit in a proper way to all sentient beings will benefit and strengthen our practice at the same time it helps others.

The prefix *maha* in Mahayana means great. As a vehicle, or *yana*, the Mahayana is considered great because its path has seven great qualities, as outlined by Maitreya in the *Ornament of the Mahayana Sutras*: great field of concern, great practical application, great wisdom, great diligence, great skill in means, great accomplishment, and great enlightened activity. The first five of these, especially the first quality, the great field of concern, can also apply to all followers of the Mahayana path, whether they follow the Paramitayana or Vajrayana traditions. The great field of concern means our concern is not for ourselves particularly, nor for only our family or friends; rather, our concern is for all sentient beings without exception. Therefore, all our practices—whatever we practice, including dedication—should always be performed for the sake of all sentient beings without exception.

Appendix 1
Practice Questions

The questions presented here have arisen frequently during teachings I've conducted on the preliminary practices. I offer these answers to you so they can serve as a guide as you undertake the preliminary practices at home. However, should you have further questions, don't hesitate to ask your guru, as the ngöndro should be guided by your lama.

Watching the Mind

Question: The teachings emphasize the significance of engaging in virtuous deeds. It appears that some students find it easier than others. How can I approach increasing my virtuous deeds?

Answer: We may think that since other people are performing virtuous deeds, then I, too, need to follow and repeat their actions. There are two motives for doing this.

The first motive is unhappiness or jealousy that arises when we see others practicing virtue. With jealous feelings, we try to replicate their virtue or even outdo them, which is a mistake. This is not a real practice of Dharma. The virtuous deed performed in that case is merely Dharma practice in a superficial sense, because it stems from jealousy.

The second motive is without any jealousy; we just follow someone's action and practice because we are following the crowd. Although such action does not result from any negative thought, it is not real Dharma

184 | APPENDIX 1

practice either, because it lacks any pure motivation, given it is due to merely imitating others.

These two motives derive from paying attention to others' ways of doing things without focusing on our own mind. We need to focus and watch our own mind. Imitating others means we are not watching our own mind. We should shift the emphasis, deemphasizing what others are doing, and focusing on the observation of our own mind. This is crucial.

The way we focus determines if we are watching our mind properly. If we focus outside ourselves, there is no way for us to focus on our own mind. But if we direct our focus toward our own thoughts, feelings, and reactions, it means we are watching our own mind. Dharma practice is neither physical nor verbal, but mainly a mental practice. Thus, we need to focus on our own mind.

MOTIVATION

Question: How can we ensure our motivation is pure? Is there a method to do so?

Answer: There are ways to check if our motivation is pure. If we are thinking, "I need to do this practice because I need to accumulate merit, gain liberation, attain buddhahood, become a better person," and so on, then that means deep down in our mind, we have strong selfish thoughts. Although we wish to do all those good things, they are based on our own self-interest. If this is the case, we are not really doing genuine Dharma practice. Whatever we do, it should not be motivated by our own selfish thoughts. We can question ourselves: Is our action based on selfish thoughts, or is it based on pure thoughts, such as the thought of renunciation, infinite loving-kindness and compassion, and aspirational and engaged bodhichitta?

To determine if our motivation is truly genuine and pure, first we need to know the reason why we need to develop those pure thoughts. Until we have developed those pure thoughts, we will not be able to gain liberation and enlightenment. Understanding this can encourage us to find the right method to practice with pure motivation.

The real method to ensure our motivation is pure is to recognize the defects of samsara. When we know the consequences of having the wrong motivation, it naturally helps us generate the right motivation. For example, when we know there is a problem, it helps us to look for the right remedy or method. In this context, we need to know that the right method to be liberated from samsara is the thought of renunciation, because the thought of renunciation is the genuine wish to gain liberation from the whole of samsara. If we wish to gain liberation, then we must have this thought.

Moreover, one must generate genuine loving-kindness and compassion to help all sentient beings. To do this, we need to think how kind and important others have been to us, how without them, we cannot survive. One person is not able to survive in this world alone. There is no way we can survive without others. We rely on others from the moment we are conceived until the moment we die. We cannot be conceived by ourselves; we need to be conceived in our mother's womb. As soon as we are born, we rely on others for clothes, shelter, food, transportation, and so on. Because of the kindness and work of others, we have been able to survive until now. So, we need to repay their kindness. The only way to repay their kindness is through our practice. Such thoughts can help us do more and more virtuous deeds and genuinely practice loving-kindness, compassion, and other positive thoughts.

And last but not least, the main pure motivation is to have bodhichitta, which is the enlightened mind for the sake of all sentient beings, without exception.

Question: How can I enjoy doing Dharma practices—ngöndro and all the other practices, such as sadhana recitation, meditation, and so on? I have noticed that most of the time, I am excited to start a new practice, then after some time, I lose interest and start feeling it is a drag to do it every day. For those practices that come with a commitment, I even feel that I have to force myself to do them each day to keep my commitment.

Answer: We can find inspiration to practice by reading and understanding the biographies of the great practitioners. What they have done is great, and through their great practice, they have gained great benefits and realizations. They have gained the ultimate realization, which is

186 | APPENDIX 1

buddhahood. So, we should also have the courage to practice and to follow in the footsteps of these great practitioners of the past and the present to gain temporary and ultimate benefits for the sake of all sentient beings.

Further, remembering the benefits of ngöndro practice in particular will boost our mental strength and energy to put more effort into the practice with great joy. For example, in our worldly life, if we see profits in doing business, although we might need to face great difficulties, we are willing to bear hardships because of the profits that we will reap. Similarly, if one can see the temporary and ultimate benefits of doing Dharma practice, and in this case ngöndro, then it will really help us bear the difficulties and challenges that arise doing the practice; it will help us make effort with great joy.

The fourth of the six perfections, the perfection of diligence, is not just making an effort in a mundane sense. Putting effort into virtuous deeds or Dharma practice with great joy, which is sealed with bodhichitta, is the definition of the perfection of diligence.

COMMITMENTS

Question: Is there a commitment if I were to do the uncommon ngöndro practices?

Answer: Generally, those who are doing Vajrayana practices hold refuge vows, bodhichitta vows, and Mantrayana vows. To hold these three vows, you will need to keep the samayas or precepts of these three types of vows, and this is the main commitment. Then, based on these commitments, you perform the common and uncommon ngöndro practices according to the Vajrayana tradition.

COMMENCING NGÖNDRO

Question: I am thinking of starting to practice ngöndro. Must I do the practice every day?

Answer: Start the practice, be it common or uncommon ngöndro or both, on an auspicious day, such as a new moon or full moon day. Once you have started ngöndro practice, it is better to maintain the practice daily, and if possible, to do two to three sessions every day.

Question: What is the right way to practice? Do we start off with common ngöndro and then move forward to uncommon ngöndro? Or do we start off with both at the same time?

Answer: You should start off with the common ngöndro practice since it is the basis of the uncommon ngöndro, which itself is also a basis for further practices. It is difficult to say we have to perfect the common ngöndro practice before pursuing the uncommon ngöndro practice. But based on the common ngöndro practice, we should then engage in the uncommon ngöndro practice.

While performing the uncommon ngöndro practice, it will be beneficial to commence one's session with contemplation and reflection of the four common ngöndro.

Counting the Numbers of Practices

Question: Am I required to count the numbers of times I do each of these ngöndro practices?

Answer: Yes, you may count how many times you do the practice. However, by saying this, it does not mean we should focus on the numbers without focusing on our visualization. We count the number of times we recite these practices, yet at the same time, we must do this together with the proper visualization for our ngöndro practices.

Question: Must I achieve the targeted numbers of recitations, such as one hundred thousand or one hundred ten thousand?

Answer: It is good to achieve the targeted numbers, which are often one hundred thousand or one hundred ten thousand times with proper visualization. Proper visualization is the most important. If we recite while we're distracted or without proper visualization, then our practice will not be very effective. You can have a targeted number to achieve, but

188 | APPENDIX 1

at the same time, we must do the practice with pure motivation, proper visualization, and appropriate dedication.

Ideally, we should continue the practice until there is a genuine sign of progress. We can observe some general, genuine signs that show our progress in the practice in the body and mind. Physically, one's body becomes lighter. Mentally, we will have a better or clearer visualization. Further, we will have the ability to control negative thoughts and will be a happier person. We will have less clinging and less attachment to the mundane world and the five sense objects perceived through the eye consciousness, ear consciousness, nose consciousness, tongue consciousness, and body consciousness. Ideally, one needs to count the number of times one recites these practices and do it until there is a genuine sign.

Nevertheless, most practitioners, including advanced ones, typically perform more than one hundred thousand or one hundred ten thousand recitations of each ngöndro practice. For example, Dagmo Trinley Paljor, the aunt of His Holiness the Forty-First Gongma Trichen, who was a great practitioner, performed six hundred thousand prostration and refuge practices and twenty million guru yoga practices.

Question: Can I recite a multiplication mantra so that my ten prostrations performed today are equivalent to one hundred prostrations? I heard there is a multiplication mantra that can do that. What about practices done on holy days when merit multiplies? Does that mean the ten mandala offerings we do on a holy day will become one million or more?

Answer: Reciting the multiplication mantra and doing practices on holy days can multiply our merit; we can receive more benefit, that is for sure. But when in the context of counting our ngöndro practices, up to for example one hundred thousand times, then we should count as usual even if we recite the multiplication mantra or do it on a holy day.

Timeframe for Completing Ngöndro

Question: Must I complete the ngöndro practices within a given timeframe?

Answer: It is better not to set a certain date to finish reciting each of these practices one hundred thousand times—such a timeframe, especially if it is short, will incline one to rush through the practice without proper visualization. Instead of rushing to complete the practice, one should focus on doing the proper practice—with proper motivation, visualization, and dedication. If one is not hurriedly trying to meet an arbitrary deadline, one will not feel pressurized by time; one will feel more relaxed, and with this relaxed calm mind, then of course, one will be able to do the practice properly.

Having said that, if one wants to set a timeframe, then set it with a realistic mindset, allowing a longer period of time so that one can properly practice in a relaxed and joyful way.

Staying Motivated

Question: I am busy with work and family commitments. I feel discouraged that I am sometimes too tired at the end of the day to do prostrations or even other ngöndro practices. Please advise what can I do to stay motivated and be persistent in embarking on and continuing this practice.

Answer: You must think about the benefits of practicing ngöndro as well as the downsides associated with not practicing ngöndro. By considering these things, it will help us to stay motivated to practice; we will want to put more effort into it.

After a long day of worldly activities, our body and mind are easily tired; if we practice at night, it may be difficult for us to focus. The ideal time to practice is in the morning; after a good night's sleep, the mind is fresh, and physically you are not tired. At this time, you will have better focus, and this is the best time to practice. Try to spend an hour in practice, or if you have a busy life, then allocate whatever amount of time you can afford to practice. Once you have started ngöndro practice, it is important to continue with it daily.

190 | APPENDIX 1

PROSTRATIONS

Question: I am physically unable to do a full prostration. Can I still do the uncommon refuge practice?

Answer: When we do ngöndro practice, especially the refuge practice, we typically do a full prostration—which involves lying down fully in front of the merit field that you visualize. For this practice there should be some representation of the merit field physically present, like a statue or thangka painting, but most important is to visualize the merit field. In front of these, not only do you recite the refuge prayer, but you also do prostrations. In the Sakya tradition, prostration is not a must at the time of refuge practice. If you do the prostration, it is more meritorious, but it should be done according to your physical ability. If you cannot do a full prostration, then try doing a half prostration, which involves only going down to one's hands and knees. If you cannot do a half prostration, then you can mentally visualize that you are prostrating.

THE SIGNS OF PROGRESS

Question: Do we expect any signs after doing ngöndro practice, especially for completing one full set or more?

Answer: If you do the ngöndro practice with the right motivation at the beginning, with the right focus and visualization in the middle, and with the right dedication at the end, in this way it becomes a complete ngöndro practice. Such ngöndro practice is very effective and beneficial, it will definitely be the right remedy to remove suffering and the causes of suffering. In other words, it will be the right remedy to gain liberation from samsara and to attain the state of full enlightenment.

Through the general practice, you can have genuine signs indicating the practice is progressing. For example, after doing the refuge practice properly, you may feel the place where you are doing the practice, when you are there, is more comfortable and conducive to practice, so you will have more faith and devotion to the guru and Triple Gem.

After practicing the Vajrasattva meditation and recitation properly, you will feel happier to do virtuous deeds or Dharma practice. You will have clearer visualization. You may have dreams of taking a shower or bathing, signifying purification.

After accumulating merit through the practice of mandala offering, you will have more devotion and faith in the guru; you can feel the guru as the real deity or as a combination of all the objects of refuge. The place where you are doing the practice becomes more conducive and comfortable, and in your dreams, you will meet your guru and your guru will appear in a pleasing mode. Such appearances will be perceived by other practitioners. You might also have dreams of sitting on a throne, wearing beautiful ornaments, and so on.

I have not read any commentaries that mention the signs of proper guru yoga practice, but I believe through the proper practice of guru yoga, it is the same as above: you would have more devotion and faith to the guru and the Triple Gem, you would receive all blessings in your own mental continuum, gain more realization, reduce your own negativities and obscurations, and so on. In the past, there were many great masters who focused on the practice of guru yoga and attained liberation and enlightenment.

Graduation from Ngöndro

Question: After I have finished one set of ngöndro practices, does that mean I have graduated and can move on to other "higher" teachings?

Answer: Ngöndro practice is essential; it is the foundation of all the practices. Take for instance, when you build a high-rise building; first it needs to have a very solid foundation. Without a solid foundation, one cannot build the remaining floors of the high-rise building. Similarly, first we should have a strong practice of ngöndro, and after that, one's main practice is more effective, powerful, and meritorious.

Actually, there is no certain limit to how many times one should do these practices, although we say recite them one hundred thousand times each. In reality there is no such limit. In the past, the great masters spent many, many years, most of their lives, doing ngöndro practices. There are practitioners who mainly focus on ngöndro practice, while there are

192 | Appendix 1

practitioners who do ngöndro practice and then their main practice. I do not think there is a so-called graduation from ngöndro practice—not until we have attained liberation and enlightenment. Anyway, ngöndro practice is essential and based on it, one can have a better practice of any deity that one wishes to focus on, after receiving the empowerment of that deity from a genuine guru.

Whether our practice is profound or not depends on us. It depends on how we practice, not what we practice. If we know the proper way to practice ngöndro, then this preliminary practice becomes a profound practice. If we do not know how to properly engage in deity practice, although it is the main practice, it is not profound.

It is good to continue the ngöndro practice, and one can add the main practice on top of that later on.

The precision of the Visualizations

Question: When it comes to visualization during the uncommon ngöndro practices, especially in visualizing the field of refuge, how accurate do our visualizations need to be? Must we visualize them as a certain size and precise appearance, such as how all the lineage masters and deities look exactly in the image of the refuge tree I received during my vow ceremony or in the text I received?

Answer: In general, doing proper visualization is essential whether you are doing ngöndro practice or the main deity practice. The clearer our visualization is, the more effective and beneficial our practice becomes. So, we should try to make our visualization as clear as possible. Now, how do we have a clearer visualization? If we have been engaged in mundane activities for the whole day, at the end of the day, we may feel very tired physically and mentally. We have to avoid such conditions; our body must not be tired and our mind must be fresh and clear. Once we know how to visualize properly, with a fresh and clear mind, we will be able to do a proper visualization.

Another method is to look at and focus on an image, such as an image of the refuge tree, which depicts the masters of the Sakya lineage that have come before us. We try to visualize this, and as we keep practicing, our visualization will be clearer. Sometimes, however, the way the image is painted and the way we need to visualize is different, because the image that we see in a painting, for example, is a two-dimensional form, while the way we need to visualize is as a three-dimensional form. So, we should know that there can be a difference in this aspect from the teachings we have received or by studying this carefully.

We should visualize the object in a three-dimensional form, in the nature of light, even if it might be different from the image we see in a thangka painting or picture.

The Guru and Visualization

Question: I have a number of different teachers and gurus. When I am doing the ngöndro refuge visualization and guru yoga, which teachers should I visualize?

Answer: When you do a general Vajrayana practice of the highest yoga tantra without focusing on a specific deity, you can visualize your guru in the form of Vajradhara. As to whom to visualize as the guru, you may choose the one for whom you have the greatest faith and devotion as the main guru, while the other gurus you have received empowerments and teachings from, regardless of their tradition, absorb into the main guru who is in the form of Vajradhara. It is important to think that all the gurus from whom one has received teachings, regardless of tradition, have the same nature.

About Refuge Practice

Question: Do I have to recite the refuge prayer and prostrate at the same time?

Answer: Many people do recitation and prostration at the same time, but in our Sakya tradition, it is not compulsory to do both at the same time. Whether you are reciting the refuge prayer with prostration or without prostration, most important is that you must do it with the right visualization.

Question: Can I use tools when performing physical prostrations, such as a prostrating board, gloves, knee guards, and elbow guards?

Answer: You can use these tools. Many prefer to use some kind of cloth or gloves so that they will not touch the floor with their bare hands, and because it helps them glide their whole body forward on the floor.

General and Deity-Specific Ngöndro

Question: I am already doing a deity practice that includes the uncommon ngöndro. Can I still do ngöndro as a separate practice? Is there a difference between the two?

Answer: If you are doing the general ngöndro practice of the highest yoga tantra tradition, then it is already covering all the deities of the highest yoga tantra. Based on that, you can do whatever deity practice you want. But if you are doing Hevajra ngöndro practice, yet you want to do Vajrayogini practice, then you will have to do the Vajrayogini ngöndro practice. In other words, for different deity practices, you will need different ngöndro practices. This is because the refuge field, the mandala offering, and the guru yoga practice will differ. Therefore, it is better for you to do the general ngöndro practice of the highest yoga tantra tradition, and based on that, the specific deity practice as you wish, considering you have already received the necessary empowerment or initiation of that deity.

Integrating Ngöndro with Daily Life

Question: How do we integrate and apply all these ngöndro practices in our daily lives?

Answer: There are many ways we can integrate practice of ngöndro with our daily lives. I will briefly mention a few here.

Through the practice of renunciation, we can reduce pride and arrogance about mundane qualities. Ngöndro generally can help us reduce other negative thoughts as well.

By meditating on the difficulty of obtaining a precious human life, we will not waste this precious human life; with practice we know how rare and difficult human life is to obtain and how much potential we have if we use our lives meaningfully. This understanding helps us use our life in an effective way without wasting time. This is how contemplating the occasion of a precious human existence applies to daily life.

By understanding impermanence and death, we really come to feel that worldly activities are impermanent and therefore not as important as we thought. That understanding helps reduce attachment to worldly things and reduces our irritability with ordinary beings.

As the Buddha said in a sutra, "Pondering impermanence is like making offerings to the buddhas. Pondering impermanence is prophesized and blessed by the buddhas. The most excellent perception of all is that of impermanence. Thinking of impermanence has infinite benefits." This helps us to perceive the reality of relative truth directly and ultimate truth indirectly. Perceiving impermanence will lend us more enthusiasm and urgency in our practice, so we are willing to make more effort in practice with great joy and without any delay.

Pondering the law of cause and effect really helps us accept what needs to be done and avoid what needs to be abandoned in our daily lives. It helps us to realize that we cannot bribe the law of karma, cannot change the law of karma, and cannot deceive the law of karma, and that the law of karma is fair to each and every one of us, without discrimination. We should imagine that the law of karma is somehow witnessing all our actions without exception. This will help us to do more virtuous deeds and to abandon nonvirtuous deeds, because we understand that all wish to gain happiness and alleviate suffering.

By practicing genuine refuge, we will not take refuge in worldly gods in our daily life. We will abstain from taking the wrong path. Whatever practice we do will become more meritorious due to the refuge vows. As part of the refuge precepts, we vow not to harm anyone, and in our daily lives that will prevent us from harming others. These are some examples for how to integrate refuge practice in our daily lives.

196 | APPENDIX 1

The practice of *bodhichitta*, the awakening mind, will help us to calm and control our minds. It will make a great impact on our minds. When our minds are controlled and influenced by bodhichitta, this has a great impact on our physical and verbal activity. When we can control our minds through bodhichitta practice it means we can control all our activities, because mental activity is the principal activity. If the principal activity is controlled, then all other activities will be controlled. Through the practice of bodhichitta we develop positive minds; with positive minds we develop positive activities via body and speech. Positive states of mind cannot motivate us to do negative physical or verbal actions. These are just some of the ways that practice can really change our daily lives.

Through the practice of refuge and bodhichitta, we are more protected from obstacles and evil spirits. Taking refuge and generating bodhichitta are excellent protection.

Through the practice of Vajrasattva meditation and recitation, we are better motivated not to commit any nonvirtuous deeds; and even if we do, we will confess them immediately with the four powers. As a result, our practice will become better. We will be able to visualize more clearly. Our body, speech, and mind will feel lighter and fresher, and become more active, making us feel great joy in practice.

We can accumulate great merit and blessings from mandala practice. We will also be able to accumulate more meritorious deeds in our daily lives.

The practice of guru yoga will help us to develop stronger devotion to the guru, and to serve the guru with genuine perception and right motivation through our body, speech, and mind, without any obstacles and without any resistance in the mind.

MIXING DIFFERENT NGÖNDRO LINEAGES

Question: I have been introduced to more than one ngöndro lineage practice. Can I combine the practices? For example, if I complete the mandala offering accumulation, can it be counted toward both the Sakya ngöndro and Kagyü ngöndro? And some of the visualizations are different for different lineages; can I create one to fit all these different lineage practices?

Answer: There are several different schools of Tibetan Buddhism, and they have different ngöndro traditions. It is better to do one tradition of ngöndro practice because the visualizations of the refuge field, the guru or deity, and so on vary from school to school. Whichever ngöndro lineage you have decided to pursue, you should follow that from the beginning until the end. That is more effective and more beneficial. Conversely, combining the refuge practice of one lineage with the guru yoga of another lineage will not be helpful.

Ngöndro and Enlightenment

Question: Can we gain liberation or even full enlightenment by just relying on ngöndro practices?

Answer: Based on the common ngöndro practices, we practice the uncommon ngöndro. It is possible for us to gain liberation and even perfect enlightenment just by practicing the uncommon ngöndro. This is because in the refuge practice, we visualize the refuge field in the form of a deity. Many accomplished masters and practitioners have attained liberation and enlightenment through guru yoga practice, which is part of the uncommon ngöndro.

Appendix 2
Mandala Offering Illustrations and Figures

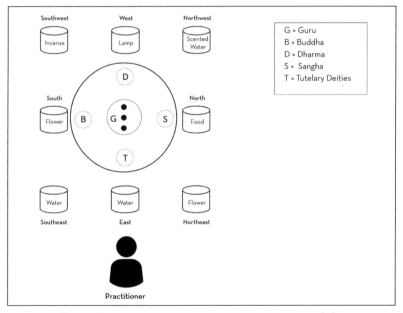

Fig. 2. Key to setting up a propitiation mandala.

The Propitiation Mandala

Set up the propitiation mandala on a square table or on an elevated place. If you already have a shrine, you may set up the propitiation mandala on or near the shrine. If you do not have a shrine, the propitiation mandala is sufficient. The objects surrounding the mandala should ideally be in a square shape. The offerings are water for drinking (*argham*) in the east, water for cleansing the hands and feet (*padyam*) in the southeast, flowers (*pushpe*) in the south, incense (*dhupe*) in the southwest, lamps (*aloke*) in the west, scented water (*gandhe*) in the northwest, and food (*naividya*) in the north. A flower is placed in the northeast, in Tibetan *chamzin metog*, literally meaning a flower held at a corner, to serve as a marker.

Ideally, the practitioner would be seated opposite the propitiation mandala, with the east direction of the mandala closest to the practitioner, so that the practitioner and shrine are facing each other.

One is required to change the grains or rice used for the practice mandala every session or every day. However, one does not need to change the offerings used in the propitiation mandala. For a food offering, either a food torma or real, clean food, such as cookies or nuts, can be used.

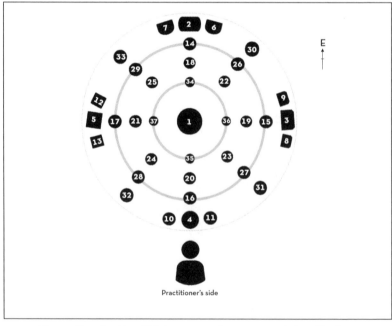

Fig. 3. Key to the thirty-seven-heap mandala offering.

The Thirty-Seven-Heap Mandala for Highest Yoga Tantra Deity Practice

Cleaning the mandala plate

- Before starting the mandala practice, clean the plate by applying scented water on the mandala plate. One could add saffron to the clean water for this purpose.
- Having taken up the offering mandala in one's left hand, take up some grain with the fingers of the right hand. While reciting the hundred-syllable Vajrasattva mantra, clean the mandala with the right wrist clockwise until it is clear of dust and dirt (however many times are required to clean the plate) while thinking that all the negative deeds, obscurations, faults, and downfalls imprinted on one's mental continuum are purified. It is essential to have a very clean mandala plate before proceeding to the practice.
- In actuality, it is not the mandala that needs to be cleaned. Rather, cleaning the mandala is for the sake of purifying the obscurations of defilements and knowledge in one's mental continuum.
- It is taught that how well the mandala is cleaned will indicate how well one's mental continuum will be purified. One should refrain from cleaning the mandala with other means, such as a cloth, and just use one's wrist alone.

The thirty-seven-heap mandala practice

- With the three doors—body, speech, and mind—engaged together, one begins the mandala practice by physically arranging the heaps of grains or offering substance, verbally reciting the words, and mentally visualizing the meaning of the words. It is important to maintain an undistracted mind rather than merely focusing on the physical actions while performing the mandala offering practice.
- The grains or offering substance should be placed on the

202 | APPENDIX 2

mandala by allowing them to flow through the tips of the five fingers or from the top of the fist, through the thumb and forefinger. They should not flow from the wrist end of the palm, as this is disrespectful.

- The central heap should be higher than the surrounding ones.

The vajra ground

- Start by pouring scented water in the middle of the mandala plate. Using the middle and ring fingers, smear the water from the center outward, drawing and anointing the plate thoroughly without leaving any gaps. Move the fingers all the way around to the northeast, which is toward the right side of the plate, and then down around the edge of the plate, forming a square shape in a clockwise direction.
- If one offers a dry mandala, one will be reborn in a very dry place and one's mental continuum will be devoid of the moisture of compassion. Hence it is essential to offer with scented water.
- Having poured some scented water on the mandala plate, pick up some grains or whatever offering substance one is offering and recite, "*Om vajra bhumi ah hum / shi yong su dakpa wangchen ser gyi sa shi*; the universe is wholly pure, of great power, with earth of gold." With the index and middle fingers of the right hand beginning at the center, draw a square starting with drawing a line diagonally to the left of oneself, away from oneself to the edge of the mandala plate, without leaving any gaps, taking it all the way around to the northeast.
- While performing this, visualize that the vajra ground, comprising the three mandalas, is created. The lowest mandala is the air mandala, blue in color, with an immeasurable diameter. On top is the water mandala, which is a golden liquid ocean. On top of that is the pure golden earth mandala.
- Both the water and earth mandalas have the same diameter. However, the air mandala is twice as deep as the water mandala, while the water mandala is twice as deep as the earth mandala.

The vajra fence

- Next, recite, "*Om vajra rekhe ah hum / chi chak ri khor yuk gi kor wai*; the outermost limit is surrounded with an iron fence," while making a circle, starting from the northeastern point in a clockwise direction.
- Visualize a circle of iron mountain or iron fence rising on top of the earth mandala around the edge of the diameter.

Mount Meru

- Recite "*Ü su hum*; in the center is *hum*," and place a heap of rice in the center (heap 1).
- Visualize the blue letter *hum* arising there. Then recite, "*Ri gyalpo ri rab*; King of Mountains, Mount Meru," and visualize the mountain as a square arising in the center of the mandala, in the middle of a vast sea. The base of Mount Meru is ringed with eight terraces, of which four are above and four are below water, surrounded by an ocean.
- Mount Meru is surrounded by seven separate golden mountains that are round in shape. Outside these mountain bands are the four continents, one on each side of four sides of Mount Meru. The east side is made of white diamond, the south side is blue lapis lazuli, the west side is red ruby, and the north side is yellow gold.
- Both the uppermost terrace of Mount Meru and the innermost square band of golden mountains are half of the height of the summit of Mount Meru. The remaining square of the mountain squares each progressively decreases in height by half.
- Beyond the continents is the iron mountain or iron fence of the outer limit.
- Between the outer limit and the continent, between the continents and the concentric squares of golden mountains, between each of the squares and between the inner square of golden mountains and Mount Meru, are oceans. The ocean between the innermost band and Mount Meru is twice as wide

as the ocean between the first and second band. The width of the subsequent oceans progressively decreases by one half. The ocean possesses qualities such as being clear, cool, refreshing, smooth, tasty, good for the throat, and not harmful to the stomach.

- An exquisite city is on the summit of Mount Meru. In the center is the Heaven of the Thirty-Three. Upon the four steps of Mount Meru and on the summit of the seven bands of golden mountains are the divine realms of the guardian kings of the four directions. In the sky above Mount Meru are other gods from the desire realm: Yama, Tushita, Nirmanarati, and Heaven of Controlling Others' Emanations, respectively. From the Brahmaloka up to Akanishta are the form of realm gods. Those divine realms of perfect design are instantly manifested.

Continue to recite the name of each of the objects, and place the grains on the associated place on the mandala plate, with the following visualizations.

The four continents

- "*Sharlu Phakpo*; eastern continent Purvavideha" (heap 2): A great white continent made of diamonds, semicircular in shape.
- "*Lho Dzambuling*; southern continent Jambudvipa" (heap 3): A great blue continent made of sapphires, trapezoidal in shape.
- "*Nubpa Langchö*; western continent Aparagodaniya" (heap 4): A great blue continent made of rubies, circular in shape.
- "*Jang Draminyen*; northern continent Uttarakuru" (heap 5): A great yellow continent made of gold, square in shape.

The eight subcontinents

Each of the pairs of subcontinents are placed on either side of their main continent. They are of the same color, shape, and element as the main continent, except they are half the size of the main continent.

- *"Lu dang Luphak*; eastern subcontinents Deha and Videha" (heaps 6 and 7)
- *"Ngayab dang Ngayabshen*; southern subcontinents Camara and Aparacamara" (heaps 8 and 9)
- *"Yoden dang Lamchokdro*; western subcontinents Satha and Uttaramantrin" (heaps 10 and 11)
- *"Draminyen dang Draminyen Gyida*; northern subcontinents Kuru and Kaurava" (heaps 12 and 13)

The four precious objects

- *"Rinpochei riwo*; Jeweled mountain" (heap 14): Visualize that the three eastern continents are covered with many very beautiful high mountains made of jewels and precious gems, such as rubies, sapphires, emeralds, diamonds, pearls, coral, and so on.
- *"Paksam gyi shing*; Wish-fulfilling trees" (heap 15): Visualize that the three southern continents are thickly wooded with extremely beautiful, jeweled trees whose trunks, branches, leaves, and flowers all made of different jewels and seven precious substances—golden roots, silver trunks, lapis lazuli branches, crystal leaves, red pearls for flowers, jade petals, and diamond fruits that bestow all wealth and wishes.
- *"Döjoi ba*; Wishing-granting cows" (heap 16): Visualize that on the three western continents are many beautiful cows with blue jewel-like horns and sapphire hooves, as well as an inestimable tail that is as if made from a wish-fulfilling tree. Their urine and droppings are gold. Each hair pore of the cows provides an inexhaustible source of whatever one desires.
- *"Mamopai lotog*; Unploughed harvest" (heap 17): Visualize that on the three northern continents, even though the land has never been ploughed, fine crops spontaneously grow and can be harvested repeatedly. Upon harvest, the fields are again filled with ripened crops.

The seven precious emblems

The seven precious emblems symbolize the seven factors of enlightenment.

- "*Khorlo rinpoche*; Precious wheel" (heap 18): Visualize that the sky above the eastern continents is filled with countless precious thousand-spoked wheels made of gold from the Jambu River. It rises into the sky, can fly long distances in a day, and has the power to conquer all four continents. A precious wheel symbolizes the quality of mindfulness.
- "*Norbu rinpoche*; Precious jewel" (heap 19): Visualize that the sky above the southern continents is filled with countless precious jewels that can bestow all wishes. The jewels, made of blue lapis lazuli and hexagonal in shape, emit five colors of light rays, preventing untimely death and infectious disease. When it is hot, the rays are cooling; when it is cold, the rays are warming. Precious jewels symbolize the quality of joy.
- "*Tsunmo rinpoche*; Precious queen" (heap 20): Visualize that the sky above the western continents is filled with mini countless precious queens with great qualities. They possess beautiful form and eight tactile qualities: an agreeable mind; the ability to give birth to many sons; being of similar class; a high status; no jealousy toward other women; no idle speech; no wrong views; and if without home or kitchen, will not fall under the power of sense objects. The queens can eliminate the sorrows, hunger, and thirst of beings wherever they dwell. A precious queen symbolizes the quality of tranquility.
- "*Lönpo rinpoche*; Precious minister" (heap 21): Visualize that the sky above the northern continents is filled with countless precious ministers who have the power to execute without fail any order of the emperor in accordance with the Dharma. They are also able to perceive treasures hidden under the ground. A precious minister symbolizes the quality of concentration.

- "*Langpo rinpoche*; Precious elephant" (heap 22): Visualize that the sky above the southeastern area is filled with countless great white precious elephants with six tusks. Their limbs and trunks cover the earth and resemble snow mountains, and they possess the knowledge of movement and the power to overcome all enemies. Precious elephants symbolize the quality of wisdom.
- "*Tachok rinpoche*; Precious supreme horse" (heap 23): Visualize that the sky above the southwestern area is filled with countless white precious horses called "the All-Knowing." The saddles and bridles are made of divine jewels. They are able to go around the world in half a day and know how to accomplish whatever their master desires. A precious supreme horse symbolizes the quality of energy.
- "*Makpön rinpoche*; Precious general" (heap 24): Visualize that the sky above the northwestern area is filled with countless precious generals, who are clever and skilled. They can turn back all acts of war that beset the country, are untiring and not discouraged, know the emperors' thoughts, and are able to overcome all enemies without harming them. A precious general symbolizes the quality of equanimity.

Then, recite:

- "*Terchen poi bumpa*; Great treasure vase" (heap 25): Visualize the sky above the northeastern area is filled with countless treasure vases that can gather all desirous qualities without exhaustion. The vases are made of gold, encrusted with jewels, and adorned with *kalapatra* leaves; they have a round belly, long neck wrapped with fine ribbons, drooping lip, and flat base. They are decorated with wish-fulfilling trees and divine cloths on their handles.

The eight goddesses

These eight goddesses are visualized as having two arms.

- "*Gekmoma*; Goddess of Grace" (heap 26): Visualize that the sky above the southeastern area is filled with countless goddesses of grace, white in color, both hands holding a five-pronged vajra on either side at the level of the hips, elegantly poised.
- "*Threngwama*; Goddess of Garlands" (heap 27): Visualize that the sky above the southwestern area is filled with countless goddesses of garlands, yellow in color, holding a garland of flowers in their hands raised to their foreheads.
- "*Luma*; Goddess of Melody" (heap 28): Visualize that the sky above the northwestern area is filled with countless goddesses of melody, white in color with a reddish tinge, and holding a lute in their hands, which they play.
- "*Garma*; Goddess of Dance" (heap 29): Visualize that the sky above the northeastern area is filled with countless goddesses of dance, green in color and dancing with a vajra in each hand.
- "*Dukpöma*; Goddess of Incense" (heap 30): Visualize that in the southeastern area countless goddesses of incense appear on the outer mountains of that region, white in color, and holding vessels with burning incense.
- "*Metokma*; Goddess of Flowers" (heap 31): Visualize that in the southwestern area countless goddesses of flowers appear on the outer mountains of that region, yellow in color, and holding vases of flowers.
- "*Marmema*; Goddess of Light" (heap 32): Visualize that in the northwestern area countless goddesses of light appear on the outer mountain of that region, pink in color, and holding lamps.
- "*Drichabma*; Goddess of Perfume" (heap 33): Visualize that in the northeastern area countless goddesses of perfume appear on the outer mountains of that region, green in color, and holding conch shells filled with fragrantly scented water or perfume.

The sun and moon

- *"Nyima;* the sun" (heap 34): Visualize a sun disc in front and above the first row of the seven rows of mountains surrounding Mount Sumeru, or within the innermost band of golden mountains. The sun disc is made of fire glass, like a magnifying glass; a warm light is pervading brightly in all directions, eliminating gross and subtle darkness of all the continents.
- *"Dawa;* the moon" (heap 35): Visualize that the moon, made from water crystal jewels, is within the innermost band of the golden mountains, shining brightly with a cooling light, eliminating gross darkness of the continents.

The auspicious symbols

- *"Rinpochei duk;* Precious umbrella" (heap 36): Visualize that in the sky above the innermost band of mountains in the south are one hundred thousand white ceremonial parasols. The handles are made of gold, with one thousand golden spokes, lapis lazuli tips, and pearl ornaments on their crests, and they are made of divine cloth, with jewels dangling down around their perimeter. Precious umbrellas symbolize protection given by the Dharma.
- *"Choklé nampar gyalwai gyaltsen;* Victory banner" (heap 37): Visualize that the sky above the innermost band of mountains in the north are many banners of victory. They are made of divine substances and adorned by a great variety of cloths. They have a wish-fulfilling jewel as a crest ornament and handles of gold. They are completely victorious over all unfavorable conditions in all directions. Victory banners symbolize that one is able to conquer all delusions and becomes a Dharma holder.

Continue pouring a large handful of grains or whatever offering substance one is using over the entire mandala while reciting: *"Lhadang mi paljor phun sum tsok . . . ;* These offerings of the riches of gods and men . . ." Visualize the thirteen main places—that is, Mount Meru, the four main continents, and eight subcontinents—with the entire sky above them filled with the eight auspicious articles (parasol, golden fish, vase, lotus flower, white conch shell, eternal knot, banner of victory, and golden wheel); the eight auspicious materials (elephant bile medicine, curds, mirror, *durva* grass, wood-apple fruit, vermillion powder, right coiling conch shell, and white mustard seed); the seven lesser riches of the emperor (sleeping couch, throne, cushion, sword, shoes, snakeskin, and robe); and the five objects of enjoyment of the sense faculties (mirror, fruit, cloth, cymbal, and scented water).

In brief, the mandala is filled with all requisites and riches desirable to gods and humans, of great delight, and fully replete with nothing missing.

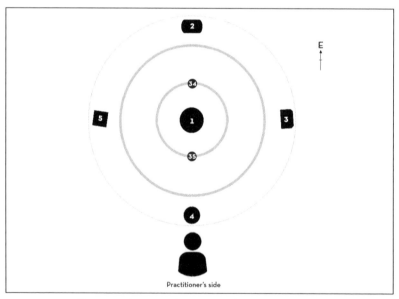

Fig. 4. A key to the seven-heap mandala.

The Seven-Heap Mandala

First, clean the plate and commence the offering practice from "*Om vajra bhumi ah hum / shi yong su dakpa wangchen ser gyi sa shi*; the universe is wholly pure, of great power, with earth of gold" (heap 1), up to the four main continents, "*Jang Draminyen*; northern continent Uttara-kuru" (heap 5), as instructed for the thirty-seven-heap mandala offering. Then continue the yoga by placing grains or other offering substances on the sun and moon heaps while reciting: "*Nyima*; the sun" (heap 34) and "*Dawa*; the moon" (heap 35), with visualizations as described in the thirty-seven-heap mandala.

Next, pour handfuls of grains or offering substances over the whole mandala plate while reciting, "These offerings of the riches of gods and men, perfectly and utterly complete with none omitted, to the greatly kind root guru and lineage gurus who are glorious and holy, to all the deities in the mandala of the tutelary deity, to the buddhas and bodhisattvas, to the protectors who guard the holy Dharma, to the wealth deities of the desire realm and their *yaksha* retinue: to all these together I make these offerings. Through compassion for the purposes of beings, please receive them. Having accepted them, please bestow your blessings." The visualization is as described for the thirty-seven-heap mandala.

NOTES

1. According to the *Fortunate Eon Sutra* (*Bhadrakalpika Sutra*), 1,002 buddhas will appear during the *kalpa*, or eon, in which we presently live. A kalpa is an almost inconceivably long period of time. The historical Buddha Shakyamuni, who lived in India, was the fourth buddha of our eon. It is called a "fortunate" eon because so many buddhas will appear.

2. Buddharakkhita, Acharya, trans. *The Dhammapada: The Buddha's Path of Wisdom* (Kandy, Sri Lanka: Buddhist Publication Society, 1985), 51.

3. *Shravaka* means "one who hears and proclaims," and refers to a follower of the Lesser Vehicle who strives to attain the level of an arhat. *Shravakayana* thus refers to the "Vehicle of the Shravakas" or "Vehicle of the Hearers."

4. Aggregates (Tibetan: *phung po*; Sanskrit: *skandhas*) refer to the five aggregates of clinging: form, feeling, perception, mental formations, and consciousness. Henceforth, the abbreviations "Skt." and "Tib." will be used to refer to Sanskrit and Tibetan terms, respectively.

5. The vows (Tib. *sdom pa*) are, for example, the vows of refuge, bodhichitta, and Mantrayana. Precepts (Tib. *bslab bya*, literally "trainings") are the rules that must be kept after taking vows.

6. The four empowerments (Tib. *dbang bzhi*) are the vase empowerment, secret empowerment, wisdom empowerment, and precious word or fourth empowerment. The four empowerments are part of the anuttarayogatantra empowerment. Generally speaking, the

214 | THE FUNDAMENTAL PRACTICES

three lower tantras—kriyatantra, charyatantra, and yogatantra—have no four empowerments.

7. For example, at the crown of a Lotus-family deity such as Hayagriva, there appears the small head of Buddha Amitabha who is the lord of the Lotus clan; at the crown of a vajra-family deity there is a small head of Buddha Akshobhya who is the lord of the Vajra clan, and so on.

8. In some texts, these four might be presented in a different order.

9. *Dharma* is a Sanskrit term with many meanings. As a lowercased term, it can also mean phenomena, but when capitalized, *Dharma* refers to the Buddha's teachings.

10. Translations in this book are my own, unless otherwise noted.

11. *Bardo* is a term commonly used to denote the intermediate state between death and rebirth, but in reality, bardos are occurring continuously throughout both life and death. They are junctures at which the possibility of liberation, or enlightenment, is heightened. In this context, *bardo* refers to the intermediate state between death and rebirth.

12. *Dharmakaya* means "absolute body" or "truth body." Upon attaining buddhahood, enlightenment manifests at three levels, known as the three bodies, or *kayas*, of a buddha. Dharmakaya is one of the three bodies attained. See chapter 9 for more detail on the kayas.

13. *Rupakaya* is the form body of a buddha, of which there are two types: nirmanakaya and sambhogakaya. See chapter 9 for more detail.

14. *Samadhi* means "meditative absorption" or "concentration," and can be used in the context of either the name of a practice or the state of meditation.

15. *Pratyekabuddhas* are solitary realizers, followers of the Lesser Vehicle who attain the level of pratyekabuddha arhat by themselves in solitude. *Pratyekabuddhayana* is the vehicle of solitary realizers.

16. *Bodhisattvacharyavatara* 5.16.

17. *The Excellent Path of the Two Accumulations* was originally published by Sakya Tenphel Ling in Singapore in 1979. It is based on the text by Venerable Dezhung Tulku Rinpoche, who compiled the practice based on many Lamdré sources, particularly from text by

Gatön Ngawang Lekpa, together with supplementary notes by His Holiness the Forty-First Gongma Trichen. The revised text includes additional explanations from His Holinesss, with further clarifications from the ngöndro commentary by Ngaklo Rinpoche, Jampa Ngawang Lodrö Rinchen, titled *The Lamp of the Path of Knowledge: The Instruction Stages of All Liberation that Are the Common and Uncommon Preliminaries of the Path of Anuttarayoga Vajrayana.*

INDEX

A

accumulation of merit and wisdom, 25, 53
  guru yoga and, 178, 179
  importance of, 47, 165–66
  mandala offering and, 166–70, 174–75
  six paramitas and, 168–69
afflictive emotions, 1, 131
  as enemy, 105
  five paths and, 125
  freedom from, 63, 64, 71
  self-cherishing and, 119
  tainted offerings and, 166
aggregates, 28, 213n4
  suffering and, 71, 72, 83
Akanishta realm, 123, 204
alaya consciousness, 24, 140, 169
anger, 106, 119, 140
Angulimala, 160
animal realm, 76–77, 80, 107
antidote, power of, 162
anuttarayogatantra, 159, 163
appearances
  clinging to ordinary, 120
  illusory and karmic, 102

as projection of mind, 169
  relative truth and, 46
Ashvaghosha, 179
aspirational bodhichitta, 67, 147, 148–49
Atisha, 6, 9, 173
attachment (desire), 106, 119
  impermanence and, 91, 92
  suffering and, 71, 83
  to this life, 59, 60, 63–64, 84, 96, 195
attainments (*siddhis*), 26
auspicious symbols, 209
Avalokiteshvara, 151

B

bardo, 90, 99, 214n11
Bari Lotsawa Rinchen Drakpa, 12
bhumis, 26, 148, 151, 165, 168
birth, suffering and, 77–78, 83
blessing (*chinlab*), 28–29
  Dharma teachers and, 34
  guru yoga and, 48, 178
bodhichitta
  benefits of practicing, 149–50, 196
  bodhisattvas and, 150–51

218 | THE FUNDAMENTAL PRACTICES

cultivating, 2, 66–68, 130, 147–57
as essence of Dharma, 149–50
exceptional practice of, 157
four aspects of precepts of, 154–55
importance of, 22, 25, 37, 48, 113
prerequisites for practicing, 156–57
proper way to practice, 151–56
relative, 66–67, 125, 147–48, 156
ultimate, 147–48, 156–57
vows of, 25, 36, 67–68, 148,
    149–50, 157
bodhisattva levels, 151
Bön tradition, 5
Buddha
  having faith in, 120–21, 138–39
  as object of refuge, 114, 117, 122–23,
    126–28, 132, 142
  refuge precepts for, 136–37
  ultimate qualities of, 128
buddha nature, 1, 104
Buddha Shakyamuni, 1, 51, 213n1
  authentic teachings of, 3–4, 49–50,
    124
  brief biography of, 17–19, 64
  enlightenment of, 19, 64, 141
  mahaparinirvana of, 94
  as nirmanakaya buddha, 24, 49,
    64, 123
  taking refuge in, 126–28
Buddha Vajradhara, 24, 25, 26, 39, 193
Buddhadharma, 123–25. *See also*
  Dharma
buddhahood
  cultivating bodhichitta and, 152–53,
    155–56
  expedient path to, 23
  great compassion and, 65–66
  guru yoga and, 178
  as intent of Dharma, 61
  ngöndro and, 1, 2–3, 197

refuge vows and, 140, 142
buddhas
  making offerings to, 136
  three kayas of, 24, 122–23
Buddhist teachings
  authenticity of, 49–50
  four reliances and, 44–46
  Kangyur and Tengyur, 29–30, 124
  as provisional and definitive, 20–21,
    33, 46
  purpose and goal of, 19–20, 61–62
  three yanas of, 20–23
  transmission to Tibet, 4–6

C

Calling the Guru from Afar, 41
Chakrasamvara Tantra, 52
Chandrakirti, 45, 66
Chanting the Names of Manjushri
  (Manjushrinamasangiti), 24
Chittamatra school, 157
clairvoyance, 82
clear faith, 120
common preliminary practices, 1–2,
  47–48, 52–53, 69. *See also* ngöndro; *specific practices*
compassion, 22, 49
  bodhichitta and, 151, 152–53, 154
  as causal motivation, 132
  cultivating immeasurable, 64–66,
    99–100, 130, 185
  four immeasurables and, 143, 145
  prayer of, 151
  of qualified teacher, 37
  refuge and, 121–22, 132
  as source of ultimate qualities, 66
confession, practice of, 160–63
confident faith, 120–21
consciousness
  as beginninglessly pure, 104

eight kinds of, 24
as unbroken continuum, 103
continents and subcontinents, 204–5

D
Dagmo Trinley Paljor, 188
death. *See* impermanence and death
dedication, 181–82
demigod realm, 80, 108
desire. *See* attachment
desire realm, 81
desire-realm gods, 81–82
Dhammapada, 19
Dharma
  listening to and following genuine,
    134–35
  as object of refuge, 114, 117, 123–25,
    142
  refuge precepts for, 134–35, 137
  two types of, 124–25
Dharma practice
  aspirational bodhichitta and,
    67–68
  to benefit sentient beings, 65–66
  as only protector at time of death,
    95–96
  right motivation for, 2, 59–61,
    185–86
  understanding impermanence and,
    91–92
Dharma teachers
  authenticity of, 50
  importance of, 33–34
  relying on qualified, 134
  types of, 34–35
  See also guru
dharmakaya, 110, 122, 166, 214n12
disharmony, creating, 106
Dölpopa Sherab Gyaltsen, 14

Drakjor Sherab (Ngok Lekpai
  Sherab), 6
Drogön Chögyal Phakpa, 10, 11, 173,
  178
Drokmi Shakya Yeshé (Drokmi
  Lotsawa), 7–8, 9, 12, 39
Dromtönpa, 60
Dzongpa lineage, 13

E
eager faith, 120
eight goddesses, 207–8
eight unfavorable conditions, 87–88
Eight Verses of Mind Training, 129
Eleven Yogas of Vajrayogini, 12–13
empowerment (*wang*)
  bodhichitta vows and, 157
  four empowerments, 37, 213n6
  receiving, 26–28, 35, 38
  refuge and, 126
  samaya and, 163
  Vajrasattva practice and, 159–60
emptiness (*shunyata*)
  direct experience of, 25–26, 125
  realizing view of, 165
engaged bodhichitta, 67–68, 147,
  148–49
equalizing oneself and others, 156
equanimity, four immeasurables and,
  143, 146
*Excellent Path of the Two Accumula-
  tions, The*, 179, 214n17
exchanging oneself and others, 156

F
faith
  refuge and, 138–39
  three types of, 120–21
fear, refuge from three types of,
  118–20

220 | THE FUNDAMENTAL PRACTICES

Fifty Verses on Guru Devotion, 179
five certainties, 122–23
five paths, 25, 125–26
form realm, 81
formless realm, 81
Forty-First Sakya Trizin, Ngawang
  Kunga (His Holiness Kyabgon
  Gongma Trichen Rinpoche),
  14–15, 54, 173
four immeasurables, 143–46
four maras, 105
four noble truths, 70
four reliances, 44–46
four seals, 81
four thoughts that turn the mind to
  the Dharma, 1–2, 48, 174

G

Gatön Ngawang Lekpa Rinpoche
  (Jamgön Ngawang Lekpa), 55,
  172, 214n17
Gayadhara, 8
generosity, 23
Geshé Langri Thangpa, 129
god realm, 80, 81–82, 108
Gorampa Sönam Sengé, 11–12, 116
grand guru, 35
greed, 106
guru
  devotion for, 39–42, 48, 175, 178
  different types of, 34–35
  importance of, 33–34, 177
  relying on qualified, 134
  types of offerings for, 40
  visualization of, 193
Guru Padmasambhava, 4, 5, 9
guru yoga, 2, 48, 113
  benefits of, 179, 191, 196
  mandala offering and, 175–76
  practice of, 177–78

prerequisites for, 179
guru-student relationship
  holding pure view of guru, 45–46
  how to evaluate a guru, 42–44
  how to maintain, 38–42
  importance of, 35–36
  qualities of a student, 38
  qualities of qualified guru, 36–38

H

happiness
  bodhichitta and, 152
  transient nature of, 71–72
harm, avoiding, 141
harsh words, 106
hatred, harboring, 106
hell realm, 74, 80, 106, 107
Hevajra tradition, 7, 12, 27–28, 48,
  52, 163, 164, 179
higher realms, 77–82, 108, 167
Hinayana, 2
human realm, 77–80, 108
hungry ghost realm, 75–76, 80, 106,
  107

I

idle talk, 101, 106
ignorance, 76, 106, 119
impermanence and death, 48, 91–97
  benefits of pondering, 91, 96–97,
    195
  certainty of, 92–94
  Dharma practice and, 95–96
  in god realm, 81–82
  suffering and, 78–79, 83
  uncertainty of time of, 94–95
instructions (*tri*), 29

J

Jambhala, 22

INDEX | 221

Jamgön Ngawang Lekpa. *See* Gatön
  Ngawang Lekpa
jealousy, 80, 131, 183
Jetsun Drakpa Gyaltsen, 10, 59–60
Jonang tradition, 13–14
joy, four immeasurables and, 143, 146

K

Kalachakra Tantra, 14
karma, law of, 48, 99–111
  benefits of pondering, 195
  brief description of, 99–102
  four essential factors in, 100–101
  liberation and, 104–5
  negative karma, 106–7
  neutral karma, 109
  positive karma, 107–9
  rebirth and, 102–5
  transforming activities into positive
    karma, 109–10
Khenchen Migmar Tsering, 97
Khön clan, 4–5, 8–9
Khön Könchok Gyalpo, 8–9
Khön Sherab Tsultrim, 8–9
killing, 100–101, 106, 107, 108
knowledge, obscuration of, 1, 168
Kublai Khan, 11

L

Lamdré tradition, 2, 7–8, 10, 12, 28
  bodhichitta vows in, 157
  four authenticities and, 49–50
  guru yoga and, 179
  ngöndro and, 49–50, 52
Lamp for the Path to Enlightenment
  (Atisha), 6
liberation
  law of karma and, 104–5
  renunciation of samsara and, 62–64
lineage guru, 35

Lopön Sönam Tsemo, 10
Lotsawa Rinchen Sangpo, 6, 12
loving-kindness, 22, 49
  bodhichitta and, 152–53, 154
  cultivating immeasurable, 64–66,
    99–100, 130, 185
  four immeasurables and, 143,
    144–45
  prayer of, 151
lower realms, 73–77
lying, 106, 107

M

Madhyamaka school, 12, 14, 157
Mahayana (Paramitayana), 2
  bodhichitta and, 22, 149–50
  characteristics of, 21–22
  compared with Vajrayana, 22–23,
    25–26
  qualified teacher of, 36–37
  refuge and, 117–18, 119, 132–33
Mahayana Sutralamkara (Maitreya),
  56
Maitreya, 56, 59, 168, 182
Mal Lotsawa Lodrö Drakpa, 12
mandala offering, 2, 48, 113, 165–76
  actual practice of, 174–75
  benefits of practicing, 191, 196
  cleaning mandala plate, 201
  counting accumulations in, 173–74
  guru yoga and, 175–76
  merit accumulation and, 166–70
  offering mandala and materials,
    172–73
  propitiation mandala, 170–71, 173,
    199–200
  seven-heap, 210–11
  thirty-seven-heap, 200, 201–10
  visualization in, 167–70, 174
Manjushri, 10, 22, 51–52, 59, 151, 178

222 | THE FUNDAMENTAL PRACTICES

Marpa Chökyi Lodrö, 7–8, 39
meditative absorption, suffering and, 82
mental afflictions, transforming, 26, 55, 63, 124, 168
mental practice
  bodhichitta and, 196
  mental preparedness and, 58
  ngöndro and, 53–54
  refuge vows as, 128, 140–41
  visualization as, 128, 129, 132–33
  watching our minds, 183–84
Milarepa, 10, 39
mind (*sem*), 23–24
  importance of taming, 51, 129–31
  protecting from negative thoughts, 141
  samsara as prison of, 62–63
Mongol Empire, 11
moral conduct
  importance of, 60, 124
  of qualified teacher, 36–37
motivation
  bodhichitta, 66–68
  compassion and loving-kindness, 64–66, 132
  importance of right, 54, 59–61, 184–86
  mandala offering and, 167, 168
  for ngöndro practice, 58, 189
  renunciation and, 62–64
  for taking refuge, 129–32
Mount Meru, 203–4
multiplication mantra, 188

N
Naktso Lotsawa Tsultrim Gyalwa, 6
Naropa, 13, 40, 53, 157
negative karma
  nonvirtuous deeds and, 106–7

purification of, 2, 101, 159–63
  as temporary, 104
Ngakchang Sungkyi Palwa, 13
Ngok Lekpai Sherab. *See* Drakjor Sherab
Ngok Loden Sherab, 6
ngöndro (preliminary practices)
  advice on commencing, 186–87
  counting accumulations in, 55, 173–74, 187–88
  dedication of merit in, 181–82
  different lineages of, 196–97
  enlightenment and, 197
  general vs. deity-specific, 194
  graduation from, 191–92
  importance of, 47, 49–51
  integrating with daily life, 194–96
  overview of, 1–3, 47–49, 52–53, 113
  preparing for, 56–58
  proper visualization in, 132–33, 187–88, 192–93
  quantity vs. quantity in, 53–54
  receiving transmission for, 56
  Sakya tradition and, 48–52
  signs of progress in, 190–91
  timeframe for completing, 188–89
  See also specific practices
Ngor lineage, 13, 15
Ngorchen Kunga Sangpo, 11, 13
nirmanakaya, 24, 49, 64, 122, 123, 165
nonvirtuous deeds, 106–7
  purification of, 160–63
nonvirtuous friends, abandoning, 134
Nyingma lineage, 5

O
obscurations
  purification of, 2, 159–63, 168
  purity free from, 122
  two kinds of, 1

INDEX | 223

offerings
  for guru, 40
  to Triple Gem, 136
  types of, 166
old age, suffering of, 78
oral transmission (*lung*), 29, 164
Ornament of the Mahayana Sutras,
  182

P

Paramitayana, 20, 21. *See also*
  Mahayana
Parting from the Four Attachments,
  10, 13, 30, 52, 59–60
path of accumulation, 125, 150, 151
path of application, 125
path of meditation, 125
path of no more learning, 125–26
path of seeing, 125, 148, 165
Perfection of Wisdom, 155
permission (*jenang*), 28
phenomena
  conditioned nature of, 72–73, 83
  fear of clinging to ordinary, 120
pith instructions (*mengak*), 29–30, 35
pratimoksha vows, 25, 36, 113, 116, 157
Pratyekabuddhayana, 117, 118, 214n15
precepts of refuge
  five precepts, 116
  general, 133–36
  specific for the Triple Gem, 136–39
precious human birth, 48, 85–90, 195
  cause for attaining, 86
  eighteen qualities of, 87–89, 167
  examples of difficulty attaining,
    89–90
  great benefits of, 85–86, 90, 108
  rarity of, 85–90
precious objects and emblems, 205–7
preliminary practices. *See* ngöndro

pride, subduing, 129, 130
prostrations, 190, 193–94
pure realms, in mandala offering, 167
purity, twofold, 122

R

realization, Dharma of, 124
rebirth
  continuum of consciousness and, 103
  karma and, 99, 102–3
refuge
  as basis for Buddhist path, 142, 157
  benefits of taking and practicing,
    114–15, 139–43, 190, 195, 196
  compassion and, 121–22, 132
  four immeasurables and, 143–46
  general precepts of, 133–36
  importance of, 2, 48, 51, 113, 114
  in Mahayana tradition, 117–18, 119,
    132–33
  objects of, 25, 122–26, 128–32
  proper motivation and, 129–32
  proper practice of, 126–32, 193–94
  prostrations and, 190, 193–94
  reasons for taking, 118–22
  renunciation and, 116
  specific precepts for Triple Gem,
    136–39
  from three fears, 118–20
  three types of faith and, 120–21
  types of vows, 115–18
  visualization for taking, 126–27,
    128, 129, 132–33
regret, power of, 161–62
relative truth, 46, 104
renunciation
  Dharma practice and, 2, 59–61
  generating thought of, 62–64, 185
  suffering and, 70, 77
  taking refuge and, 116

224 | THE FUNDAMENTAL PRACTICES

resolve, power of, 162–63
rimé movement, 14
Rinchen Sangpo, 6, 12
Rongtön Sheja Künrig, 11
rupakaya, 110, 122, 165, 214n13

S
Sachen Kunga Nyingpo, 9–10, 52,
  59, 141
sadhanas, 29
Sakya Monastery, 9–10, 13
Sakya Pandita, 10–11, 28, 31, 66, 135,
  149, 173, 178
Sakya tradition
  authentic lineage and teachings of,
    4, 12–13, 49–50
  early history of, 4–12
  Lamdré tradition and, 7–8, 12
  in modern world, 14–15
  ngöndro practice in, 48–52
  subschools of, 13–14
Sakya Trizin (Sakya Throne Holder)
  Khön clan and, 4, 9
  in modern world, 14–15
samadhi, 110, 214n14
samaya
  fourteen root vows, 163–64
  importance of keeping, 37, 40–41,
    138
  purifying broken, 160
  types of, 163, 186
samboghakaya, 24, 122–23, 165
samsara, shortcomings of, 48, 69–84
  fear of suffering and, 118–19
  renunciation and, 62–64, 185
  suffering in higher realms, 77–82
  suffering in lower realms, 73–77
  three kinds of suffering and, 70–73,
    83

Sangha
  as object of refuge, 114, 117, 125–26,
    142
  refuge precepts for, 137–38
  types and levels of, 125–26
Sarma schools, 5–6
self-cherishing, refuge from thoughts
  of, 119–20
sentient beings, limitless
  boundless love and compassion for,
    99–100, 121–22
  cultivating bodhichitta for, 151–56
  four immeasurables and, 143–46
  mandala offering for, 167, 168
  practicing Dharma for, 65–66
  taking refuge for, 129–30, 132
seven-heap mandala offering, 210–11
seven-limb prayer, 157
sexual misconduct, 106
Shakya Chokden, 12
Shangtön Chöbar, 10
Shantarakshita, 4, 5
Shantideva, 85–86, 133, 140, 148–49,
  150, 152, 153, 155, 162
Shravakayana, 21, 23, 213n3
  refuge and, 117, 118
  vows of, 25, 36, 113, 116, 157
shrine setup, 57–58
  for mandala offering, 170–71,
    199–200
sickness, suffering of, 78
six paramitas, 22, 168–69
six realms, 73–82
skillful means, 26
Songpa Kunga Namgyal, 11
stealing, 106, 107, 108
suffering
  fear of, 118–19
  limitless compassion for, 65
  samsara and, 62–63

suffering of change, 71–72, 73, 77
suffering of conditioned nature of
phenomena, 72–73, 83
suffering of suffering, 71, 73
sun and moon, 209
support, power of, 161

T

Teaching of Akshayamati, 44
ten favorable conditions, 88–89
thirty-seven-heap mandala offering,
200, 201–10
Tilopa, 40
*Treasury of Abhidharma (Abhi-
dharmakosha)*, 125
*Treatise Distinguishing the Three
Vows*, 66, 149
Triple Gem
faith and, 120–21
guru as, 48, 179
making offerings to, 136
never abandoning, 135–36
as object of refuge, 2, 114, 117,
122–26, 133
refuge precepts for, 136–39
visualization of, 126–27
Triple Tantra, 30
*Triple Vision (The Three Levels of
Spiritual Perception)*, 30, 48, 49,
51, 52, 69, 83, 93
Trisong Detsen, 4, 170–71
Tsar lineage, 13, 15
Tsarchen Losal Gyatso, 13

U

ultimate truth, 46, 104, 147
uncommon preliminary practices, 48,
52–53, 113
transmission for, 56
See also ngöndro; *specific practices*

V

Vaibhashika, 20
vajra fence, 203
vajra ground, 202
vajra master, 35
Vajra Verses, 49
Vajrasattva practice, 2, 48, 113, 159–64
benefits of, 190–91, 196
four powers in, 160–63
prerequisites for, 159–60, 164
samaya and, 163–64
Vajrayana, 2, 21
brief description of, 23–26
importance of lineage in, 37
origins of, 24
qualified teacher of, 37–38
refuge and, 116, 117, 120
secret teachings of, 30–31
special characteristics of, 22–23
tantric teachings of, 3–4, 163
transmission in, 26–30
Vajrayogini, 12, 52, 53, 173
valid cognition (*pramana*), 103
Vasubandhu, 123, 125
Vikramashila, 6, 7
Vinaya tradition, 12, 129, 135
qualified teacher of, 36
virtuous deeds, 107–9
dedication of, 181–82
proper motivation and, 129–30,
183–84
refuge vows and, 139
Virupa, 7, 10, 12, 49, 50, 51, 52, 157
visualization
guru and, 193
importance of proper, 187–88,
192–93
mandala offering and, 167–70, 174
taking refuge and, 126–27, 128, 129,
132–33

226 | THE FUNDAMENTAL PRACTICES

vows, 213n5
  keeping three levels of, 25, 186
  purifying broken, 160
  teachers bestowing, 34
  types of refuge, 115–18

W

Way of the Bodhisattva, The (Shantideva), 85, 133, 140, 148–49, 152,
  153, 155, 162
wealth, suffering and, 72, 73, 79–80
wheel of Dharma, three turnings of,
  19, 20–23
wisdom
  buddhahood and, 23, 168
  cultivation of, 22

different approaches to, 25–26
overcoming conceptual mind, 141
of qualified teacher, 37
reliance on, 46
ultimate, 122, 124
worldly activities, suffering of ceaseless, 83
wrong views, 106

Y

Yaktön Sangye Pal, 11
yanas (vehicle, path), three, 21–23,
  24, 25
Yeshé Ö, 5–6

About the Author

His Holiness the Forty-Second Sakya Trizin, Ratna Vajra Rinpoche, holds the esteemed position of the forty-second Sakya throne holder within the Sakya school of Tibetan Buddhism. He is renowned for his profound knowledge and the clarity of his teachings, making him one of the most well-regarded lineage holders in the Tibetan Buddhist tradition. He hails from the acclaimed Khön family, known for producing successive generations of exceptional Buddhist masters. From a young age, His Holiness received extensive teachings, empowerments, and transmissions in both sutra and tantra from his father and numerous other esteemed teachers. After completing rigorous philosophical studies at Sakya College in India, he earned the *kachupa* degree. He began embarking on meditation retreats at the age of twelve, including the Hevajra retreat, a key tantric practice within the Sakya school. With great humility, he travels extensively to offer teachings and empowerments to students worldwide upon their request.

What to Read Next

The Bodhisattva Path from Ground to Fruition
Commentary on Sakya Paṇḍita's Clarifying the Sage's Intent
His Holiness the 42nd Sakya Trizin

Discover profound teachings on the Buddhist path from His Holiness the 42nd Sakya Trizin, Ratna Vajra Rinpoche, one of Tibetan Buddhism's most prominent leaders.

Freeing the Heart and Mind
Part 1: Introduction to the Buddhist Path
His Holiness the Sakya Trichen

The first book by His Holiness Sakya Trizin, the head of the glorious Sakya lineage.

Freeing the Heart and Mind
Part 2: Chögyal Phagpa on the Buddhist Path
His Holiness the Sakya Trichen

Explore two seminal Sakya texts with an incomparable teacher.

The Sakya School of Tibetan Buddhism
Dhongthog Rinpoche
Translated by Sam van Schaik

Since its 1976 publication in Tibetan, Dhongthog Rinpoche's history of the Sakya school of Tibetan Buddhism has been a key reference for specialists in Tibetan studies. Now English readers can consult it as well through Sam van Schaik's authoritative, fully annotated, and accessible translation.

Ornament to Beautify the Three Appearances
The Mahāyāna Preliminary Practices of the Sakya Lamdré Tradition
Ngorchen Könchok Lhundrup
Translated by Cyrus Stearns
Foreword by His Holiness the Sakya Trichen

Ornament to Beautify the Three Appearances is the first book of a two-volume set of works written by Ngorchen Könchok Lhundrup (1497–1557) to explain the Lamdré teachings, the most important system of tantric theory and practice in the Sakya tradition of Tibetan Buddhism. This volume is translated by Cyrus Stearns with a foreword by His Holiness the Sakya Trichen.

About Wisdom Publications

Wisdom Publications is the leading publisher of classic and contemporary Buddhist books and practical works on mindfulness. To learn more about us or to explore our other books, please visit our website at wisdom.org or contact us at the address below.

Wisdom Publications
132 Perry Street
New York, NY 10014 USA

We are a 501(c)(3) organization, and donations in support of our mission are tax deductible.

Wisdom Publications is affiliated with the Foundation for the Preservation of the Mahayana Tradition (FPMT).